Media Leaks and Corruption in Brazil

Analyzing the political consequences of the most extensive corruption investigation in recent Latin American history, Operação Lava-Jato, *Media Leaks and Corruption in Brazil* answers two central questions about the contradictory effects news media has on political systems. First, how can political actors in a seemingly well-functioning democracy quickly override checks and balances, and replace a head of state with a corrupt vice-president? Second, how can very active news media, while ostensibly performing the role of the watchdog, still fail to deliver media accountability to the public?

Combining a quantitative view of the media sphere with case studies of the leaks, legal actions, and alliances forming and breaking in the Brazilian Congress, Mads Bjelke Damgaard demonstrates that the media's attention to leaks and investigations of corruption paved the way for Dilma Rousseff's impeachment. By timing the disclosure of information in scandals, actors with inside information were able to drive the media agenda and let some scandals escape from the limelight. The book delivers an in-depth study of how scandals become political weapons in a time of media personalities and post-politics.

This book will interest scholars of Latin American Studies and Brazil, and the broader fields of media studies, democracy studies, and journalism studies.

Mads Bjelke Damgaard is PhD fellow in the Department of English, Germanic and Romance Studies at the University of Copenhagen, Denmark. He has previously worked at the University of Southern Denmark as well as the Department of Cross-cultural and Regional Studies, Science of Religions Section at the University of Copenhagen. When living in Rio de Janeiro and Brasília, he was visiting PhD fellow with the Universidade de Brasília and has collaborated with the media research group LEMEP (Laboratório de Estudos de Mídia e Esfera Pública) of the state university UERJ in Rio. He has previously published on corruption and Brazil in the King's College-based journal *Brasiliana* and the journal *Ephemera – Theory & Politics in Society*.

Routledge Studies in Latin American Politics

www.routledge.com/Routledge-Studies-in-Latin-American-Politics/book-series/
RSLAP

Media Leaks and Corruption in Brazil

The Infostorm of Impeachment and the Lava-Jato Scandal

Mads Bjelke Damgaard

Routledge
Taylor & Francis Group

NEW YORK AND LONDON

First published 2019
by Routledge
711 Third Avenue, New York, NY 10017

and by Routledge
2 Park Square, Milton Park, Abingdon, Oxon, OX14 4RN

Routledge is an imprint of the Taylor & Francis Group, an informa business

© 2019 Taylor & Francis

Library of Congress Cataloging-in-Publication Data
A catalog record for this title has been requested

ISBN: 978-1-138-48548-8 (hbk)
ISBN: 978-1-351-04930-6 (ebk)

Typeset in Times New Roman
by Wearset Ltd, Boldon, Tyne and Wear

Contents

Illustrations

Figures

Tables

Abbreviations

Brazilian Accountability Institutions

MPF	Ministério Público Federal (Public Prosecutors' Office)
PF	Polícia Federal (Federal Police)
PGR	Procurador-Geral da República (Prosecutor-General)
STF	Supremo Tribunal Federal (Supreme Court)
STJ	Supremo Tribunal da Justiça (Supreme Tribunal of Justice)
TCU	Tribunal das Contas da União (Tribunal for the Accounts of the Union)
TSE	Tribunal Superior Eleitoral (Superior Electoral Court)

Brazilian Party Abbreviations in 2016

DEM	Democratas*
PCB	Partido Comunista Brasileiro
PCdoB	Partido Comunista do Brasil
PDT	Partido Democrático Trabalhista
PEN	Partido Ecológico Nacional*
PFL	Partido da Frente Liberal
PHS	Partido Humanista da Solidariedade
PMDB	Partido do Movimento Democrático Brasileiro*
PMN	Partido da Mobilização Nacional
PP	Partido Progressista*
PPS	Partido Popular Socialista
PR	Partido da República
PRB	Partido Republicano Brasileiro
PROS	Partido Republicano da Ordem Social
PRP	Partido Republicano Progressista
PRTB	Partido Renovador Trabalhista Brasileiro
PSB	Partido Socialista Brasileiro
PSC	Partido Social Cristão
PSD	Partido Social Democrático
PSDB	Partido da Social-Democracia Brasileira

PSDC	Partido Social-Democrata Cristão*
PSL	Partido Social Liberal*
PSOL	Partido Socialismo e Liberdade
PT	Partido dos Trabalhadores
PTB	Partido Trabalhista Brasileiro
PTC	Partido Trabalhista Cristão
PTN	Partido Trabalhista Nacional*
PTdoB	Partido Trabalhista do Brasil*
PV	Partido Verde
SD	Solidariedade

Note

* In 2017, several parties were discussing or had filed official name changes: PMDB → MDB; PP → Progressistas; PSDC → Democracia Cristã; PSL → Livres; PEN → Patriotas; PTN → Podemos; PTdoB → Avante and DEM → Centro Democrático.

1 Introduction

In March 2014, a case of corruption was uncovered in Brazil that would go on to shake the country's democratic institutions to their very core. Through blind luck, a few arrests snowballed, and the case became the largest investigation of political corruption ever in Brazil – a country already infamous for dirty politics. However, the corruption investigation, known as Operation Lava-Jato, did not merely result in trials and sentences for the culprits. The Lava-Jato case had many impacts – but the most profound impacts went well beyond the individuals investigated in the case.

Spinning off from the explosive political atmosphere developing along with the Lava-Jato probe, the elected President Dilma Rousseff became the target of dozens of petitions for impeachment, and was ousted in 2016, six months after the installment of impeachment proceedings. In this atmosphere, much-needed political and economic reform was obstructed indefinitely, and the difficulties of constructing governable majorities in Congress kept the state's fiscal policies in disarray for three years in a row.

Meanwhile, scores of federal representatives, senators, and governors became targets in an avalanche of new investigations precipitated by the Lava-Jato probe. Rousseff's vice-president stepped in and picked a cabinet from the ranks of these congressmen, but four of the minister were forced to resign on corruption charges, with two of these in prison at the time of writing.

With no elections held, and despite the absence of criminal charges against the impeached president, the political program of the Brazilian government could change completely overnight, disrupting social conquests of the last decade and manifesting the prevalent Latin-American trend toward (or back to) neo-liberal economic politics. The Lava-Jato scandal not only made this sea change possible, but also precipitated the fall of a whole generation of politicians, and obliterated the citizens' already negligible trust in political authorities. Furthermore, targeting the top construction companies of the country as well as the continent-leading state oil company Petrobras, the scandal brought investments and public works in an already retracting economy to a standstill.

Since 2014, evidence and material of the Lava-Jato probe have continuously been made public to journalists by the prosecutors and the regional court of Curitiba, but in addition to this, the same journalists have been fed morsels (and sometimes torrents) of information in the form of leaks. Like the WikiLeaks and the leaks of the Panama and Paradise Papers, the Lava-Jato leaks have been continuously curated by journalists, and like these other famous leaks, the sources remain undisclosed. The accumulated data material, over the course of three years, is by now enormous, much like the internationally known leaks, reaching terabytes of data at the time of writing. In contrast to the international leak cases, however, the journalists of the Brazilian news media have not been in complete control of the material pertaining to the case.

The unauthorized leaks of key information in the case were distributed to different media outlets, probably for a variety of strategic reasons and from various sources with access to the investigation. The timing of the disclosure had a great impact on the political atmosphere. In contrast to instantaneously publicized data dumps such as the Panama Papers, the Lava-Jato case unfolded and leaked over the course of several years, adding a new episode to a crescendo of political drama each time new leaks appeared. In 2016 alone, the leaks of the Lava-Jato operation had profound consequences.

The consequences, however, were far more profound than, say, the disclosure of the Panama Papers in the same period, involving political and business elites of many other countries, including elites in the rest of the so-called BRIC countries. While the Panama Papers, detailing international tax evasion schemes, also made international headlines and meant public disgrace and interrupted careers for some European bank executives as well as the Icelandic prime minister, it barely piqued the interest of Russian and Chinese political authorities, and the systemic issues revealed with the leaked documents were virtually ignored around the world. The disclosure of corruption in the Brazilian political and economic elite, on the other hand, had critical consequences for the whole political paradigm of the nation, for the state apparatus and economy, as well as the balance between the branches of government. The ousting of the president, and ascension of the vice-president with congressional support from the former opposition, especially, was a surprising and monumental turnover: Surprising because erstwhile President Dilma Rousseff was not at that point investigated in the Lava-Jato probe, but instead was impeached on charges of being personally responsible for delays in transfers of funds between the National Treasury and public banks. Yet, in the crucial vote for her impeachment, held in the lower House of Congress on April 17, scores of federal representatives spoke of Rousseff's corruption. This belied the fact that the Rousseff administration had early on refused to interfere in the Lava-Jato investigations, even as it reached the political and business elite of Brazil.

The impeachment was a monumental event, because it resoundingly broke the governance model of welfare capitalism in Brazil, spearheaded for 13 years by the Worker's Party. By indicting, charging and sentencing key figures of the Worker's Party cadre, including the ex-President Lula, the party image was severely tarnished and the left wing of Brazilian politics was in tatters.

Finally, the probe and consequent trials broke with the established pattern of impunity common in Brazilian political corruption cases. The operation came to herald – perhaps prematurely – the end of one of the mechanics that made the particular Brazilian hybrid regime of coalitional presidentialism work in practice. Grafting and directing contracts within public procurements to political allies may have been the oil that greased the wheels and made the government coalitions work. Now, with a host of politicians under scrutiny and with an empowered judiciary and prosecuting branch of government, such a mode of striking political deals may have been curbed. This, to be sure, is good for democracy, but the chances of future consensus among the key players in the political arena looks very uncertain at the time of writing, six months before the 2018 general elections. What kind of majority will govern Brazil in the years to come? What are the tools that can ensure stable coalitions in the future? Questions such as these are still unanswered, in consequence of the turmoil launched with the Lava-Jato case. In this political chaos of corruption scandals, recession, and paralysis of important reform measures, it is pertinent to consider the role played by scandals in catalyzing political transformations.

The Conundrums of the Corruption Probe

Social and political scientists are normally keen on explaining societal change, and have developed large repertoires of theory to account for the changes seen in contemporary societies. Every once in a while, these repertoires fail to deliver answers. One such moment is arguably the Lava-Jato case. In a period of less than two years, so many events conspired to change the political scene that established academic perceptions about Brazilian society and politics couldn't keep up. In this book, I will focus on one of the theoretical challenges posed by this surprising turns of events: The democratic problem of too much visibility. The accountability overload and excessive corruption disclosure produced cascades of public signals in the news media – and with these cascades, news media ended up disregarding relevant information about the corruption of the political actors grabbing the reins of the federal government. With this preliminary statement of the theoretical challenge, I have already introduced one of the concepts that could increase the scientific understanding of the conundrums posed by the Lava-Jato case.

After the media storm of the Lava-Jato scandal and the impeachment of Dilma Rousseff, several accepted truths about Brazilian democracy capsized, posing the following questions to researchers: First, how could political actors in a seemingly well-functioning democracy quickly override checks and balances, ousting the president Rousseff and putting a corrupt vice-president in her place? Second, how could the nation's very active media, while they ostensibly were performing the role of the watchdog, still fail to deliver media accountability to the public? Third, political scientists had more or less agreed that the executive branch of the Brazilian system held too much power relative to the other branches. That notion was completely undermined with the impeachment proceedings. How could an elected president not maintain even a third of the congressmen as allies, given the budgetary and formal powers of the executive branch? Fourth, it is generally supposed that the independence of the judiciary is a bedrock of the rule of law, but in this case, it seems that independence of the judiciary is apt to mutate into political interests. Could it be that there is such a thing as too much independence, or in other words, that the Brazilian system of checks and balances is, in itself, neither balanced nor checked properly?

These tendencies – the bypassing of democracy, the accountability failure in plain sight, the impotence of the presidency, and the imbalance of the judiciary – are now appearing as issues on the agenda in Brazil. At the same time, each of these tendencies poses questions relevant to democracies across the globe, especially in the age of virally spreading information, 24/7 news, and media personalities grabbing the positions as leaders of the world's largest democracies. Therefore, the case of Brazil is a valuable lesson, not just to scholars, but to anyone interested in the state of democracy today.

Finally, the Lava-Jato investigation came as a big surprise in itself, because corruption scandals have been the norm since the military dictatorship ceded the reins of the country to civilians in the 1980s. Since then, barrages of scandals and disclosure of corruption have reached front pages of newspapers, the airwaves, and the evening TV news, but accused politicians were rarely convicted. The de facto law of impunity was notoriously hard to break, even as public prosecutors, little by little, gained political independence from the 1990s and onwards. But the astounding success (which to many spectators should be interpreted as the astounding excesses) of Lava-Jato has broken that vicious cycle, it seems. In order for readers not familiar with the recent Brazilian history of political corruption, I will present a small tour of the environment of media and politics since the country's transition, in the mid and late 1980s, to democracy.

25 Years of Media Exposés

The censorship institution of the military dictatorship, which had repressed free journalism in Brazil in the 1970s (Kucinski 1991), petered out with the gradual opening of democracy in the 1980s. As the generals stepped down, a new era was inaugurated in press-state relations, and this era was characterized by an explosion of corruption scandals during the civilian presidency of José Sarney, attributable both to high levels of corruption and the newfound freedom of press (Lattman-Weltman and Abreu 2001: 12ff.). Arguably, the heyday of Brazilian investigative journalism was the 1992 disclosure of corruption within the government of Fernando Collor de Mello. The young president was the first to be elected in free elections after the military left the presidential palace in Brasília. Collor moved into the Palácio de Planalto in 1990 on a wave of support for his image as the "hunter of maharajas," the broom that could sweep out the overpaid and corrupt public servants still lingering in the country's bureaucracy. However, Collor was exposed himself as corrupt by his brother in the weekly magazine *Veja* in 1992. He resigned before impeachment proceedings were finalized, in face of a massive wave of popular protests in the streets (Figueiredo 2010). His vice-president, Itamar

Franco, stepped in, but he struggled to find a cure for the four-digit inflation that Collor had left behind, hollowing out the economy.

Only in the middle of the 1990s did the Brazilian government manage to stop the hyperinflation marring the period after the return to the democracy. Fernando Henrique Cardoso (former Minister of Finances in the Itamar Franco administration) was the name of the new president who headed the team of technocrats behind the successful Plano Real that ended the spiral of inflation (Skidmore et al. 2010: 343). Cardoso's team worked within the boundaries of orthodox economics and the so-called Washington consensus until his second term was up in 2002. Under Cardoso, many corruption scandals surfaced, but his appointed prosecutor-general of the republic decided to shelve the vast majority, and only let 60 out of 600 cases of grand political corruption pass into court rooms.

At the end of his second period, Cardoso was unable to end a recession, and this gave the leader of the opposition, the union boss and socialist Lula, his first win in a presidential election, despite running in every election since the first free election in 1989. Lula represented (and had founded) the Worker's Party PT, and as a former steel worker and union leader he had an image of being close to the common people. However, in his successful bid for the presidency he still had to convince the economic elites, both in Brazil and in the international organizations such as IMF and the World Bank, that he would maintain Brazil on the path of orthodox economics. Lula managed to combine that pressure from the international financial markets with his socialist ideologies, inaugurating several very successful cash transfer programs and lifting millions of citizens out of poverty without draining the public coffers (ibid.: 346). The neo-developmental model of the Lula administrations (Bresser-Pereira et al. 2014) and the transfer programs were lauded across the world, as the country joined with other developing giants under the abbreviation of "BRICS." The middle class expanded enormously in Lula's two terms as president. However, he and his party came under severe fire in a corruption scandal known as the *Mensalão* case.

The Mensalão scandal (named for the neologism used to describe the big monthly payments to parliamentarians) drew headlines throughout the country in 2005 and 2006. Money was allegedly pulled from slush funds of Lula's PT and dealt out to congressmen in order to sway votes. While Lula remained unscathed, and succeeded in getting re-elected in 2006, central members of his inner circle in government and the party were indicted and went on trial, after many delays, in 2012. Sectors of the electorate became disappointed with the corruption in PT, a party used to defending ethical politics loudly. However, in contrast to the Cardoso period, federal prosecutors had by then obtained independence to pursue investigations into national political elites. The laws that made this possible were signed by Lula, and – undeniably – constituted a great step in constructing a functioning set of checks and balances in the Brazilian democracy.

The trial of the Mensalão case before the Supremo Tribunal Federal (the Supreme Federal Court) was big news: The exceptional number of defendants, their political positions close to the presidency, the vast amount of documents, and the potential to seriously harm the governing party fueled the intense interest of the media. As the trial progressed, the adamant will of the majority of judges to condemn political corruption severely were also hailed as a historical event in the media, a milestone in the country's continuous struggle against corruption (Damgaard 2015, Michener and Pereira 2016, Power and Taylor 2011: 33). The trial happened to be the first time after the transition to democracy that a minister was sentenced for corruption in the Supreme Court – even the case of Collor had ultimately been filed away.

Lula had more or less left the political scene by the time of the Mensalão trial, recovering from cancer, and left the presidency to a former minister of Mines and Energy, later chief of staff in the cabinet, Dilma Rousseff. Rousseff had initiated her presidential period in 2011 with a grand gesture of cleaning out the ranks, by sacking all ministers denounced in the press. Combined with impressive growth rates in the economy and a continuously flourishing middle class, Rousseff managed to remain relatively popular, even as her party was the target of scathing critique in the media coverage of the Mensalão trial.

Two international milestones dominated the political arena in the years following the Mensalão case. Brazil prepared to host the World Cup in 2014, and the Chinese economy began to slow down after decades of rapid growth. This was gradually felt in the Brazilian sectors of commodities, especially soy and mineral exports, and eventually meant reduced tax income and empty public coffers. On the domestic scene, a wave of protests against a bus fare increase picked up steam and erupted into massive street protests in June 2013. The protests saw millions in the streets of the large capitals, numbers not seen since the 1980s and early 1990s. The protesters were not united under any single banner, as the multitude in the streets branched off from the topic of public transportation fares (Cardoso and di Fatima 2013, Saad-Filho 2013). However, the mainstream media quickly cast the protests as being focused on corruption and governmental overspending, especially on the World Cup prestige construction projects (Avritzer 2016). Somehow, in the media discourse interpreting the June protests, the supposed milestone of the Mensalão trial was not proof that the law of impunity for political corruption had been broken.

The Initial Phase of the Operation Lava-Jato and the Chain of Plea Bargains

In 2014, on March 17, another exception to the law of impunity appeared: The first phase of the Lava-Jato operation caught a big fish with ties that went to the top of the political scene. That morning, a money launderer (a so-called *doleiro*) named Alberto Youssef, working out of Curitiba, Paraná, was apprehended by Federal Police officers. Youssef had been identified as a key actor in a criminal network linked to the gas station Posto da Torre in the hotel sector of central Brasília. The police operation was code-named *Lava-Jato*, literally "Jet Wash," referencing both the car wash (*lava a jato*) in that gas station and implying that the amounts of money laundered surpassed the value of a jet (Netto 2016: 28).

The operation that apprehended Youssef was not what caught the eye of Brazil's media, however. While the case was covered briefly on March 18, it was not linked to Petrobras before it became known that a former director of Petrobras, Paulo Roberto Costa, was in cahoots with Youssef. Costa, who headed the oil giant's Supply Department until 2014, happened to be arrested in the same case a few days later, and that became the first tremor that set off the avalanche. On March 20, Costa was apprehended by the Federal Police, because he, on the morning of Youssef's arrest, had called on his family to destroy evidence in his office and remove large amounts of money. The ex-director's family members were nearly caught red-handed by the police, who rapidly accessed surveillance tapes from the very same morning and eventually stopped the destruction of evidence (ibid.). Costa, being one among the select group of people being called by politicians to lead the large state companies, had much to tell the police once he decided for a plea bargain.

Plea bargains (in Portuguese: *delação premiada*) are a relatively new measure in criminal investigations in Brazil (importing it recently, like other countries, from the common law system of the United States). Plea bargains were only effectively introduced into the category of legal evidence in probes into criminal organizations with the law 12.850 of 2013. In corruption cases, the evidence emerging from plea bargains can be vital, because corrupt deals are struck, in their very nature, between very few people, producing as little material evidence as possible. With this legal measure in hand, the team of police agents and prosecutors that conducted the Lava-Jato investigations reminded the Petrobras director that he could obtain a reduced sentence by spilling the beans. Costa, used to the luxury of the federal capital and up-scale neighborhoods of Rio de Janeiro, took the bait and revealed a number of things about the procurement processes of Petrobras. He also mentioned the structure of payments that followed subcontracts, and when the *doleiro* Youssef also opted to plea bargain, the prosecutors were stunned as they gradually unraveled the practice and extent of corruption in the state company.

There is another reason for mentioning plea bargains at this point, beside the fact that it was the plea bargains of Costa and Youssef that really started the avalanche of the operation. As the investigations developed, it became a firm principle of the Lava-Jato task force and the Prosecutor-General (directing inquiries in cases pertaining to parliamentarians, ministers and governors) that plea bargains can only be negotiated when the testimony incriminates individuals on higher organizational rungs. That is, each defendant admitting to corruption charges and negotiating a plea bargain must deliver names and evidence not only of those who moved the money, but also those who asked for it, and those who paid. This is sensible from the perspective of the investigations, because that is the only way to get to the top of the chain of command – and if a defendant keeps certain things to himself, a reduction in sentence would harm the spirit of the Rule of Law. However, when this desire to get to the top of the chain of command becomes manifest, defendants will have incentives to lie, because they are more likely to obtain a plea bargain if they implicate business leaders and political leaders above them.

Despite this potential problem for the quality of information in investigations, the plea bargains of Costa and Youssef went on to trigger a cascade of new bargains. Youssef implicated the former Samsung employee Julio Camargo, and once he was arrested, Camargo pointed to an executive by the name of Augusto Mendonça, who had been his colleague in the construction company Toya Setal. Mendonça implicated, in turn, the Petrobras manager Pedro Barusco, who also decided to strike a plea bargain. Barusco identified more subcontractors of Petrobras that had paid kickbacks for contracts, and the executives and managers of these companies named more directors of Petrobras, who then implicated more construction company leaders with direct or indirect ties to the most influential Brazilian politicians. Some (but not all) of the plea bargains were negotiated while the defendant was being held indefinitely in prison under the law of "preventive arrests," that is, imprisonment without sentence aiming at avoiding destruction of evidence or even new crimes. To some experts, the indefinite span of preventive arrests could be construed as a way of forcing persons into admission of guilt. At the time of writing, the former minister of Finances in the Lula administration, Antônio Palocci, and the former President of the Lower House of Congress, Eduardo Cunha, have both been held captive in Curitiba for a year, and both of them are attempting to settle plea bargains. The stakes of this chain of plea bargains are now so high that only implicating a president or an ex-president is sufficient to make a deal go through. Hopefully, there will be ample evidence, and not merely allegations, to back up such revelations about masterminds in the heart of the political system.

The point, in sum, is that allegations about corruption have been feeding the investigations, for good and for worse. Allegations have pointed police agents to new targets and caches of evidence, and insofar as this has been the case, it has surely been for the better. However, the incentive to denounce others has had consequences outside of the courts, creating a very peculiar atmosphere of news. Plea bargains are constructed through the negotiation between a defendant, his lawyers, and the public prosecutors. Many individuals had access to such plea bargains and the documentation surrounding it, even before a judge validated the material as suitable for trials and investigations. In a number of high-profiled cases of the Lava-Jato probe, the material has been leaked to the press before the ink was dry on the paper containing the terms of the plea bargain. This plea bargain law is thus not merely a great innovation in the judiciary system, but the successful use of the law in the unfolding Lava-Jato scandal also had ramifications for the media system and the way investigative journalism works today in Brazilian news rooms. During the course of this book, I will present some of the many consequences of plea bargains and media leaks in the political system.

The plea bargains laid bare a system of political negotiation that went beyond the system of distributing coalition goods and "pork" (amendment expenditure) to parties supporting the president (Raile et al. 2011). Not only can Brazilian presidents wield extended powers to allocate state expenditures to specific projects in exchange for votes in Congress, but an astonishing amount of top-level public office positions are also governed, ultimately, by the executive branch of the State. It is estimated that more than 20,000 leading positions in public companies, agencies and other state entities are appointed by the political system. In the case of Petrobras, Paulo Roberto Costa and other directors admitted that they were politically appointed (and later maintained in their positions) by government coalition partners. In this way, each directorate was allocated to a political party, and the contracts in the business areas of these directorates yielded kickbacks for the parties. Earlier suspicions of the "auctioning off" of state enterprises and private-public operations (Power and Taylor 2011: 264) were now documented, as the Lava-Jato investigations revealed this practice not only in Petrobras, but also in the state energy company Eletrobras, in nuclear plants, and in the health sector.

Colluding in tenders, a cartel of 16 companies had informally distributed subcontracts of Petrobras and other state companies, fixing prices and planning kickbacks for directors and for the politicians backing them. In November 2014, CEOs and presidents of seven of these companies were arrested, based on the information provided by the chain of testimonies initiated by Paulo Roberto Costa. That became the start of Operation Lava-Jato, and in the course of this book, the various consequences of this investigation will be described.

Theorizing Information Flows and Media Leaks in Accountability Processes

Little did the federal police agents that arrested Costa in March 2014 know that three years hence, the operation would have changed the political landscape of Brazil. Neither could they foresee how they themselves would be hailed as heroes, and then cast as anti-heroes, by media, segments of the population, and even ex-presidents and presidents. As pointed out above, the Lava-Jato case, from 2014 to 2017, had any number of unforeseen and surprising results. To reiterate, some of those results prompt the central questions of this book: How could the nation's media fail to produce accountability to the public despite extensive coverage of the political machinations and maneuvers? And how could political actors in a seemingly well-functioning democracy quickly override checks and balances, ousting the president Rousseff and putting a corrupt vice president in her place?

These questions require crossing the disciplinary boundaries of media studies, accountability research, and institutional theory. The deficits of Brazilian accountability institutions are well known (for an overview, see Macaulay 2011 and Power and Taylor 2011), and concerns about media's problematic influence on public opinion and politics have been voiced for a century (e.g., Lippman 1922). The particular problems of the Brazilian media system in relation to democracy have been articulated and discussed by many influential authors (Avritzer 2016, Chaia and Teixeira 2000, 2001, Lattman-Weltman and Abreu 2001, Lima 2004, 2006, 2009, Mesquita 2014, Miguel 1999, 2003, Porto 2011). The democratic problems arising from the Lava-Jato scandal cannot be reduced to either the field of media discourse or an institutional field, however. Rather, the consequences appeared precisely in the interstices of the media sphere and the web of accountability mechanisms. The deficits of accountability, transparency, and public visibility were nested within both organizational fields, compounding the democratic problems and at the same time imbuing the Lava-Jato investigations with unusual political potential.

Therefore, this book will establish a theoretical framework that can address the intersection of media studies and accountability research, taking into consideration the complex interplay between these social and organizational fields. I will argue shortly that both the study of political scandals and accountability theory can benefit from incorporating the concept of informational cascades. By viewing interactions between media organizations, the public agenda, accountability agencies and political actors as essentially informational processes, evolving in dynamic sequences, the framework established here aims at improving the theoretical understanding of processes wherein media scandals and fragile accountability institutions are used instrumentally.

Accountability has been conceived along two axes: the horizontal axis and the two vertical dimensions of electoral accountability and societal accountability (Mainwaring and Welna 2003). The horizontal axis encompasses the constitutionally configured checks and balances of democratic systems, such as veto powers of executives, judicial review of courts, investigative and overseeing capacities of various government agencies and courts, as well as the legislative instruments of oversight, investigative commissions, and, last but not least, the impeachment instrument (Smulovitz and Peruzzotti 2000: 153). Accountability actors on the vertical axis include all citizens, in principle, but in particular, various collective forms of non-governmental actors, such as civic organizations and NGOs. The organizations of civil society that can mobilize citizens' demands for accountability are important actors, as are political parties in their representative capacity, and media actors. The main electoral accountability body, included under the umbrella of vertical accountability, is the constituencies of elected governmental actors. Together, the mesh of institutions and actors constitute a "web" of accountability institutions (Mainwaring and Welna 2003: 29) or "accountability networks" (Waisbord 2000: 210). In the Brazilian web of institutions, bodies, and agencies, each actor might be more or less tuned into the processes of the others, and problems may arise in both the lacunas and the overlapping areas of the web (Power and Taylor 2011).

The processes whereby information circulates between the horizontal accountability institutions, on one hand, and media organizations, on the other, are particularly interesting in the Lava-Jato case. Here, the main problem in the web of accountability arises from an institutional relation crossing the vertical-horizontal divide. The extant literature on media exposés in the Latin American media has emphasized how media can (and should) activate accountability mechanisms (e.g., Porto 2012: 40, Smulovitz and Peruzzotti 2000: 152, Waisbord 2000: 211). Knowing that exposés and disclosure of corruption might activate horizontal accountability mechanisms, both political actors and civic actors have incentives for pushing information to media actors. As Peruzzotti and Smulovitz say:

once the media was revealed as an effective mechanism for controlling and accelerating public decisions, civil society organizations used this discovery to gain access to an alternative route to justice, to get attention from the public authorities, and to informally judge presumed illegal activities. In some countries, this new role has led to the emergence of a strong and sometimes threatening investigative journalism.

(2006: 18)

However, Peruzzotti also warned that exposés and scandals could be considered a tool in struggles between political elites, with Latin American media covertly taking sides in such struggles:

given their privileged access to inside information [the press and the opposition could choose what to disclose]. Political scandals were thus largely seen as intraelite games, the outcome in each case fundamentally depending on the postures and maneuvers adopted by media and political elites. The citizenry and society at large only played a passive role as "public opinion.... Can the Latin American media be considered independent? Is the image of a fourth estate adequate to describe the workings of journalism in the region? Do media exposés and denunciations help to strengthen democracy and governmental accountability? Or are they an instrument of the "politics by other means" that ultimately feed political cynicism and apathy?

(Peruzzotti 2006: 255–256)

Peruzzotti's suspicion of "politics by other means" was already voiced in Latin American media studies of the 1980s and 1990s:

Against popular and media-centric approaches that conclude that the news media have exceptional powers in bringing down ministers or presidents, it is necessary to analyze the balance of congressional forces, the configuration of the judiciary system, and the response of organized interests to gauge the consequences of media exposés. Especially in countries where the news media have not historically kept a distance vis-à-vis powerful interests but offer channels for doing *politics by other means*, it is a mistake to examine the relations between press and accountability independently from larger political dynamics.

(Waisbord 2000: 222–223, emphasis added)

The critical perspective of Waisbord (and other related critiques concerning unsubstantiated media accusations, e.g., Smulovitz and Peruzzotti 2000: 154) casts doubt on the effectiveness of Latin American media in creating accountability. These authors highlighted that exposés, in fact, sometimes express the vested interests of elites rather than the ideals of watchdog journalism. Though Waisbord analyzed several of the problems of these horizontal-to-vertical information flows and the sub-politics of sources and journalists (Waisbord 2000: 93), the matter largely stands as it did in the 1990s. Then, Waisbord observed that "closeness between journalists and official sources is also indispensable for the media to delve into official wrongdoing" and that this proximity "results from the organization of news-making and a journalistic culture that highly prizes official news" (ibid.). A decade later, Porto echoed this, and also called to attention the problem of "[c]ollusion between journalists and officials [that] frequently prevents watchdogs from barking even when evidence of wrongdoing is available" (Porto 2011: 111). Moreover, Porto noted the related problems of counter-denunciations stemming from such closeness: "Journalists' dependence on officials also allows some sources to avoid denunciation, while at the same time ensuring that the media will publicize accusations against rivals" (ibid.).

In a nutshell, these problems cannot be grasped within the paradigm of accountability theory, as this theory is not equipped to analyze exactly how media systems are invested – politically and economically – in the production or omission of scandals. Furthermore, the fundamental element here is actually not the accountability mechanisms and institutions, but rather the flows of information that are generated and disseminated by those institutions. For these reasons, I will establish a line of analysis centered on the flows of information. Theoretically, the reason for highlighting information flows of scandals in relation to accountability is the following: The production of accountability, in at least two senses of that word, depends on distribution of information. The vertical accountability of political actors, whether in the sense of electoral accountability or societal accountability, depends on constituencies and civic actors having access to accurate information about politicians and public office holders. Horizontal accountability, meanwhile, depends on information distribution in another sense: Interventions made through horizontal mechanisms of checks and balances (e.g., overseeing or auditing governmental agencies) require an element of transparency and publicness, and thus of distribution of information. If the results of horizontal accountability mechanisms are not made sufficiently public, actors caught in improbity may simply continue in other areas of public life, or even the very same office, while waiting for a final verdict or while dragging out trial and audit processes. Massive delays (Falcão et al. 2014: 57, 81) of investigations, verdicts, and appeals at the top level of politics are commonplace.

Because of the many opportunities for delaying and annulling legal processes, voters and other social actors need media or other forms of information distribution in order to become aware that horizontal accountability mechanisms have been activated or stonewalled. The effective and just application of horizontal accountability (such as trials or impeachment) is thus theoretically linked to the vertical dimension (electoral processes especially) through information distribution.

The work of prominent scholars analyzing scandals (such as Allern and Pollack 2012, Maier 2011, Pujas 2002, Thompson 2000, Tumber and Waisbord 2004) fails as starting points for analyzing the Lava-Jato case, although these works predict, like the accountability theory cited, that scandals generally have reputational and symbolic costs for the denounced (e.g., Balán 2011, Peruzzotti and Smulovitz 2006: 11, Seligson 2002, Thompson 2000: 245). However, while these authors observe that elites trigger scandals to inflict this reputational harm on political opponents, that does not systematically explain the ways in which accountability institutions and media work to inflict such damage. The academic literature on scandals has a lot to offer, but it rarely provides models of the entanglement of judiciary and political institutions, nor of the information flows in public spheres that set these institutions in motion. Furthermore, most of this literature has been conceived in times where digital and viral around-the-clock recycling of news and large-scale leaks were still in their infancy.

The literature on scandals suggests that the usual route taken is the "Indirect activation of horizontal mechanisms" where "claimants organize and mobilize but also […] reach the media or the media reaches them" (Peruzzotti and Smulovitz 2006: 18). That is clearly not the pattern of many cases emerging from the Lava-Jato investigations. Here, the accountability institutions – prosecutors, courts, audit agencies – have fed media with information so that horizontal mechanisms have activated vertical accountability actors, which is the opposite of the relation theorized in much research. Moreover, the reputational costs predicted are only inflicted when information about corruption is reproduced and acted upon in very specific ways – but that reproduction does not necessarily lead to action in accountability institutions, nor extensive coverage in the media.

In sum, the critique of exposés, though two decades old, has stopped short of investigating the systematic links between legitimate and leaky sources of accountability institutions, journalists, and editors. Furthermore, the intra-elite perspective needs to be unpacked, as it glosses over the important information flows between media and accountability actors, which might be just as problematic as corrupt political elites denouncing each other. The trajectory of information in public spheres is a crucial factor in the evolution of the scandal, but hitherto, models of scandals have not systematically treated information flows as analytical components. The same goes for studies of accountability. To remedy the shortcomings of accountability theory, scandal studies and the intra-elite struggle perspective, I will present an approach tailored to examining how diverse representations of corruption in the media came to impact upon the political agenda, coalition formation and judicial processes. Information disclosure in scandals and accountability processes together form sequences of information flows, or informational cascades, defined in the following.

Informational Cascades

Recent theoretical work on information sequences in public spheres has uncovered the pitfalls inherent in certain sequences of signals. This structure is called informational cascades, and according to Hendricks and Hansen (2016), such cascades emerge in groups of actors acting upon their knowledge of the sequence of public signals rather than private knowledge of information. I will briefly show how this theory of information and social psychology can generate insights into the dissemination of corruption news in Brazil. When deciding how to act,

> agents may choose to base their action not only on their private information, but also on the information extracted from their peers – social proof.... An informational cascade ... may easily occur when a number of people doubt the accuracy of their own information, and subsequently observe the preceding decisions and actions of others in the hope that it can lessen the doubt. This course of action then leads to each individual making the rational choice of following in his or her predecessors' footsteps, independent of his own preceding information.
>
> (Hendricks and Hansen 2016: 52, 62)

Doubt about course of action is not the only reason for choosing to act upon public signals, however. Scarcity of private information is another reason for people to pay close attention to social proof. This also goes for media actors. As described above, information on corruption publicized or leaked from accountability institutions can pass into journalistic production in one newsroom and, if it is treated as highly important there, it might then spread quickly to all other news media. A scoop might spread simply because one media actor signals the importance of the disclosed information. In other words, a scoop on a front page will likely be replicated by competitors in the same news market. The information might then be recycled many times over in the sphere of media, where different media outlets monitor and circulate news from competitors and reproduce and respond to other outlets' exposés to the degree that such news items are considered relevant to their own target audience. When response-coverage add new layers to an exposé, this can in turn be recycled by other outlets, multiplying the coverage.

The information disclosed by one or more media outlets can be distorted or misrepresented in various ways (potentially leading to states of dis- or misinformation, which is defined in Chapter 5). Some information, furthermore, might bear the connotation of corruption, contextually signaling political transgression, but not actually spell it out in so many words. So, in the public spheres of modern media, "informational cascades may turn out to be extremely powerful instruments if controlled in such a way as to manipulate public signals, so false information is spread instead of true knowledge" (ibid.: 22).

Due to organizational constraints in media (deadlines and labor resources, as well as physical attributes of newspaper space or broadcast news program duration), some information will be included while other may be disregarded at each broadcast or deadline. Some aspects might be highlighted, at the news room or in the editing process, producing particular frames interpreting the information concerning corruption (Entman 1993). The same goes for the following instances where information about corruption is disseminated – meaning is added or subtracted, texts are interpreted, framed and modified in innumerable ways. But crucially, as long as the basic bit of information – about political transgression – remains intact and is consistently present across media and the subsequent sites of dissemination, members of the various media audiences might consider this information as multiple instances of the same public signal. In other words, when there is a preponderance of one frame, signals are accumulating and that might lead audiences (as well as media professionals) to disregard information speaking to the contrary. Because of the evolving dynamics of scandals, disclosure of corruption is not a one-shot public signal, and the scandal coverage thus produces accumulated signals. This has consequences for how new information is likely to be treated later on:

> Information keeps accumulating until a preponderance of evidence supports one action or the other by just enough to outweigh one individual's private signal. At this point a cascade starts and new information stops accumulating.
>
> (Bikhchandani et al. 1998: 158)

In situations where private knowledge is very limited for the majority of actors, such as a national corruption scandal, these actors must make decisions based on public signals. Looking to peers or the media actors who supposedly holds privileged information, a "preponderance of evidence" might then sway these actors.

Thus, at the level of the audience, the effects of the media system's circulation and shared coverage are reinforced because media consumers often have a range of media outlets (and technological platforms) at their disposal. The everyday experience of (re)-circulated coverage (especially salient in moments of political scandal) is one aspect of our living media-saturated lives (occurring while we are also often influenced by local opinion leaders) (Lazarsfeld et al. 1944). If people recurrently glean information about a scandal from one or several media – be it printed news, broadcasting platforms, web-based news portals, weekly magazines, Twitter or Facebook – then their opinion will not be formed based on a single news text (see Miguel 2015 for a critique of the ideological weight of news items), but rather the aggregate stack or sequence of information. So, in so far as the analysis of cascades is situated at this level of aggregate news coverage, it is thus hardly compatible with framing studies (in the vein of Entman 1993 or Iyengar 1990). As the informational cascade accumulates signals, news items with divergent interpretive frames, for all the potential to sway individual opinion, are submerged in the wave of news repeating the initial signal crashing upon the cognitive shore of the audience.

Because each informational cascade is unidirectional and creates herd-like behavior, the phenomenon has been likened to financial bubbles, where information-driven markets come to over-valorize certain bits of information. In relation to the field of theories of media studies, the informational cascade approach is linked to agenda-setting theory (Wiewiura and Hendricks 2017). As predicted by agenda-setting theory (Ghanem 1997, McCombs 2005, McCombs and Shaw 1972), the salience given to news topics by media outlets will influence audience members' perceptions of the relative importance of those topics. To this, the informational cascade approach adds a framework for analyzing the networked sequences of information flows, and the power of specific sequences to attract the attention of an entire media sphere – or conversely, the potential to generate pluralistic ignorance of information (Hendricks and Hansen 2016). Because informational cascades can emerge in the audiences of news media just as well as between media actors, the pluralistic ignorance phenomenon also bears on how audiences are apt to interpret, recycle or reproduce information, based on the sequence of signals observed in news media.

Sampling of Material

To investigate the cascade, it is necessary to start where information emerges: The newsrooms with privileged access to the national political arena. This point of departure means that the media material sampled for this inquiry is not exactly representative of all Brazilian media, nor of the average Brazilian's news consumption. More likely, the material of this book reflects what the members of the nation's political elite are reading and watching. This focus on what have been termed legacy media – such as newspapers and weeklies – has more to do with the special access of information that journalists of the traditional news media continue to sustain, than with the tradition inherited from earlier studies of scandals.

The newsrooms of the prestigious legacy media of Brazil unite considerable agenda-setting power due to their privileged position at the top of the information food chain, and in consequence of their vertical integration on the media market (Matos 2008, 2012). In the perspective of information distribution, vertical integration of media outlets means recycling of the same news in a range of media platforms: The largest media conglomerate, the Grupo Globo, controls much of the regional media in both TV, radio, and print, as well as the most-viewed national channel, the second-most viewed news channel, the third-largest newspaper (*O Globo*) and weekly magazine (*Época*) and the national newspaper of economic issues (*Valor*), as well as the most visited online news site (Porto 2012, Newman et al. 2015: 40). The Marinho brothers, who inherited the executive positions from their father, control the Globo conglomerate. The media business empire of the Marinhos is only challenged on the market for news production by the evangelical bishop Edir Macedo (who owns the broadcasting network Rede Record), by the Saad family running the Bandeirantes network, by the Mesquita family (owning the newspaper *Estado de S. Paulo* and the news agency Broadcast), by the Frias brothers (controlling the newspaper *Folha de S. Paulo* and the UOL online platform), and by the Civita family managing the Abril group with the flagship weekly *Veja* (which is traditionally the most-read weekly magazine, ahead of *IstoÉ* and Grupo Globo's *Época*). The rest of the Brazilian regional and metropolitan newspapers and broadcasts get their national political news mainly from the news agencies and mother-organizations behind those news outlets. According to Abramo:

Not only the penetration of [Rio- and São Paulo-based] newspapers is much higher than the press from other regions, but they also tend to dominate what the other newspapers publish. Upon analyzing the credited sources of stories published by the newspapers (about 14% of stories are credited to news agencies), it is found that the news agencies associated with two newspapers (*Folha* and *Estado*) are responsible for 90% of all agency-credited news published by the newspapers ... Adding the Globo agency, the percentage is 95%. This does not count news items that are simply appropriated by a newspaper without credit, a very common phenomenon.

(2007: 99)

What Abramo shows is that the news selection criteria are determined by the media organization structure, and also in many cases by the regional news values. That is, news emerges in the regional and local spheres of media according to the organizational links to national media organizations and news agencies, but, crucially, the coverage is then modified by local relevance and political ties. This means that regional media will publish material on national corruption if a local politician is implicated, or, in many cases, will actively omit such information because of personal ties to media owners (ibid.: 101), a tendency which is especially salient in the area of radio broadcasting (Boas and Hidalgo 2011: 871).

The vertical integration of news media organizations is also apparent online. The major content providers of political news (both newspapers and broadcasters) each maintain online platforms, and the newsrooms produce content for several media types, frequently recycling material to their sites. The result is a media system that is highly concentrated in the hands of a few owners, and tightly controlled by these. Journalists working with national political news obtain access to information about political corruption through a limited number of sources; sources that are often involved in investigations.

Because these newsrooms of legacy media are usually first to report on disclosure of corruption, and their news are subsequently filtered down to affiliated regional media and spill over to broadcast media, I consider these newsrooms the first potential instances in an informational cascade. Due to this position among Brazilian news media, it is worthwhile to analyze the overall distribution of these media outlets' coverage of the scandals in the Lava-Jato case and the impeachment. Their coverage patterns are likely to be echoed in the vertically integrated media ecology. Such a quantitative research approach is operationalized in the fifth chapter of this book where I sample media material that, in total, forms the largest corpus of news on corruption that has yet been analyzed in the Brazilian context: A quantitative dataset of every news item and political commentary from the web and the printed versions of *Folha de S. Paulo* and *Estado de S. Paulo* dealing with national corruption cases during a seven-month period (from October 2015 until the ousting of Rousseff in May 2016). The dataset comprises 8,200 news items and metadata about each item. On top of this, the fifth chapter also analyzes a dataset comprising six months of front pages of both

Folha, Estado and *O Globo* (October 2015 till April 2016), with more than 1,300 items describing corruption and political transgression.

Combined, these two datasets serve as proxy for the entire landscape of Brazilian news discourse, and they cover with great granularity the period until the impeachment of President Rousseff. The first dataset dwarfs the many quantitative studies of Brazilian news media's treatment of corruption and politics produced in recent years, including those by Biroli and Mantovani (2014) (n=236), Makhoul (2009) (n=252), Lemos and de Barros (2016) (n=351), de Paiva et al. (2017) (n=932), and even Feres Júnior and Sassara (2016) (n=6,032). The size of this corpus compares to the annual corpus in the monumental ten-year study (n=107,248) by Mancini et al. (2017) that sampled news items on corruption from three different European media contexts. In other words, the sample of the two São Paulo dailies in this study's seven-month period outsizes the average corruption coverage of three large European countries combined.

Plan of the Book

The book can be read as a tour of the different stages in the informational cascade emerging in the public spheres of Brazil, triggered by the Lava-Jato investigations. As the chapters progress, I move from the initial moments where corruption is disclosed, via the particular accountability processes that sustain the media attention, and on to the aggregated macro-level of months of scandal and media exposés. In the final chapter, the empirical consequences of the cascade, as well the theoretical contribution of this movement, are summed up. For the sake of orientation, I will briefly present the arguments of each chapter.

The next chapter provides an overview of Brazil's media system, historically and organizationally, with special attention paid to the vertical concentration of media conglomerates, and the continuing political importance of television and a few prestigious newspapers. The chapter then briefly reviews the style of political journalism called *denuncismo*, detected by researchers since the 1990s. This scandalizing and often criticized off-the-records journalism is now gradually giving way to another style, because the newsrooms covering the national political arena are attuned to the workings of the accountability processes and official investigations. Information flows from these processes provide the base for a new way of writing news about political corruption, in which prosecutors, magistrates, and police agents are positioned as protagonists in scandal narratives. Bearing this in mind, I argue that corruption is a malleable discursive construct, rather than merely a legal or objective fact, and that the news frames are particularly important in defining what corruption means. Framing theory, however, is not useful for the purposes of this book, because salience transfer effects are unlikely to be encountered in this context.

The third chapter analyzes the political repercussions of leaks of the Lava-Jato investigations, by process-tracing the contribution of leaks to the disintegration of the coalition government led by Dilma Rousseff. In this chapter, I argue that the disclosure of corruption constitutes an especially powerful and dramatic style of interaction between judiciary, political and media systems. Leaks of information can be harnessed by political and institutional actors to great effect, and in a fast-paced media environment, leaks fundamentally erode journalistic boundary control and paradoxically provide powerful (and potentially anti-democratic) access to the media for those institutional actors with inside knowledge. These actors are concealed, despite having vested political interests, while the media outlets represent disclosure as ostensibly increasing transparency.

The fourth chapter describes the accountability institutions in Brazil relevant in the Lava-Jato probe. On the basis of this, five case studies demonstrate the complex interplay of political actors, prosecuting authorities, and judicial institutions in court trials during the period from 2015 to 2017. The outcome of those accountability processes was not purely the punishment of political transgression, as several trials ended in impunity. Rather, several macro-level changes and various side-effects surfaced in the political arena due to legal processes spawned during the Lava-Jato investigations. In a discussion of the outcomes of the legal processes, the chapter argues that political actors use legal action and corruption denunciations strategically to wage political war through the institutions of law and the repressive power of the state, which has been termed "lawfare." Lawfare encompasses the ways that legal (or quasi-legal) discourse and processes are abused as instruments for subjugating political subjects. Crucially, the mechanisms of the State, in this case checks and balances if not accountability institutions, also drive the media agenda.

The fifth chapter introduces the concept of informational cascades and adapts it to corruption scandals. An informational cascade is an aggregate phenomenon that coalesces out of actions of political, economic, and media actors and institutions. Based on a large-*n* sample of news items from mainstream print and web media, a content analysis demonstrates how information about corruption was shaped and passed on in cascades in the public spheres of Brazil. From political elites, through mainstream media and on to the stock markets of Brazil, the informational cascade repeated the signal of crisis and instability and created the conditions for the ousting of Rousseff.

The final chapter concludes the book by joining the strands of the preceding chapters: Despite the principally distinct discursive fields concerning political transgression, and the fact that Rousseff was not investigated for corruption then, the media climate of the Lava-Jato scandal created the conditions for replacing Rousseff with her vice-President, Michel Temer. At that point, Temer had been implicated by five different individuals in testimonies of the Lava-Jato probe. While the legality of the proceedings was observed, I argue that the legitimacy of the impeachment was thoroughly impaired as Temer and his party were participants in the graft of the state companies and benefitted from the corruption. In the conclusion, I answer the oft-asked question whether the impeachment could be considered a coup d'état or a legit constitutional act, contending that the legitimacy of the process was merely façade. Finally, I consider how the lessons of the Lava-Jato probe, the leaks, and the lawfare may inform current academic discussions on accountability, post-politics, and media systems.

References

Abramo, C.W. (2007) "Brazil: A Portrait of Disparities" *Brazilian Journalism Research*, vol. 3(1), 93–107.
Allern, S. and Pollack, E. (eds.) (2012) *Scandalous! The Mediated Construction of Political Scandals in Four Nordic Countries*. Göteborg: Nordicom.
Avritzer, L. (2016) *Impasses da democracia no Brasil*. Rio de Janeiro: Civilização Brasileira.
Balán, M. (2011) "Competition by Denunciation: The Political Dynamics of Corruption Scandals in Argentina and Chile" *Comparative Politics* vol. 43(4), 459–478.
Bikhchandani, S., Hirshleifer, D., and Welch, I. (1998) "Learning from the Behavior of Others: Conformity, Fads, and Informational Cascades" *Journal of Economic Perspectives*, vol. 12(3), 151–170.
Biroli, F. and Mantovani, D. (2014) "A parte que me cabe nesse julgamento: A Folha de S. Paulo na cobertura ao processo do Mensalão" *Opinião Pública*, vol. 20(2), 204–218.
Boas, T. and Hidalgo, D. (2011) "Controlling the Airwaves: Incumbency Advantage and Community Radio in Brazil" *American Journal of Political Science*, vol. 55(4), 869–885.
Bresser-Pereira, L.C., Oreiro, J.L., and Marconi, N. (eds.) (2014) *Developmental Macroeconomics. New Developmentalism as a Growth Strategy*. New York: Routledge.
Cardoso, G. and Fatima, B. di (2013) "Movimento em rede e protestos no Brasil. Qual gigante acordou?" *Dossiê Mídia, Intelectuais e Política*, vol. 16(2), 143–176.
Chaia, V. and Teixeira, M. (2000) "Máfia dos Fiscais e as estrelas de cidadania" *Observatório da imprensa, ed. 63, Mídia e política*, 31–37. Retrieved from http://observatoriodaimprensa.com.br/primeiras-edicoes/mfia-dos-fiscais-eas-estrelas-da-cidadania/.
Chaia, V. and Teixeira, M. (2001) "Democracia e Escândalos Políticos" *São Paulo Perspectivas*, vol. 15(4), 62–75.
Damgaard, M. (2015) "Narrating the Mensalão Trial: Configurations of Corruption" *Brasiliana*, vol. 3(2), 197–234.
Entman, R. (1993) "Framing: Toward Clarification of a Fractured Paradigm" *Journal of Communication*, vol. 43, 51–58.
Falcão, J., Hartmann, I.A., and Chaves, V. (2014) *III Relatório Supremo em Números: o Supremo e o tempo*. Rio de Janeiro: Escola de Direito do Rio de Janeiro da Fundação Getulio Vargas.
Feres Júnior, J. and Sassara, L. (2016) "Corrupção, Escândalos e a Cobertura Midiática da Política" *Novos Estudos*, vol. 35(2), 205–225.
Figueiredo, A.C. (2010) "The Collor Impeachment and Presidential Government in Brazil." In M. Llanos and L. Marsteintredet (eds.), *Presidential Breakdowns in Latin America* (111–127). New York: Palgrave Macmillan.
Ghanem, S. (1997) "Filling in the Tapestry. The Second Level of Agenda Setting." In M. McCombs, D. Shaw, and D. Weaver (eds.), *Communication and Democracy: Exploring the Intellectual Frontiers in Agenda Setting* (3–14). Mahwah, NJ: Lawrence Erlbaum Associates.
Hendricks, V. and Hansen, P.G. (2016) *Infostorms. Why Do We "Like"? Explaining Individual Behavior on the Social Net*. 2nd edn. London: Springer.

Iyengar, S. (1990) "Framing Responsibility for Political Issues: The Case of Poverty" *Political Behavior*, vol. 12(1), 19–40.

Kucinski, B. (1991) *Jornalistas e Revolucionários nos tempos da imprensa alternativa.* São Paulo: Editora Pagina Aberta.

Lattman-Weltman, F. and Abreu, A.A. de (2001) "Controles Midiáticos: Investigação e Denuncismo na Construção da Visibilidade Pública Democrática." Paper presented at ANPOCS 25th conference at Caxambu, Minas Gerais, October 17, 2001.

Lazarsfeld, P., Berelson, B., and Gaudet, H. (1944). *The People's Choice: How the Voter Makes Up His Mind in a Presidential Campaign.* New York: Columbia University Press.

Lemos, C. and Barros, A. de (2016) "Lutas simbólicas na arena midiática: o poder de agência do Ministério Público e as controvérsias sobre a PEC 37" *Opinião Pública*, vol. 22 (3), 702–738.

Lima, V.A. da (2004) "Sete teses sobre mídia e política no Brasil" *Revista USP*, São Paulo, no. 61, 48–57.

Lima, V.A. da (2006) *Mídia. Crise Política e Poder no Brasil.* São Paulo: Perseu Abramo.

Lima, V.A. da (2009) "Revisitando as sete teses sobre mídia e política no Brasil" in *Comunicação & Sociedade*, vol. 30(51), 13–37.

Macaulay, F. (2011) "Federalism and State Criminal Justice Systems." In T. Power and M. Taylor (eds.), *Corruption and Democracy in Brazil. The Struggle for Accountability* (218–249). South Bend, IN: University of Notre Dame Press.

McCombs, M. (2005) "A Look at Agenda-Setting: Past, Present and Future" *Journalism Studies*, vol. 6(4), 543–557.

McCombs, M. and Shaw, D. (1972) "The Agenda-Setting Function of Mass Media" *Public Opinion Quarterly* vol. 36, 176–187.

Maier, J. (2011) "The Impact of Political Scandals on Political Support: An Experimental Test of Two Theories" *International Political Science*, vol. 32(3), 283–302.

Mainwaring, S. and Welna, C. (eds.) (2003) *Democratic Accountability in Latin America.* Oxford: Oxford University Press.

Makhoul, F. (2009) *A cobertura da revista Veja no primeiro mandato do presidente Lula.* Master's thesis, São Paulo: PUC-SP.

Matos, C. (2008) *Journalism and Political Democracy in Brazil.* Lanham, MD: Lexington Books.

Matos, C. (2012) *Media and Politics in Latin America. Globalization, Democracy and Identity.* London: I.B. Tauris.

Mesquita, N.C. (2014) "Media and the Quality of Democracy: The Different Impacts of the Media on Regime Support in Brazil." In R. Figueiras, P. Espírito Santo, and I.F. Cunha (eds.), *Democracy at Work: Pressure and Propaganda in Portugal and Brazil* (13–38). Coimbra: University of Coimbra Press.

Michener, G. and Pereira, C. (2016) "A Great Leap Forward for Democracy and the Rule of Law? Brazil's Mensalão Trial" *Journal of Latin American Studies*, vol. 48, 477–507.

Miguel, L.F. (1999) "Mídia e Eleições: A Campanha de 1998 na Rede Globo" *Dados*, vol. 42(2), 253–276.

Miguel, L.F. (2003) "A Eleição Visível: A Rede Globo Descobre a Política em 2002" *Dados*, vol. 46(2), 289–310.

Miguel, L.F. (2015) "Quanto vale uma valência?" *Revista Brasileira de Ciência Política*, no. 17, 165–178.

Netto, V. (2016) *Lava-Jato: O juiz Sergio Moro e os bastidores da operação que abalou o Brasil.* Rio de Janeiro: Editora Sextante.

Newman, N., Levy, D., and Nielsen, R.K. (2015) *Reuters Institute Digital News Report 2015*. Oxford: Reuters Institute for the Study of Journalism, University of Oxford.

Paiva, A.L. de, Garcia, A., and Alcântara, V. (2017) "Disputas Discursivas sobre Corrupção no Brasil: Uma Análise Discursivo-Crítica no Twitter" *Revista Administração Contemporânea*, vol. 21(5), 627–647.

Peruzzotti, E. (2006) "Media Scandals and Social Accountability. Assessing the Role of Scandals in Argentina." In E. Peruzzotti and C. Smulovitz (eds.), *Enforcing the Rule of Law. Social Accountability in the New Latin American Democracies* (249–271). Pittsburgh, PA: University of Pittsburgh Press.

Peruzzotti, E. and Smulovitz, C. (eds.) (2006) *Enforcing the Rule of Law. Social Accountability in the New Latin American Democracies*. Pittsburgh, PA: University of Pittsburgh Press.

Porto, M. (2011) "The Media and Political Accountability." In T. Power and M. Taylor (eds.), *Corruption and Democracy in Brazil* (103–126). South Bend, IN: University of Notre Dame Press.

Porto, M. (2012) *Media Power and Democratization in Brazil. TV Globo and the Dilemmas of Political Accountability*. London: Routledge.

Power, T. and Taylor, M. (eds.) (2011) *Corruption and Democracy in Brazil*. South Bend, IN: University of Notre Dame Press.

Pujas, V. (2002) "Explaining the Wave of Scandal: The Exposure of Corruption in Italy, France, and Spain." In R. Kuhn and E. Neven (eds.), *Political Journalism: New Challenges, New Practices* (149–167). London: Routledge.

Raile, E., Pereira, C., and Power, T. (2011) "The Executive Toolbox: Building Legislative Support in a Multiparty Presidential Regime" *Political Research Quarterly*, vol. 64(2), 323–364.

Saad-Filho, A. (2013) "Mass Protests Under 'Left Neoliberalism': Brazil, June–July 2013" *Critical Sociology*, vol. 39(5), 657–669.

Seligson, M. (2002) "The Impact of Corruption on Regime Legitimacy: A Comparative Study of Four Latin American Countries" *The Journal of Politics*, vol. 64(2), 408–433.

Skidmore, T., Smith, P., and Green, J. (2010) *Modern Latin America*. Oxford: Oxford University Press.

Smulovitz, C. and Peruzzotti, E. (2000) "Social Accountability in Latin America" *Journal of Democracy*, vol. 11(4), 147–158.

Thompson, J.P. (2000) *Political Scandal: Power and Visibility in the Media Age*. Cambridge: Polity Press.

Tumber, H. and Waisbord, S. (2004) "Introduction" *American Behavioral Scientist*, vol. 47, 1143–1152.

Waisbord, S. (2000) *Watchdog Journalism in South America. News, Accountability, and Democracy*. New York: Columbia University Press.

Wiewiura, J. and Hendricks, V. (2017) "Informational Pathologies and Interest Bubbles: Exploring the Structural Mobilization of Knowledge, Ignorance, and Slack" *New Media and Society*, vol. 20(3), 1123–1138.

2 The Media System and Political Journalism of Brazil

This chapter provides background knowledge for readers unfamiliar with the Brazilian media system. First, the chapter sketches out the general market structure of news media and the national media ecology. Such an outline of the media system (Hallin and Mancini 2004, 2012) and its relation to the Brazilian state cannot, however, sufficiently explain the particular way that scandals emerge or come to be narrated in the sphere of media, and I will therefore review the literature concerning Brazilian political journalism and, in particular, the type of scandalizing coverage known as *denuncismo*. On the basis of this review, I will furthermore discuss the common framings of corruption found in scandal coverage and argue that the *denuncismo* in political journalism is supplanted in the Lava-Jato case by coverage attuned to official sources. This case and the impeachment process were both hotly contested issues and were framed and interpreted in a range of ways by various political actors. The largest news media, however, all displayed a propensity for framing the corruption scandals through the same set of frames, based on the prosecutor's disclosure of information. Because of that monolithic framing, this chapter argues that framing is ultimately unhelpful as a methodological approach for the study of this particular media system and scandal context. The argument and the media system outline prepares the ground for the following chapters.

I will briefly sketch out how the different genres and technologies are located in the landscape of Brazilian news media, in order to show which media are most important in political scandals, and to what extent these media reach the population. Before turning to online news media and television, I will start with the historical emergence of print media and the limited national reach of newspapers.

Brazil has had a considerably shorter history of a print media-based public sphere than many other nation-states, because of the nation's colonial origins and because the Portuguese crown banned printing until 1808 (Azevedo 2006: 92, Sodré 1977). In consequence, a public sphere, in the sense originally and powerfully analyzed by Habermas (1989 [1962]), did not develop in Brazil in a way comparable to European public spheres. Furthermore, slavery, poverty, and illiteracy stunted the growth of a market-based system of mass print media for decades, and even in post-colonial times, Brazil saw limited circulation of newspapers compared to other Western media systems (Albuquerque 2010, Hallin and Papathanassopoulos 2002).

Perhaps it is not meaningful to even speak of a "mass press" in the Brazilian case, given the low circulation relative to other nations. However, television eventually emerged as mass media in Brazil in the 1960s, and its reach overlapped and intersected with that of the Brazilian state, ruled by the military dictatorship. When the television technology was introduced in the 1950s, few had access and broadcasting did not significantly impact political events. Following the coup d'état of 1964, the military leaders came to see television as an instrument fit to edify and modernize the nation, and placed the cornerstones of the modern media system by investing in broadcasting infrastructure across the country. Thereby, the generals also paved the way for the first TV moguls of Brazil. When democracy was reintroduced in the 1980s, the Brazilian media system was dominated by the broadcasting conglomerates that prospered during the dictatorship, and the political elite, to this day, continues to have strong ties to media conglomerate owners.

The alliances between media and groups within the political elite is characteristic of the Brazilian media system's history. Newspapers were tied to individual political projects in the first half of the nineteenth century, and the crown maintained prerogatives for restricting freedom of press (Sodré 1977). In the second half of the nineteenth century, (relatively) large-scale industrial print runs of newspapers emerged (such as *Estado de São Paulo*, founded in 1875 as *A Província de São Paulo*; *Jornal do Brasil*, founded in Rio de Janeiro 1891; and *Correio do Povo*, founded in Porto Alegre in 1895). *O Globo* and *Folha de São Paulo* (then *Folha da Manhã*) were both founded in 1925 (Azevedo 2006: 93). The relative circulation of such newspapers reached an apogee in the 1950s but declined soon after, so that "[i]n the early fifties, the newspaper industry in Brazil was selling 110.6 copies per 1,000 people, a penetration figure that, by the end of the 1960's, had declined to 45.4 copies" (Carro 2016: 4).

The period of the military dictatorship (1964–1985) had other important newspapers than the above-mentioned, such as *Jornal do Brasil*, *Jornal do Comercio*, *A Notícia*, and *Correio da Manhã* (Sodré 1977), and weeklies such as *Revista da Semana*, *Fon-Fon*, *O Cruzeiro*, and *Manchete*. In face of censorship, an alternative press also developed, with *O Pasquim* leading the pack ahead of *Opinião*, *Repórter*, *Movimento*, and *Pif-Paf*, among others (Kucinski 1991). While a few survived the 1980s (*O Pasquim* until 1991, *Manchete* until 2000, and *Jornal do Brasil* until 2010 as print, continuing as a digital publication), the structural conditions of the media system during the dictatorship were obviously different than the period after the transition to democracy.

Simultaneous with the transition to democracy, the market of news shifted decisively toward television. UNESCO figures of newspaper circulation in 1996 were 40 per thousand Brazilians, the lowest of the countries considered by Hallin and Papathanassopoulos (2002: 177). By 2000, it was up to 60.6, but in 2009 down to 45.3 newspapers sold per 1,000 adult citizens (Albuquerque 2012: 78). Such a penetration ratio of print media of course depends on the population size, which complicates the picture. In the two decades from 1990–2010, while the economy, the middle-class, and the literacy rates grew, and while the newspapers doubled their print runs, the booming Brazilian population outgrew the newspapers:

[f]uelled in part by this new-found readership, paid circulation expanded at an average year-on-year growth rate of 4.42 percent between 1991 and 2000. However, the relatively fast pace of expansion achieved during the 1990's, would decrease significantly through the following decades. Through the 2000's and 2010's (so far), the country's population increased at a much faster pace than the paid-for dailies circulation. In fact, between 2011 and 2014, circulation shrunk at an average rate of 4.31 percent year-on-year, while the number of inhabitants in the country continued to rise. Consequently, newspaper readers are becoming an increasingly smaller share of the Brazilian population ... [Circulation figures] went further down to 36.7 copies in 2014.

(Carro 2016: 4)

Ratios between population and newspaper print runs notwithstanding, the recent absolute decline of print is visible when comparing figures from IVC (the Brazilian Institute for Verification of Circulation), in five-year intervals (2005, 2010 and 2015). The latest yearly figures have also been included in the table below.

The latest years of decline of already low-circulation papers have left Brazil with three traditional, prestigious, quality newspapers with national reach: *Folha de São Paulo* and *Estado de São Paulo* (located in the ideological space between liberal and conservative viewpoints), and the Rio-based *Jornal O Globo*, culturally liberal but orthodox in its economic editorial opinions (Fonseca 2005, Lattman-Weltman and Chagas 2016). In practice, relatively few newsstands in Rio de Janeiro offer the São Paulo papers and vice-versa. The economy-oriented *Valor Econômico*, created in 2000 by *Folha* and the Globo group (but recently bought out by Globo), accompanies this trio nationally, with a distinct appeal to the business elite (thus, it has considerably lower circulation of 40,000 printed copies). In an already small market by global standards, the print runs of the

Table 2.1 Print runs of Brazilian newspapers, 2005–2016

Newspaper	2005	2010	2015	2016
Folha de S. Paulo	309,383	295,558	175,441	154,700
O Globo	276,385	257,262	183,404	181,000
Extra	267,225	248,119	136,000	128,000
Estado de S. Paulo	231,165	212,844	149,241	146,000
Zero Hora	174,617	No data available	144,191	122,365

Sources: 2005 figures reported in Albuquerque 2012: 78; 2010 figures reported in Porto 2010: 113; 2015 and 2016 figures reported in Instituto Verificador de Circulação 2016. Figures for *Extra* in 2015 and 2016 reported in Rocha Filho 2016.

national newspapers have in effect been cut in half in the last two decades. The São Paulo-based newspapers have also cut staff lately in their newsrooms in consequence of the revenue loss from direct sales and the accompanying declining revenue from advertisement sales (Becker and Waltz 2017: 119, note 9).

In addition to the trio of nationally distributed newspapers, many daily newspapers are printed and circulated in regional capitals or states. These newspapers are often purely advertisement-financed, or very subsidized, and are referred to as "popular papers" by most scholars, because the focus of these papers are sports and celebrity content (Lattman-Weltman and Chagas 2016: 341). The landscape of regional newspapers changes frequently, and in 2016 comprised *Extra, Super Notícia, Meia Hora, Zero Hora, Aqui, Destak, Agora São Paulo, Diário Gaucho, Expresso* and *Metro São Paulo*. Though these papers account for a large part of the total national circulation, they rarely produce content about national politics themselves, but instead reproduce material from the news agencies of *Folha, Estado* and *Globo* (Abramo 2007). For that reason, the regional and popular papers are not included in the analyses of this book.

Despite the relatively large print runs of the market leaders among the popular newspapers, the weekly magazines of Brazil are probably the only print media which could be properly termed "mass" media. While the daily newspapers of Brazil in their (relatively late) heyday reached hundreds of thousand readers, the weekly magazines (especially *Veja*) have, at various points of modern media history, seen print runs of more than one million copies. *Veja* was founded in 1968, published by the Abril group, in the format of the US weekly magazine *Time*. The *Veja* editor and founder Mino Carta left the magazine in 1976 to launch *IstoÉ* (publicized by the Editora Trés [Porto 2010: 114]) as a competitor to *Veja*, and the Globo conglomerate launched a weekly magazine (*Época*) as another rival to *Veja* in 1998. For the last decades, the three have been the dominant weeklies, with political content inclining toward anti-PT views (Biroli and Miguel 2012: 39ff.).

On the opposite wing of the political spectrum, a few weekly and monthly magazines provide a counter-weight to *Veja* and the others. Mino Carta left *IstoÉ* in 1981 and a decade later founded yet another magazine, the *CartaCapital*. *CartaCapital* started as a monthly magazine in 1994 but has been weekly since 2001 and caters to a left-leaning audience in contrast to *Veja, Época,* and *IstoÉ*. In 2014–2016, *CartaCapital* had only a few competitors for that target audience, most prominently the printed magazines *Caros Amigos* and *Revista Piauí*, and the purely digital news sites with prominent blogs such as *Brasil 247, Jornal-GGN,* and *CartaMaior* (Carvalho and Albuquerque 2017).

Both the weekly magazines, the large national newspapers, and the main broadcasters also mirror their printed content online, albeit to different degrees. Currently, the news sites based on print newspapers and magazines all employ more or less the same business model: Reading a limited number of articles each month is free of charge for readers, but beyond that, each site maintains a paywall to avoid cannibalizing on their print products. The number of print subscriptions has recently been declining (since 2014 this trend has become visible across the board, see Instituto Verificador de Circulação 2016), and *Folha* paywall subscribers are now more numerous, for the first time ever, than the print subscribers (Folha de S. Paulo 2016).

The current market leader of the online news media is, if one tallies up visitors across websites, Globo. The conglomerate hosts the online news service G1 and the web version of GloboNews (the conglomerate's 24-hour news channel). Both reproduce, or "shovel" (a term defined as "repackaging content produced for other media" [Paterson and Domingo 2008: 7]) material from their news broadcasts onto the online platforms. The journal *O Globo* also shovels most material onto the site oglobo.globo.com, and the conglomerate's weekly magazine *Época* does the same. The most-visited Globo platform is the G1 site (Newman et al. 2015, 2017) which mostly relies on content about politics produced in Brasília and affiliated regional newsrooms. Many political news items on G1, especially commentary spots, are simply edited material from the Globo news program *Jornal das Dez* or from the evening broadcast *Jornal Nacional*.

Likewise, the main competitor of Globo, the broadcaster Rede Record produces shovelware on the R7 online platform by recycling material from their repertoire of programs. A similar pattern is true of the national market leader, *UOL*. The UOL platform has been the most visited Brazilian site in a decade (only surpassed in visits by Google, Facebook, and YouTube). Founded back in 1996 by the Grupo Folha, *UOL* was an early player on the stage. The political news of the UOL site is provided by direct links to the online version of *Folha de S. Paulo*. *Valor Econômico* and *Estado de S. Paulo*, like the rest of the national papers, maintain news sites with material mirrored from their print versions, but to some degree extend this by providing additional material that gets cut in the print version.

Possibly because of the links to *UOL*, *Folha* also boasted the largest number of page views in the peak period dealt with in this book, March 2016. According to IVC research, *Folha* reached just below 100 million page views in each week of March, with an apogee of 155 million weekly page views for the third week. The closest competitors that week were *Estado*'s news page *Estadão*, at 47 million page views, *ClicRBS* at 42 million, and *O Globo* at 39 million. After *UOL* and *Folha*, the most-accessed internet news sites were ones tied to the Globo conglomerate (in addition to the *O Globo* site, the news site G1, that used to be market-leader) (Newman et al. 2017: 107).

There are few born-online news media platforms in Brazil with access to the circles of political power, but a number of journalists have set up smaller news sites for political news, gossip, and punditry. This kind of entrepreneur journalists are usually former employees of the above-mentioned mainstream papers. Most notably, two former leading *Veja* journalists started the blog *O Antagonista* with specific focus on the Lava-Jato case, and they have managed to break news ahead of mainstream news a few times. The left-wing allied blogsites *Tijolaço* and *Jornal GGN*, through their political ties, also have access to sources within the political elite. In addition to these journalistic entrepreneurs, a few online media sites aggregate and produce news with political content that can claim national outreach: The prolific alternative news page *Midia NINJA* excel at grassroots reporting, commentary, and networked journalism, but although important in the younger audience bracket, this alt-news channel has not been in the leak-loop and does not get access to any political scoops (Becker and Waltz 2017). The American web media outlet *BuzzFeed* has lately been investing in the Brazilian market, setting up a local newsroom and working with the aim of getting traffic to the site through original journalistic content. What is true of other media contexts (Harder et al. 2017, Welbers et al. 2018) is also true of Brazil: legacy media outlets are able to influence the online news agenda to a considerable degree.

Radio is a less-used and less-researched news source in Brazil, but it still survives as a "niche" in certain segments and rural areas of Brazil (Meneguello 2010). Compared to other countries in a survey conducted by Reuters in 2014 (Newman et al. 2015), the Brazilian consumption of radio as a news source was neither high nor low: 39 percent of urban Brazilians say they get some news from the radio. Because of the regional limitations of the radio industry, radio as a news media has not been considered important in the literature dealing with contemporary politics (with exceptions such as Chaia 2001). Historically, radio stations were linked to regional political leaders, earning them the nick-name of *coroneis eletronicos* (Lima and Lopes 2007, Nunes Leal 1997, Motter 1994), although this term also refers to the owners of broadcast media.

As mentioned, the audience penetration of televised news surpassed that of printed news. As television, locally launched in 1950, grew into the mass media of the 1960s and 1970s, the military authorities actively subsidized and groomed the growing television industry as a nation-building, ideological instrument, and broadcast news became the primary source of popular knowledge about the political arena (Biroli et al. 2011, Biroli and Miguel 2013, Lima 2004, 2009, Miguel 1999).

TV Globo only had its hegemony challenged in the early 1980s (Matos 2012a, Porto 2012: 70) with Silvio Santos's Sistema Brasileiro de Televisão (SBT) and eventually, in the 1990s the Rede Record entered the scene, gradually conquering larger shares of viewership (from 4 percent of the evening slot audience in 1996 to 17 percent in 2008 [ibid.: 72]). Globo has remained comfortable at the top of the broadcast market for decades, while TV Record and SBT have been vying for second place (Porto 2010: 111). But despite this continued dominance of Globo after the transition to democracy, in the 25 years from 1989 to 2014, the media market has changed substantially: The broadcast market grew both in terms of producers and diversity, with satellite and cable services entering the market after the Cable Law of 1995. Furthermore, all of the main Brazilian outlets allied with multinational media groups in this period: Grupo Abril (that publishes Veja and a range of other magazines) teamed up with MTV, Rupert Murdoch's News Corporation partnered with Globo, and Folha's online portal UOL partnered with BBC (Azevedo 2006: 1010, Matos 2012b: 866).

Apart from the three national broadcasters, five groups are dominant in the five regions of Brazil: RBS (Rede Brasil Sul) to the South; Organizações Jaime

Câmara and the regional TV Anhanguera in the Central Brazil and Eastern regions; the network Rede Amazônica de Rádio e Televisão in the Northern part of the country; the Grupo Zahran is predominant in the large states of Mato Grosso and Mato Grosso do Sul; and, finally, the media market of northeastern Brazil is dominated by the Grupo Verdes Mares (Cabral 2017: 51).

In comparison to other media types, television today still maintains the position as central news source for the population. This is (surprisingly) the case even for the urban-dwelling Brazilians with relatively good access to internet: In the survey from 2014 (*n* = 2033), 91 percent of the respondents stated that they accessed news online in the past week, but 81 percent also accessed news from TV, while radio and print news was mentioned by 39 percent and 33 percent of the respondents, respectively (Newman et al. 2015: 51). In this group, 54 percent of the respondents self-identify as more digital news consumers than consumers of traditional radio/TV/print, while 12 percent define themselves as mostly relying on traditional news sources (which puts Brazil as the country with fewest traditional news consumers in the group of countries surveyed by Reuters). So, even in urban Brazil, which compared to other surveyed populations contain more "digital" than "traditional" news consumers, reliance on TV is still almost the world's highest. Among the surveyed countries in the 2014 survey, Brazil occupied the last position in relation to internet access, having 54 percent penetration of internet for the entire population in 2014, which grew to 68 percent by 2017 (Newman et al. 2017: 106).

Even today, with this rapidly rising rate of access to internet, television reaches outskirts of Brazil where few broadband cables run and no cellular operator has yet put up an antenna. Because of the geographical challenges, reliance on TV for news can thus be assumed to be even higher in the vast rural areas, since broadband coverage is scarce, print media circulation is low and, in some places, hard to come by. Partly for these reasons, 60 percent of the total advertisement expenditure in Brazil is still allocated in television, and for similar reasons, researchers such as Porto have previously concluded that "broadcast television remains the dominant medium" (Porto 2010: 110). Though this situation may change in response to the growing consumer demand for internet access and government policies to promote it, media studies of Western countries with already high-choice media environments have shown (e.g., Harder et al. 2017, Shehata and Strömbäck 2013) that internet media platforms still attend to the agenda put forth by legacy media, and that this agenda thus maintains strong links to the public agenda of surveyed users, despite individual consumption of media being more fragmented than in earlier decades.

The evening news *Jornal Nacional* of TV Globo has remained the major newscast of the national television market (Biroli and Miguel 2013: 88), usually with two to three times the audience of *Jornal da Record* and about five times the audience of *Jornal do SBT* (Ribeiro 2017: 113). *Jornal Nacional*, in 2015–2016, was usually the most watched or the second-most watched program among all Brazilian programs, in a field dominated by popular (semi-global) entertainment formats (e.g., *Big Brother*) and the Brazilian mainstay genre of *telenovelas*. Furthermore, TV Globo reigns in the domain of 24-hour news service with their GloboNews channel. GloboNews is paid cable news, however, and because the competing Record News is available on open frequencies, Record reaches a larger audience amongst the dedicated news channels.

The complex and non-linear interplay of the technological and institutional developments of the Brazilian media since the transition to democracy has thus yielded a system of news media dominated by a few powerful conglomerates, with much vertical as well as horizontal integration between different regional outlets and different media types. The political arena is systemically closed off to all but a few dozen journalists, working in the Congress, in the Presidential palace, or in the political beat of the major state capitals such as Rio de Janeiro and São Paulo. Because of this, only a few newsrooms control the gates of the political system, and the information admitted through these editorial processes propagates through networks of news agencies and inter-media shoveling. The limited range of news agencies and organizations are owned by only a handful families, in turn, and this certainly poses barriers to the kind of material that can be published or broadcast by these conglomerates, especially in cases where owners are aligned with specific advertisers or political elites (and here, the examples are many; see Lima 2004, Matos 2012a: 52ff.). Such considerations also restrict editors, whether by direct order or by indirect pressure. In sum, Brazilian journalists refer to limited number of editors, and, ultimately, the editors of the largest media outlets have only five masters. The concentration of media is an important background condition for the emergence of intra-elite strategies that utilize media exposés and scandals for political advantage.

Denuncismo and Scandals in the Political Journalism of Brazil

The end of censorship was without a doubt a major step toward a democratic public sphere in Brazil. However, accountability is not accomplished simply because of press freedom. In this section, I will discuss the contribution of media exposés in the production of accountability in Brazil, and review the problems identified in the literature on media disclosure of corruption. The production of scandals as a political weapon is introduced here, and the term *denuncismo* and the style of political reporting associated with *denuncismo* is discussed.

Due to the military censorship, corruption scandals were often subdued in the political news of daily papers and radio in the 1960s and 1970s. Even so, large newspapers sporadically "criticized the authoritarian regime and even investigated cases that involved government officials, but watchdog journalism remained the exception" (Waisbord 2000: 25). Some of the notable exceptions to the rule of silence in this period included exposés concerning the construction of Brasília and the Rio-Niteroi bridge. As João Figueiredo, the last general-president, relinquished control, and José Sarney stepped up as the first civilian president (taking over from Tancredo Neves, who died as president-elect, on the verge of being inaugurated), scandals began to fill front pages of Brazilian newspapers. This did not necessarily mean a greater commitment to democratic ideals, however; with the gradual *Abertura* (opening), denunciations in the press served as a political instrument rather than social accountability mechanism. Thus,

> Watchdog journalism implied a commitment to determined political causes rather than to the democratic ideal of checks and balances. It responded to the political orientations of owners and reporters and functioned as a strategy to advance specific agendas. It did not intend to wrap itself around the flag of balanced reporting and the defense of public good.
>
> (Ibid.: 26)

The first free and direct presidential elections after the military rule, in 1989, highlighted the theme of anti-corruption. The winning candidate, Fernando Collor de Mello, had projected an image as a "Hunter of Maharajas," fighting the fat cats of the corrupt public bureaucracy during his campaign, but, ironically, the Collor administration fell victim to investigative journalism through disclosure of corruption. Exposés in *Veja*, *IstoÉ*, and *Folha* eventually brought enough scathing evidence to light to trigger impeachment proceedings against Collor. Matos refers to this era as the "heyday of Brazilian investigative journalism," when newsroom began establishing structures for investigations (Matos 2012a: 108), although journalists still relied to a great extent on "promiscuous relationships" with inside sources with political motivation.

Such promiscuous relationships between political sources and journalists in the political beat has been termed *denuncismo* by several authors (Lattman-Weltman and Abreu 2001, Waisbord 2000: 103ff.). This particular style of producing political scandals is distinct from investigative journalism as it

> puts in evidence the proximity of the press to government sources. The political clout of a few sources, rarely quoted or only cryptically mentioned, is often sufficient to print stories, making it unnecessary to comb other potentially knowledgeable parties or to search for alternative sources of information…. [Critique alludes] to news organizations that claim to practice investigative journalism based on groundless accusations…. The lack of solid evidence undermines the credibility of denunciations.
>
> (Waisbord 2000: 103–104)

In its most extreme variant, this style of political journalism is based on off-the-record statements from sources who often have considerable interest in the production of scandalous news items. *Denuncismo* journalism may be dressed up to look like investigative journalism, but without the in-depth research and the critical eye to the vested interests of sources. Thus, *denuncismo* coverage may simply be the product of hasty "desk journalism," such as a single rumor or a newsroom phone call turned into an article without much substantiation.

The weight of *denuncismo*, on one hand, and investigative journalism, on the other, varied historically and according to the segments of the Brazilian media.

The weekly press has increasingly given space to *denuncismo* over the last decades (Nascimento 2013), but the use of off-the-record source material is certainly not restricted to that sector of the media. As demonstrated amply in the Lava-Jato case, a denunciation may gain much traction with the media when it is transformed and recycled in various institutional forms, especially when a denunciation initiates legal processes in the accountability institutions. In this way, slander and unsubstantiated denunciations may be perceived to get reinforcement through legitimate institutional processes, which allows journalists to continue reproducing the original denunciation without questioning the underlying motives of the denunciation.

After the heyday of scandals under Collor, Brazil witnessed a decline in the force of scandals relative to the political system:

> Political changes would only come about with "scandals," which were difficult to produce as they required a continued exposition of the denounced facts, with the constant addition of revelations and new elements. Above all, the changes required the national media, highly oligarchic, to act as a filter. The emblematic episode of 1993 was the Budget scandal, in which public funds were siphoned off through parliamentary amendments to the state budget. The scandal resulted in cassations of political mandates, renunciations as well as acquittals. It also resulted in a reform of the state budget process and the law of budget amendments. In time, even this already limited tool of denunciation lost force. As the opposition leader, PT reoriented its strategy and came to prioritize … electing Lula as president over social mobilization.… In the Cardoso administration, few denunciations really lived to become scandals that could provoke significant change in the system. The production of scandals began to depend on open confrontation between allied political forces. Denunciations only prospered and had institutional consequences when utilized by allies in public disputes.
>
> (Nobre 2013: 9, translation mine)

For example, the "Senhor X" scoop of *Folha* in 1997 revealed bribes in the passing of the re-election Constitutional amendment but did not result in charges or trials. The amendment paved the way for Cardoso's second mandate as president (Waisbord 2000: 42, 136). Like other scandals of the mid- and late-1990s, it is thus not included in the list of prominent political corruption scandals at the federal level compiled by Power and Taylor (2011: 2–3), perhaps because the denunciation was obstructed and eventually filed away. Nobre, in the quote above, suggests that this has to do with the role of PT in the political system at this moment, and the strategy of the party. In this period, PT grew to become the largest party in Congress, and while PT had usually engaged in denouncing political opponents, upon conquering federal power in Lula's fourth bid for the presidency in 2002, the tables turned against the party.

Though Lula, in the beginning of his first term as president, managed to establish a truce with most mainstream media (Kitzberger 2014: 26), the weekly

Veja remained staunchly opposed and chose to radically scandalize the PT. With the onset of the Mensalão scandal in 2005 (Damgaard 2015a, Michener and Pereira 2016), a landslide of media scandals hit PT and the negative coverage continued throughout the 2006 presidential campaign, as TV Globo predominantly framed the campaign in terms of PT's scandals (Mesquita 2014, Porto 2012: 95). Nascimento (2013) reviewed the denunciations publicized in *Veja* and the two competing weekly magazines *IstoÉ* and *Época* in the six months preceding each campaign season of presidential elections (in the period 1989–2010), and he concluded "that the average number of stories containing denunciations almost tripled since 2002" (Nascimento 2013: 68), going from a weekly total average of 0.3 denunciation items to 1.3 and 1.5 in the 2002–2010 period (ibid.: 72). The focus on corruption scandals after the Mensalão scandal was not restricted to *Veja* or *Globo*, as other journals such as *Folha* eventually joined the bandwagon (Biroli and Mantovani 2014: 207).

The charge of *denuncismo* is still heard in Brazil today, but the problem of the source-journalist relations and facile accusations has been relocated, in a sense. Since the Mensalão scandal, another type of textual device than the anonymized source has been taking center stage in corruption coverage: the official document. In the prestigious newspapers' coverage of the Lava-Jato cases, institutional sources and the paper trail of official investigations are exceedingly prominent. This is perhaps the media professionals' institutional response to the charge of *denuncismo*, or perhaps it is a tendency fostered because of accountability institutions' communication strategies, as discussed in the next chapter.

The increased focus on corruption scandals, especially in the PT administration, has possibly come about as a strategy to maintain competitiveness for the Brazilian news media. As described above, the few national newspapers left have faced pressure by web media and various popular and free newspapers in metropolitan areas. To counter the economic pressures on this changing news media market, the three large daily papers have strengthened their political profile in the last decade or so, bringing about what Lattman-Weltman has termed *repartidarização* – the resurgence of the party press (Lattman-Weltman and Chagas 2016). With a stronger focus on political news, *Estado, Folha* and *O Globo* have tried to distinguish themselves from newspapers with more focus on celebrity, sports and quotidian news. This move has been to secure the share of the news consumers actually willing to pay for quality news, since the advertisement revenue of quality newspapers is moving toward internet and ad-financed free papers (Carro 2016: 20). In this media ecology, the production of scandals has become quintessential, and I will now briefly explore how denunciations of corruption are shaped and framed textually in Brazilian scandals.

Writing and Framing Corruption Scandals

If investigative journalism and *denuncismo*, at different times, became distinct but real forces in the Brazilian political landscape, it is necessary to have a closer look at the way such denunciations of corruption play out in media texts. We need to ask what actions are denounced as corrupt, and what kinds of acts are excluded from the definition of corruption? These questions take us into the territory of media studies known as framing theory, because corruption cannot be defined a priori, outside of the cultural context – nor, in the study of a scandal, outside of the media context. Information about political action is not simply information about either legitimate politics or corruption. Rather, some aspects of political action come to signify transgression of norms through particular textual strategies that highlight some perspective upon the issue. This means that "corruption" is not a static term but continuously negotiated discursively and legally.

The distinctions of what political corruption "is" differs from society to society. Indeed, the concept of corruption has evolved for millennia: In antique and classic formulations (such as Polybius or Machiavelli) corruption was conceived as particular state forms or regimes. More recently, political theory of the last four decades (originating with Nye, 1967; see Lennerfors, 2008) frequently defines corruption through a distinction between public and private roles. But the precise delimitation of public interest, collective interests, and private interests is always negotiated and contested, even in the discourse of apparently hegemonic media outlets. Thus, the concept of "corruption," depending on cultural norms, values, and negotiation models, cannot easily be subtracted from its context. Political corruption is not simply "out there," it is something defined and negotiated by a multitude of actors – by the law, but also by convention, practice, pragmatic concerns, language, and socialized norms of both the media system and the political system in question. Whether or not an act is "really" corrupt is of course a relevant question to some disciplines, law foremost of these. However, legal definitions of corruption, important as they may be, are often eclipsed in the modes of critique springing from intense coverage that characterizes scandals (Damgaard 2015). Power and Taylor (2011: 13) have similarly argued that research into corruption and illegality walks a fine line, especially in Brazil, and that it is necessary to account for both formally corrupt behavior as well as questionable, informal practices.

In this book, I set out from the premise that processes of negotiating meaning in scandals start with media's disclosure of corruption. When disclosed information indicates corruption, a journalist and his superiors (copy editors, headline and web editors, etc.) have to make a number of choices concerning their framing. They must consider the veracity of the information, the reliability of the source, the possible defense put up by the accused; in other words, the gatekeepers of the media consider varying versions of a contested reality. Media professionals consider disclosed information about corruption on the basis of background assumptions about what corruption "is" and the particular framework or understanding of politics underlining the media system into which they are embedded. Thus, news texts in corruption scandals normally work by drawing upon a well-established discursive formation wherein certain kinds of political action are considered transgressive or corrupt. By invoking these existing discourses of corruption, the coverage of a scandal also produces the reality of corruption, through "hard" news as well as public debate, public condemnations of corruption, and defenses of political actions. Together, all of this assembles a media event, which in and of itself can influence political reality (Breit 2011). As stated by John Fiske,

in a postmodern world we can no longer rely on a stable relationship or clear distinction between a "real" event and its mediated representation. Consequently, we can no longer work with the idea that the "real" is more important, significant, or even "true" than the representation. A media event, then, is not a mere representation of what happened, but it has its own reality, which gathers up into itself the reality of the event that may or may not have preceded it.

(Fiske 1994: 2)

Although I will refrain from using the concept of media event here, the insight of Fiske is an important condition of this book. Like many other studies (Anders and Nuijten 2009, Breit 2011, Damgaard 2015, Gupta 1995, Kajsiu 2014, Koechlin 2013, Lennerfors 2008), this study of corruption scandals is essentially socially-constructivist, and even relativist in its approach to corruption. This means that I will refrain from a priori judging whether one or the other act was corrupt, but instead focus on the allegation of corruption, on the denunciation, and the system-level results of this discursive activity. That move locates this book within the current of social constructivism, although it deals with political events from a realist position. This constructivist perspective means that there is more sense in registering the particular cultural repertoire of actions encompassing corruption in the actual discourse than in philosophical or political theory, thereby avoiding embedded academic ethnocentrism in the delimitation of the research object. Within this constructivist perspective, the corruption definition used here is entirely pragmatic and relational, rather than universal and substantial.

I will argue that a news text may establish various frames that convey an assessment of some political action, but if the assessment is to be understood as scandalous by audiences, the news text must indicate a transgression. Even when not explicit, such labelling can be detected intertextually or in the interpretations offered by sources presented in the news text. This could be prosecutors, whistleblowers, or commentators of various kinds, calling the transgressive action into question, representing it as morally debased and detrimental to one or more societal sub-systems (which could be political-institutional systems, the economy, the rule of law, or national development) (Damgaard 2015: 414). So, drawing upon the specific local discursive formation, which among other things outlines what concepts such as "politics," "public," and "private" signify, news texts then label a particular action as corrupt.

Labelling actions as corrupt brings me to the concept of framing. In newsrooms as well as in journalism studies, the intentional selectivity involved in packaging information for a media text is conventionally termed "framing." That is, both researchers and practitioners explicitly work with frames, albeit in distinct ways. A news media frame can be considered as both a "cognitive device used in information encoding, interpreting, and retrieving" and as a "strategy of constructing and processing news discourse" (Pan and Kosicki 1993: 57). In a classic definition proposed by Robert Entman, framing means to "select some aspects of a perceived reality and make them more salient in a communicating text, in such a way as to promote a particular problem definition, causal interpretation, moral evaluation and/or treatment recommendation for the item described" (Entman 1993: 52, emphasis removed). The academic perspectives on framing range from cognitive to constructivist approaches across discourse and symbolic environments. Some scholars therefore broaden Entman's definition, viewing frames more broadly as "structures that draw boundaries, set up categories, define some ideas as out and others in, and generally operate to snag related ideas in their net in an active process" (Reese 2007: 150). Entman and other researchers (e.g., Sniderman and Theriault 2004) predict the relationship between media frames and audience opinions. I leave the question of frames and opinion for Chapter 5, in order to continue considerations of the discursive representations of corruption in Brazilian news texts, especially the definition and attributes made salient.

In the Lava-Jato scandal, the standard reporting pattern found in the sampled Brazilian newspapers (as well as in broadcasting news) puts an emphasis on legal processes. Starting with the lead of the article, or the first sentence presented by a news anchor, the average news item assembles a story from three elements: a politician under suspicion, an accountability process in a legal arena, and a judicial or investigating actor. The basic lead or headline reads "Politician X has been indicted by the public prosecutor Y before Court Z in the Lava-Jato." While the pattern has innumerable variations, it underpins a significant number of news items.

In terms of information flows, what lies behind the emergence of this standard framing of corruption is not exactly the personal intervention of prosecutor Y, but rather that various accountability actors have begun publicizing much information about investigations and legal processes and feeding this directly to the inbox of journalists. Transforming tedious processual information into readable news stories, journalists will often utilize the metonymic relationship between specific institutional actors (say, Prosecutor-General Rodrigo Janot) and the accountability institution moving along some legal process or other. Individual political actors are normally the targets of such processes in consequence of the criminal code, while only a few processes charge the political parties of Brazil. Since the coverage of corruption is largely based on legal processes, the majority of the coverage frames corruption as an individual, rather than systemic problem. This also holds true for news items concerning denunciations that have cropped up in testimonies and plea bargains.

The journalistic framing replicates the indictment strategy of the prosecuting authorities. A similar pattern was found in *Folha*'s coverage of the Mensalão trial, where Biroli and Mantovani (2014) concluded that although the newspaper included scattered points of view opposed to the charges of the prosecutors, such as the defendants' reactions and the defense lawyers' arguments, *Folha* only presented the events of the trial through the framing of PT as the perpetrator and mastermind behind the scandal – mirroring the indictment.

The narrative projected by Brazilian news on corruption can often be reduced to this simplistic schema of suspicion or denouncement being contested in various arenas – courts and politics foremost – and this yields what can be termed a *responsibility frame* in the sense proposed by Iyengar (1990). Within Iyengar's variation of framing theory, one would predict that this kind of news is likely to be construed by audience members as signaling the individual culpability of the mentioned politician. In theory, this kind of framing would make the personal responsibility of political actors salient, rather than the systemic problems of impunity and incentives for rent-seeking in the political systems.

Opposing frames exist, of course, in the entrepreneurial media outlets and even in the mainstream media, but they are rarely found here as the main framing device. The political importance and use of such conflicting frames (or counterframes) has been explored in non-scandal contexts (e.g., Chong and Druckman 2013). Classic experimental studies have shown how framings can be used to radically alter audience responses to messages with the same informational content (Kahneman and Tversky 1979). Although it would be possible to study the relative weight of frames in the sample texts, researchers can hardly gauge the effect of the different frames found in the media, because it is not possible to artificially isolate the audience (Sniderman and Theriault 2004).

Summing up, the frames deployed by journalists and editors of the mainstream Brazilian media treated in this book are structured around the prosecutor's perspective. This means that what is defined as corrupt and what is left out of that category mostly hinges upon the legal processes and official documents. While opinion pieces and brief spurts of investigative journalism may sometimes expand the vision of the political arena, counterframes are less frequent. Because of this, it would be difficult to structure research around the effects of frames, since audiences only infrequently encounter such frames in the mainstream media. Furthermore, in the case of the Lava-Jato probe and the impeachment process, it is highly unlikely that any one journalistic framing would produce any effect at all, since the entwined scandals were so central to the contemporary public debate of Brazil, and audience members would be likely to have formed opinions before encountering specific texts. So, due to the stereotypical pattern of reporting, which is arguably founded upon the information-gathering procedure of the journalists in the political beat of Brasília, I contend that it is not fruitful to use framing theory independently to examine or explain reception effects of the Lava-Jato coverage. Still, the emergence of a hegemonic, unidirectional frame, common to several influent media actors, is interesting in itself. The following two chapters will explore two of the background conditions for the emergence of this frame, namely the leaking of information from investigations and the continuous reproduction of corruption denunciations through the steady grinding of the various accountability institutions of Brazil. These explorations can, in part, explain why the frames tend to converge and uniformly mirror the prosecutors' indictments.

References

Albuquerque, A. de (2010) "A modernização autoritária do jornalismo Brasileiro" *Alceu*, vol. 10(20), 100–115.

Albuquerque, A. de (2012) "On Models and Margins." In D. Hallin and P. Mancini (eds.), *Comparing Media Systems beyond the Western World* (72–95). Cambridge: Cambridge University Press.

Anders, G. and Nuijten, M. (eds.) (2009) *Corruption and the Secret of Law: A Legal Anthropological Perspective*. Aldershot: Ashgate.

Azevedo, F.A. (2006) "Mídia e democracia no Brasil: relações entre o sistema de mídia e o sistema politico" *Opinião Pública*, vol. 12(1), 88–113.

Becker, B. and Waltz, I. (2017) "Mapping Journalistic Startups in Brazil: An Exploratory Study." In L. Robinson, J. Schulz, and A. Williams (eds.), *Brazil: Media from the Country of the Future* (113–135). Bingley: Emerald Publishing.

Biroli, F. and Mantovani, D. (2014) "A parte que me cabe nesse julgamento: A Folha de S. Paulo na cobertura ao processo do Mensalão" *Opinião Pública*, vol. 20(2), 204–218.

Biroli, F., Miguel, L.F., and Mota, F. (2011) "Mídia, eleições e pesquisa de opinião no Brasil (1989–2010): um mapeamento da presença das pesquisas na cobertura eleitoral" *Revista Compolítica*, vol. 1(1), 67–89.

Biroli, F. and Miguel, L.F. (2012) "Orgulho e preconceito: a 'objetividade' como mediadora entre o jornalismo e seu público" *Opinião Pública*, vol. 18(1), 22–43.

Biroli, F. and Miguel, L.F. (2013) "Meios de comunicação, voto e conflito político no Brasil" *Revista Brasileira das Ciências Sociais*, vol. 28(81), 77–95.

Breit, E. (2011) *On the Discursive Construction of Corruption. A Critical Analysis of Media Texts*. Publication #227. Helsinki: Svenska Handelshögskolan and Hanken School of Economics.

Cabral, E.D.T. (2017) "Mídia Concentrada no Brasil: Até Quando?" *Revista LatinoAmericana de Ciencias de la Comunicación*, vol. 13(24), 49–59.

Carro, R. (2016) "Brazilian Newspapers: The Risk of Becoming Irrelevant," Research paper, Reuters Institute for the study of Journalism. Retrieved from https://reutersinstitute.politics.ox.ac.uk/people/rodrigo-berndt-carro-independent-journalist.

Carvalho, E.M. and Albuquerque, A. de (2017) "A Blogosfera Progressista e a releitura do modelo de jornalismo independente no Brasil." In C.J. Napolitano, M.M. Vicente, and M.C. Soares (eds.), *Comunicação e cidadania política* (305–323). São Paulo: Cultura Acadêmica.

Chaia, V. and Teixeira, M. (2001) "Democracia e Escândalos Políticos" *São Paulo Perspectivas*, vol. 15(4), 62–75.

Chong, D. and Druckman, J. (2013) "Counterframing Effects" *The Journal of Politics*, vol. 75(1), 1–16.

Damgaard, M. (2015) "Multiple Margins and Mediatized Transgression" *Ephemera – Theory and Politics in Organization*, vol. 15(2), 411–434.

Entman, R. (1993) "Framing: Toward Clarification of a Fractured Paradigm" *Journal of Communication*, vol. 43, 51–58.

Fiske, J. (1994) *Media Matters: Everyday Culture and Political Change*. Minneapolis: University of Minnesota Press.

Folha de S. Paulo (2016) "Folha é o 1° jornal brasileiro a ter circulação digital maior do que a impressa" *Folha de S. Paulo*, published on September 25, 2016. Retrieved from www1.folha.uol.com.br/mercado/2016/09/1816633-folha-e-o-1-jornal-do-pais-a-ter-circulacao-digital-maior-do-que-a-impressa.shtml.

Gupta, A. (1995) "Blurred Boundaries: The Discourse of Corruption" *American Ethnologist*, vol. 22(2), 375–402.

Habermas, J. (1989 [1962]) *The Structural Transformation of the Public Sphere*. Cambridge, MA: MIT Press.

Hallin, D. and Mancini, P. (2004) *Comparing Media Systems. Three Models of Media and Politics*. Cambridge: Cambridge University Press.

Hallin, D. and Mancini, P. (eds.) (2012) *Comparing Media Systems beyond the Western World*. Cambridge: Cambridge University Press.

Hallin, D. and Papathanassopoulos, S. (2002) "Political Clientelism and the Media: Southern Europe and Latin America in Comparative Perspective" *Media, Culture & Society*, vol. 24, 175–195.

Harder, R., Sevenans, J., and Van Aelst, P. (2017) "Intermedia Agenda Setting in the Social Media Age: How Traditional Players Dominate the News Agenda in Election Times" *The International Journal of Press/Politics*, vol. 22(3), 275–293.

Instituto Verificador de Circulação (2016) *Circulação de jornais diarias*, 2015, 2016. Retrieved from www.ivcbrasil.org.br – reproduced in Poder360, retrieved from www.poder360.com.br/wp-content/uploads/2017/04/circulacao-IVC-dez2015-dez2016.png.

Iyengar, S. (1990) "Framing Responsibility for Political Issues: The Case of Poverty" *Political Behavior*, vol. 12(1), 19–40.

Kahneman, D. and Tversky, A. (1979) "Prospect Theory: An Analysis of Decision under Risk" *Econometrica*, 47(2), 263–292.

Kajsiu, B. (2014) *A Discourse Analysis of Corruption: Instituting Neoliberalism against Corruption in Albania, 1998–2005*. New York: Routledge.

Kitzberger, P. (2014) "Demands for Media Democratisation and the Latin American 'New Left'." Hamburg: GIGA German Institute of Global and Area Studies.

Koechlin, L. (2013) *Corruption as an Empty Signifier*. Leiden: Brill.

Kucinski, B. (1991) *Jornalistas e Revolucionários nos tempos da imprensa alternativa*. São Paulo: Editora Pagina Aberta.

Lattman-Weltman, F. and Abreu, A.A. de (2001) "Controles Midiáticos: Investigação e Denuncismo na Construção da Visibilidade Pública Democrática." Paper presented at ANPOCS 25th conference at Caxambu, Minas Gerais, October 17, 2001.

Lattman-Weltman, F. and Chagas, V. (2016) "Mercado Futuro: A Economia Política da (Re)Partidarização da Imprensa no Brasil" *Dados*, Revista de Ciências Sociais, vol. 59(2), 323–356.

Lennerfors, T.T. (2008) *The Vicissitudes of Corruption. Degeneration – Transgression – Jouissance*. PhD thesis, Royal Institute of Technology, Stockholm.

Lima, V.A. da (2004) "Sete teses sobre mídia e política no Brasil" *Revista USP*, São Paulo, no. 61, 48–57.

Lima, V.A. da (2009) "Revisitando as sete teses sobre mídia e política no Brasil" *Comunicação & Sociedade*, vol. 30(51), 13–37.

Lima, V.A. de and Lopes, C.A. (2007) "Rádios Comunitárias: Coronelismo Eletrônico de novo tipo." *Observatorio de Imprensa*. Retrieved from www.observatoriodaimprensa.com.br/download/Coronelismo_eletronico_de_ novo_tipo.pdf.

Matos, C. (2012a) *Media and Politics in Latin America. Globalization, Democracy and Identity*. London: I.B. Tauris.

Matos, C. (2012b) "Media Democratization in Brazil: Achievements and Future Challenges" *Critical Sociology*, vol. 38(6), 863–876.

Meneguello, R. (2010) "Aspectos do desempenho democrático: Estudo sobre a adesão à democracia e avaliação do regime." In J. Moisés (ed.), *Democracia e confiança: Por que os cidadãos desconfiam das instituições públicas?* (201–236). São Paulo: Edusp.

Michener, G. and Pereira, C. (2016) "A Great Leap Forward for Democracy and the Rule of Law? Brazil's Mensalão Trial" *Journal of Latin American Studies*, vol. 48, 477–507.

Miguel, L.F. (1999) "Mídia e Eleições: A Campanha de 1998 na Rede Globo" *Dados*, vol. 42(2), 253–276.

Motter, P. (1994) *A batalha invisível da constituinte: Interesses privados versus caráter público da radiodifusão no Brasil.* Master's thesis. Brasília: Universidade de Brasília.

Nascimento, S. (2013) "Reportagens com denúncias na imprensa brasileira: análise de duas décadas da predileção por mostrar problemas" *Verso e Reverso*, vol. 65, 68–76.

Newman, N., Levy, D., and Nielsen, R.K. (2015) *Reuters Institute Digital News Report 2015.* Oxford: Reuters Institute for the Study of Journalism, University of Oxford.

Newman, N., Fletcher, R., Kalogeropoulos, A., Levy, D., and Nielsen, R.K. (2017) *Reuters Institute Digital News Report 2017.* Oxford: Reuters Institute for the Study of Journalism, University of Oxford.

Nobre, M. (2013) *Choque da Democracia. Razões da Revolta.* São Paulo: Companhia das Letras.

Nunes Leal, V. (1997) *Coronelismo, Enxada e voto.* Rio de Janeiro: Nova Fronteira.

Nye, J. (1967) "Corruption and Political Development: A Cost-Benefit Analysis" *American Political Science Review*, vol. 61(2), 417–427.

Pan, Z. and Kosicki, G. (1993) "Framing as Strategic Action in Public Deliberation." In S. Reese, O. Gandy, and A. Grant (eds.), *Framing Public Life: Perspectives on Media and Our Understanding of the Social World* (35–65). London: Routledge.

Paterson, C. and Domingo, D. (eds.) (2008) *Making Online News: The Ethnography of New Media Production.* New York: Peter Lang.

Porto, M. (2010) "The Changing Landscape of Brazil's News Media." In D. Levy and R.K. Nielsen (eds.), *The Changing Business of Journalism and its Implications for Democracy* (107–124). Oxford: Reuters Institute for the Study of Journalism, University of Oxford.

Porto, M. (2012) *Media Power and Democratization in Brazil. TV Globo and the Dilemmas of Political Accountability.* London: Routledge.

Power, T. and Taylor, M. (eds.) (2011) *Corruption and Democracy in Brazil.* South Bend, IN: University of Notre Dame Press.

Reese, S. (2007) "The Framing Project: A Bridging Model for Media Research Revisited" *Journal of Communication*, vol. 57, 148–157.

Ribeiro, E.F. (2017) "A redução da audiência da televisão aberta brasileira" *Temática*, vol. 13(6), 109–126.

Rocha Filho, A. (2016) "Jornalismo popular na era digital: a experiência do Extra," Paper presented at II Simpósio Internacional Jornalismo em Ambientes Multiplataforma, November 21, 2016, ESPM, São Paulo.

Shehata, A. and Strömbäck, J. (2013) "Not (Yet) a New Era of Minimal Effects: A Study of Agenda Setting at the Aggregate and Individual Levels" *The International Journal of Press/Politics*, vol. 18(2), 234–255.

Sniderman, P. and Theriault, S. (2004) "The Structure of Political Argument and the Logic of Issue Framing." In W. Saris and P. Sniderman (eds.), *Studies in Public Opinion: Attitudes, Nonattitudes, Measurement Error, and Change* (133–165). Princeton, NJ: Princeton University Press.

Sodré, N.W. (1977) *História da imprensa brasileira*. São Paulo: Graal.

Waisbord, S. (2000) *Watchdog Journalism in South America. News, Accountability, and Democracy*. New York: Columbia University Press.

Welbers, K., Atteveldt, W. van, Kleinnijenhuis, J., and Ruigrok, N. (2018) "A Gatekeeper among Gatekeepers" *Journalism Studies*, vol. 19(3), 315–333.

3 Leaks and Their Effect in Media and on Politics

Disclosure of corruption among political leaders is sure to catch the attention of any independent media system. Corruption scandals are not only excellent media material, but also the focus of intense interest in international governance. The fight against corruption has thrust the term transparency to the top of the priority lists of many international organizations and corporations, and global charters, frameworks and compliance policies are proliferating. This global focus on corruption as the evil twin of good governance does not always result in successful anti-corruption initiatives and efficient court cases that bring culprits to justice, however. Even if denounced for corruption, individuals holding positions of trust and public authority, as appointed or elected representative of citizens, can still in many cases count on impunity, due to political protection or judicial sluggishness. In other cases, scandalizing information is disclosed to great effect, when public officeholders are forced to face the pressure of courts, their own constituencies and the electorate in general.

Whether resulting in sanctions or not, the disclosure of information about corruption can be a political game-changer, even if that information turns out to be inaccurate or false. Scandals may thus wreak havoc in consolidated as well as emergent democracies, and the effects of corruption scandals, of disclosing transgressions and alleging moral misconduct, go beyond the immediate horizons of individual punishment or impunity. In this chapter, the way that such disclosure of scathing information plays out is explored. I will argue that the disclosure of corruption constitutes an especially powerful and dramatic style of interaction between judiciary, political, and media systems. Leaks of information, in particular, can be harnessed by political and institutional actors to great effect. In a fast-paced media environment, leaks fundamentally erode journalistic and editorial control and, paradoxically, provide powerful (and potentially anti-democratic) access to the media for those institutional actors with inside knowledge. These actors are shrouded as sources with vested interests, while the media outlets frame disclosure as ostensibly increasing transparency.

The chapter will proceed by first defining leaks and discussing the control of information flows in Brazilian public spheres. Subsequently, the chapter provides a description of the particular leaks that flowed from the investigations of Brazil's Lava-Jato case into the sphere of national media. The effects of these leaks in the political and judicial system are then tracked through a simplified process-tracing methodology. The outcomes traced with this methodology are relevant to research into various aspects of political systems, including the coalition formation (Balán 2011, 2014) and congressional veto-players in presidential systems (Pérez-Liñán and Rodríguez-Raga 2009), judicial intervention in the political domain (Hirschl 2008, Tate and Vallinder 1995), presidential breakdowns (Llanos and Marsteintredet 2010) as well as Latin American media-government relations (Kitzberger 2014).

The goal is not to measure how much scandalizing leaks influence political support for specific actors (Maier 2011) or overall regime legitimacy (Seligson 2002), but to identify the specific contributions of the leaks to the regime change in Brazil in 2016, including the impeachment of Dilma Rousseff and the various legal processes against her successor, Michel Temer. Thereby, this chapter expands the insights of Arantes (2002, 2011) and others (Chaia and Teixeira 2000, Porto 2011) concerning the media-savvy Brazilian prosecutors' dissemination strategies by exploring what consequences the disclosure of corruption generated besides investigations and trials.

On the background of this material, several theoretical questions emerge: How is it that disclosed information is turned into knowledge in the public sphere? How is truth determined and influenced by the mode of disclosure? What is the relationship between leaks on political corruption and the proliferation of transparency discourses in recent decades? The discussion of these questions, in the concluding sections, help explain how leaks provoke institutional rupture and possibly destabilize democratic institutions.

Existing Research on International Leaks and Brazilian Vazamentos

In this section, I will introduce some of the existing academic views about the potential democratic benefits of leaks. This means looking at both the current international research into leaks (in the sense of large amounts of data) and the research on politics of sources and information control. This section provides a background for understanding why and how leaks of information in corruption "skip the gates," that is, quickly reach the headlines of national media. The journalistic mechanisms of boundary control, which requires not only selecting the information that enters public spheres, but also fact-checking and source-checking, are challenged by the rush of the scoop when secret and scathing information is disclosed. Leaks thereby relocate some of the power of information control normally held by media, and this means that watchdogs may turn into lapdogs (Porto 2011).

The current international literature about leaks is increasingly tuned into the disclosure of very large amounts of documents; a trend probably pushed by the emergence of data storage and sharing technologies. During the past decade, leaks of vast amounts of scathing information have reached international public spheres with increasing frequency, visibility, and impact. Targeting national elites, diplomacy, and war efforts, leaks such as the Panama Papers, the Paradise Papers, and especially the prominent WikiLeaks have been lauded by scholars for fostering accountability (Russell and Waisbord 2017), for providing a corrective for imperfect institutions, a "critical safety valve" (Benkler 2014: 303) in governmental branches, and for championing free speech (Wahl-Jørgensen 2014).

The NSA documents leaked by Edward Snowden have recently been discussed by Heikkilä and Kunelius (2017), as well as Waisbord and Russell (2017), while the history of the Wikileaks platform is detailed and discussed by Benkler (2014), Chadwick (2013), Coleman (2014), Fuchs (2011), Munro (2016), and Wahl-Jørgensen (2014). Apart from the praise of the democratic potential, many of these authors also acknowledge that such a complex and hybrid assemblage of new and old media technologies and logics has very uncertain consequences in addition to the obvious potential for transparency and resistance. I will highlight the perspective of Russell and Waisbord, Benkler, and Wahl-Jørgensen, who view leaks of large amounts of data as an important new phenomenon in democracies. This kind of leak represents a novel way of doing investigative journalism, as well as a new integration between politics and media – an integration that potentially can remedy some of the flaws of accountability in modern politics (Benkler 2014).

The novelty, first off, lies in the new organizational and institutional structures emerging in order to accommodate the scale of leaks: In April 2016, the consortium behind the Panama Papers revamped the WikiLeaks model of the networked workload between freelance journalists, national quality papers and the technological aspects of servers, mass storage and encryption (Cabra and Kissane 2016, The International Consortium of Investigative Journalists 2016). The consortium of journalists disclosed the financial actions of scores of banks and hundreds of powerful and rich individuals (Drezner 2016), while the related disclosure of the Paradise Papers, publicized in November 2017, turned public the tax evasion practices of the offshore law firm Appleby. A similar combination of journalism, data leaks, and cross-media collaborations saw the light in the Football Leaks driven by the European Collaborative Investigations in late 2016. Large data dumps, in this way, have recently been assimilated by journalistic communities and editorial practices, with an organizational setup emerging along with the leaks. High-profiled Western media actors (such as the *Guardian*, *Der Spiegel*, and *El País*) have converged upon a kind of consensus and modified the constitutive framework of journalism and the production of news to manage not only the data leaks and the economic distribution of working hours, but also the economic gains of scoops strategically placed in breaking-news cycles.

Second, large-scale leaks challenge theoretical distinctions between journalistic material and, for a lack of a better word, data. Leaks exist at the border between "raw data," if there ever was such a thing, and a more classic, journalistically curated disclosure of previously hidden information. The border is blurring partly because of the divergent ideals of instantly leaking big data dumps contra journalistically curating the material as news. WikiLeaks (e.g., in the leaks of the 251,287 diplomatic cable message) originally preached radical openness built upon an open-source mindset, while other, later leak cases, such as the Panama and Paradise Papers, were disseminated in accordance with a journalistic logic. This was already a tension in the early days of WikiLeaks (Chadwick 2013), when WikiLeaks produced a video (the *Collateral Murder* video, in two versions), which is more of a documentary based on leaked footage than a leak in itself. Despite the buzz of big and raw data, researchers need to consider where to draw the line: Does the slow trickle of leads and clues followed by investigative journalists in the Watergate scandal count as a leak – or was that merely a source disclosing information and telling the *Washington Post* journalists where to look? No yardstick exists to measure leaks.

In the Lava-Jato case, anyway, both small-scale leaks and large data dumps have been disclosed, and both kinds have had political consequences. Whether or not off-the-record tips from official inside sources are theoretically distinct from data dumps of gigabytes worth of documents, and no matter the degree of journalistic pre-production, the analysis needs to account for both types, because the principal effect of a leak in public spheres cannot be predicted by either megabyte size or editing processes.

The academic literature of Brazil dealing with journalist-source relations (Waisbord 2000: 93ff.) and the public prosecutors' media relations (Arantes 2002, Porto 2011) have mostly mentioned small-scale leaks (*vazamentos*): Brazilian journalists have not seldom received access to elements of investigations from official sources, in off-the-record interviews (ibid.: 118) or even in concerted actions where whistle-blowing testimonies are recorded and transmitted live by a broadcaster (Arantes 2002: 166, 211). Investigative journalism of the 1990s (in Brazil and internationally) was rarely executed on the basis of massive databases of secret documents, however.

Today, with the introduction of cheap storage devices and processing power to facilitate searches across large swathes of documents, journalists have been given new tools to produce investigative journalism, or, rather, journalism-about-investigations (which is perhaps superseding the former, e.g., Porto 2011: 118). Journalists may thus document and demonstrate facts of corruption cases to a degree previously unheard of. A gradual opening of the judicial system has meant that a number of journalists are allowed access to a subset of non-classified case files in the same digital content management systems used by police agents, lawyers and judges, in order to cover cases. The classification of case material by courts is thus an extremely important gate, and the decisions about public access vary on a case-to-case-basis. The task-force of the Lava-Jato case and the regional court of Curitiba maintain a policy of publicizing any and all material in cases as long as that publication cannot impair investigations (Albuquerque 2017). This is not common practice in Brazil, however, and a number of cases in the Supreme Court are not known to anyone but the judges in that court.

In addition to the transparency initiatives of various Brazilian courts, various processes of the Lava-Jato probe have fed information directly to the mainstream media. At the end of this chapter, I will argue (in a more detailed manner) that the truth claims built into the discourse on leaks and exposés are strengthened with all this information at the disposal of the journalists, and I will argue for this. Here, turning to the relationship between politics and leaks in media, I will argue that the new tools and dynamics also introduce a new dynamic, without resorting to technological determinism. The new technologies of dissemination (and obtainment) of information connect accountability institutions and media in a new way.

Functionally speaking, the integration model of data-dumps and investigative journalism does not necessarily entail anything new in political arenas. Leaks of the type of WikiLeaks, Panama Papers, or Football Leaks are fundamentally disclosure with the interest of weakening political or economic actors or entire elites, calling them out in democratically dubious financial or political transactions or decisions. Quoting Thompson, '[s]candals are struggles over symbolic power in which reputation and trust are at stake' for individual actors and organizations (Thompson 2000: 245). Such disclosure was the content of Watergate, innumerable scandals after it, and many historical examples before that time (e.g., ibid.: 50). That is, contemporary data leaks are, functionally, one possible trigger event of scandals relating to transgression of the frontstage roles expected in public offices or similar (usually media-covered) elite positions.

While the effects of leaks on political systems are still embedded in the established ways of handling transgression and holding officials accountable, the media format of leaks is different: The scope is global, and the volume and extension of content is of an entirely different scale. Furthermore, as I will discuss in the following, this content is being pushed into public spheres in a qualitatively new way. The outcome – for example, media pressure and popular protests against corrupt leaders – might still be the same as for old-fashioned scandals, but the raw material and the journalistic labor of the scandal looks much different now, because of the technological affordances (Hutchby 2001). The intertwined technologies of the internet, social media, big data, search capabilities and data visualization, while not determining the emergence (and certainly not the effects) of leaks, do in fact provide some of the necessary conditions to extract and distribute the information of a scandal. Moreover, in the following sections, dealing with the dynamic of information flows, sources, and media organizations' control of information, I argue that leaks contribute to bypassing the gatekeeping role or boundary control exerted by legacy media newsrooms (Shoemaker and Vos 2009).

Information Control

I will now unpack the claim that professional journalism no longer exclusively patrols the borders of public spheres, and that every such sphere in its very publicness is, in fact, seriously challenged in this "Information Age" (or whatever epochal catch-phrase the reader might prefer). The decline of legacy media's control of the news agenda was foreshadowed in Bill Clinton-related scandals of the late 1990s (Delli Carpini and Williams 2001), but this trend is hypercharged in contemporary leaks: The affordances of a wide-ranging network of technologies, actors, and quasi-ideologies – the whole gamut of server technology, hacker communities, social media, and popular post-Watergate mythology – results in the erosion of the journalists' and editors' jurisdiction over public spheres. Leaks are one particular element in this erosion of the boundary control exercised by media professionals.

In the following, I will briefly define information control and how this control is usually exercised and negotiated in media spheres, followed by a discussion in the next section on the typical situations in scandals where information is disclosed to journalists (sometimes in the form of leaks). Based on this analysis of information disclosure settings, I can establish theoretically why leaks seem to be able to get past the gates and quickly reach the headlines of all national media outlets. I work with the label "information control" since I deal with information flows in a variety of settings, but the phenomenon has been researched before in media studies, under a different name. As early as 1950, under the heading of "gatekeeping," David Manning White theorized the relations between, on one hand, the media organizations' structures, and, on the other, the events and information that would survive selection and editing processes and ultimately make it to the news (White 1950). The primary research object of this book is not newsroom processes, however, and the following sections only deal with leaked information at the moment it reaches a media organization. Therefore, I omit the tradition and the specifics of gatekeeping theory and instead present a brief description of the obstacles in the publication of news first, and second a description of the forces that push leaked information into public spheres.

Before disclosed information can even be made to fit criteria of newsworthiness and produced as journalistic content, information has to reach a news gatherer (which is usually also a journalist, be it a freelancer, a newspaper or broadcaster employee, or a journalist working with news agency). In a way, the individuals with first-hand or authoritative knowledge constitute a kind of gate to the public sphere of the news, as these sources can decide whether to leak or not. Because the status of the source is important to journalists (Tuchman 1978: 69), some sources have an easier time pushing information. Having information from an authority or otherwise legitimated source (ibid.: 92ff.) is important to journalists, because such sources are "in-the-know" and are reliable producer of truth-claims, even when that truth is contested by other social actors. Therefore, press releases from government authorities were the staples of "objective" news gathering for decades in the United States (Shoemaker and Vos 2009: 55, Tuchman 1978: 93).

Even in the large-scale, vertically integrated, contemporary media corporations, White's insights about the forces of selection and rejection inside news organizations remain relevant; many layers of editorial selection influence the production outcome, i.e., the final printed or broadcast news product. A number of external conditions influence the selection – for example, the properties of particular events – of the news agency hierarchy, and the construction and pre-packaging of the event as newsworthy by other media professionals trying to push their texts into publication. News events themselves, the sources, the news-gathering journalists, the media organization, ideology and ownership structures all play different roles in information flows of the public sphere. Corruption scandals are a special case of information control, however, and not exactly comparable to the general processes of news selection and production. This is due to the fact that political actors implicated in a scandal will have every incentive to reduce media attention, in contrast to everyday politics where politicians want to attract the spotlight. In scandals, the parallelism of media organizations' logic of market optimization and the politician's interest in audience optimization (Landerer 2013) is inverted – a denounced politician will want as little attention as possible, while the media outlet still wants to maximize the audience.

The control of scandalous information is not just a question of sources or news objects wanting to minimize attention. The media organizations also have hierarchies determining the resources allocated to covering a scandal (or, at times, to eliminate scandalous news), meaning that journalists do not single-handedly determine what to cover, and neither does any single editor. Rather, in contemporary newsrooms, a complex set of interactions influence the process of selecting news for the next issue or the next newscast. Some of the relevant interactions, constraints, and causes include: The individual journalist's personal beliefs, identity, and professional profile position in relation to specific subsets of the news (regular columns, specific teams and tasks to which she is assigned, etc.), as well as her location in the newsroom hierarchy – all of these factors play a role in whether she can produce a news item that cuts through to publication. From time to time, a journalist might even choose not to make a news item of some bit of information in order to preserve professional relations to a source. In general, "since media trade in information, content decisions can also be driven by the need to appease suppliers, i.e., sources" (Shoemaker and Vos 2009: 77). In sum, all of this can cause a news event or bit of information to be rejected as news before it even reaches the desk of the copy editor.

Next, editors might reject material on many grounds, stemming from ideological editorial principles, such as the news media's standards of documentation or of objectivity, or stop a story on more pragmatic grounds (space constraints in the print version, or, in extreme cases, the risk of libel lawsuit). Editors might also reject stories because they operate under certain constraints set down by their superiors. In delicate political moments, editors will also consider the current editorial stance and line of opinion presented by the newspaper, in order to ensure alignment (and, as we shall see, even manipulate or omit data in order to ensure that alignment). The desire to emphasize a specific editorial line might lead to the inclusion or rejection of material handed over by journalists. The editors are also influenced by the fact that their organization, due to target group considerations, may incline toward a certain ideology and omit negative stories related to persons spouting such ideology. In Brazil, the personal relations of media conglomerate owners to political allies (which could simply be advertisers, or it could be political connections), have also led editors to remove material (see Miguel 2003: 292).

Despite the interest of implicated actors for minimizing attention, and political, editorial, and organizational reasons not to run a scandal story, leaks may still rapidly enter the public sphere as information in news items. There are a number of reasons for this: Leaks normally deal with powerful and influential individuals, and a leak about such an individual's previously secret actions is per definition newsworthy, because public office-holders are not, as a rule with some exceptions, supposed to keep secrets from their constituencies. Because of this transgression of the ideal frontstage role (Goffmann 1956) of public office-holders, leaks touch most news values: relevance, drama, scandal, negativity, conflict, human interest, proximity, and suspense (discussed originally in Galtung and Ruge 1965). Since leaks of secret information beg the question of "who else knew this," a leak generates speculation and draws in other actors (discussed in the final section of this chapter). No matter the veracity, a leak can result in repercussions for political actors and even cause a reconfiguration of the balance of power between decision-makers, which draws media attention.

In sum, many possible agents and factors contribute to obstructing or facilitating the flow of information into news at various levels: Individual levels (sources, news gatherers, and news processors such as editors), at the professional and organizational level (the routines of journalists and editors in a particular media organization set-up), the social institutional level (which at the general level determines what kind of news is no-go, what can be published and what should be avoided) and a more abstract level of the social system, culture and ideology (Shoemaker and Vos 2009: 31). However, the very secrecy of leaked information signals transgression, and disclosed transgressions are important material for news items because of the potential political repercussions, provoking speculation and coverage of reactions to the leak.

Dissemination and Disclosure

I will now explore the levels and the ways in which information is controlled, disclosed, and passed to media in scandals. Based on the media material of the Lava-Jato case, I will describe the typical situations where corruption is disclosed, or where new information about corruption emerges, and the forces that play into these situations and ensure that this information is transformed into news.

The settings and situations exhibit varying levels of information control, that is, the sources act as gates of information in relation to the journalists, to various degrees and for different purposes. However, that does not exclusively mean that sources act as obstacles by withholding information; on the contrary, many situations of corruption disclosure are specifically designed to maximize the publicity of denunciations and investigations. The Lava-Jato task force, for instance, normally host press conferences following larger police operations.

In a scandal, journalists may encounter information and elicit information from sources in several ways. This can be broken down into three groups: (1) the moments of "live," active journalism at scheduled events or in sudden, on-the-fly situations; (2) pre-packaged material sent to journalists; and (3) the special kind of source material leaking from investigations. This last group may give rise to investigative journalism based partly on insider sources, triangulated with publicly available information and information from more distant sources who may corroborate facts.

Live material comprises footage and possibly interviews from press conferences, court trials, and even investigation phases underway. The already-packaged material includes press releases from prosecuting, judging, and investigating authorities and their counterparts, the denounced or arrested individuals and their lawyers. Leaks usually either emerge from sources close to corruption, or from within the judiciary system. In the former cases, the sources are mostly clear to the eventual news consumer, while in the latter cases, the sources may be completely opaque, or the source deciding to transmit the information may be hidden. In the last case, it is usually necessary for the journalist to obscure the identity of the source for protection.

The pre-packaged information is, naturally, the most tightly controlled, and the sources act with the deliberate intention of controlling information and projecting certain framings of the material publicized: Where material is pre-packaged, the aim of the sources is always to get their version across to the media, and, possibly, to omit or de-emphasize information that could turn out to be harmful. When courts publicize material, it is often to comply with a specific policy set down to regulate and also restrict public access, meaning that such material frequently omits a lot of information deemed to be of personal nature, or potentially harmful to parallel investigations, if made public. Although pre-packaged material, in its nature, is designed to inform the press, journalists are aware of that, and will resist the framing projected by the sources, especially if the information is ultimately a denial. The framings of pre-packaged material are more likely to survive the news processing if the information comes from sources which are considered authoritative (Tuchman 1978: 69), or if the frame is consonant with the ideology and editorial line of the news outlet.

The live situations are, to various degrees, also controlled, just like the pre-packaged textual material of press releases. At one end of the spectrum, trials in court rooms are usually very ritualized and highly predictable, with the possible exception of situations where defendants go beyond the script. Information about the case will usually be accessible to interested parties and journalists either a long time ahead or not at all, in the cases of confidential cases (a small, but interesting subset of cases in the Supreme Court). Thus, the "liveness" of the trial is restricted to the spectacle of the trial (and the visual imagery of the court) because information concerning the alleged facts and accusations of the case will already have passed through the gates, and as a rule, the defense lawyers will already have decided upon a strategy of defense and made their arguments available to the press.

Another "live" setting where journalists may encounter information is the press conferences hosted by police agents and prosecutors who present phases of investigations. Such press conferences have been very common in the Lava-Jato case. They usually follow a planned script, designed to convey the facts of the police operation and explain the line of inquiry, providing easily digestible material for journalists. Likewise, the press conference situations where denounced individuals present their counter-arguments also feature tight control of information. In both situations, the speakers will usually stick to their script unless forced to respond to unexpected questions, which once in a while can turn up a nugget of information or trap the person rhetorically. The two situations differ somewhat in another sense of information control, however: When investigations are triggered and described for the first time by police authorities and prosecutors, it usually generates enough interest that editors will want to commit resources and send journalists to cover the press conference. This increases the likelihood of publication, because the resource commitment means that editors are hoping to get something in return for that investment. When a denounced person calls a press conference, it is assumed that he or she will be denying the allegations, which is less newsworthy, since it is neither surprising, unusual, nor (presumably) contributing any new information to the case. The only news criteria activated by this type of live press conferences are the sense of conflict, which is heightened by denials, and the availability of visual footage (possibly of individuals with various emotions emanating). Admissions of guilt would, of course, be surprising and more probable to pass gates; but straight admissions are also exceedingly rare (although possibly quite important for political careers; see Allern and Pollack 2012).

The live situations with the least amount of control of information are the moments where teams of reporters follow investigations, getting glimpses of arrests, and perhaps comments from investigated or investigators which have not been prepared due to the acute circumstances. Later in this chapter, a notable case of such an investigation phase is described, wherein the police force leaked the upcoming arrests to the press, in order for the TV teams to arrive in time to get material for the news. The images of such investigations and police operations may in themselves be hugely significant because they engender speculation and commentary from media pundits. The drama of live footage, where police agents with search warrants enter private homes and drag out criminals, is visually much more appealing than the stale press releases of courts and prosecutors, and thus more likely to pass gates in broadcast media.

Finally, we get to the leaks. It is necessary to distinguish between two senses of leaks: One type of leaks comes in the form of documentation – evidence, phone taps, footage, etc. – while another type is testimonies and witness accounts. What is characteristic of both types is their apparently "raw" nature, which makes them appear as inherently truthful representations of reality. Leaks of the document-evidence kind can be interpreted in many ways, allowing for speculation and extrapolation. Leaks of testimonies and plea bargains, on the other hand, seem to be of a more obviously subjective nature. However, since the information disclosed in plea bargains is revealed under severe penal restrictions, this type of information is likely assumed to contain more truthful representations of reality than denunciations and allegations presented without the restraints imposed by criminal charges and pending sentences.

When discussing leaks, I am not referring to case material publicized officially by the court in Curitiba or by the STF once dissemination could not harm the investigation. Rather, the leaks of material and information discussed here frequently came before the instauration of inquiries, before plea bargains had been finalized, or before any indictments. Several important leaks to the weekly press were based on pre-testimonies of the Lava-Jato probe, in other words, preliminary stages of plea bargains, where arrested individuals indicate the scope of their knowledge concerning corruption schemes. Such leaks could only originate with either the testifying person or the police agents obtaining the statements. In fact, the office of the Prosecutor-General of the Republic has frequently complained about the federal police agents being the source of leaks. The cases of plea bargains where police agents have been shut out of negotiations have also, however, resulted in leaks. A number of actors handle the information contained in testimonies and emerging from police investigations, including public prosecutors or police agents involved in the investigations, and in some cases (depending on the levels of confidentiality in investigations) the lawyers defending the investigated politicians and businessmen. These actors have different incentives to leak.

Lawyers would usually have little incentive to leak the information unless the media actors offered substantial rewards, which is known to happen in the UK, but is taboo in Brazilian journalism. A lawyer's professional credibility could be jeopardized if he were revealed to leak confidential information. However, the negotiation situation of plea bargains probably makes it more likely that some suspects would want to leak (or have their lawyers leak) information. This is due to the fact that when leaked information gets enough public attention, it might force the hand of the prosecutor or police agent negotiating the terms of a plea bargain: Police investigators can hardly threaten to deny a plea bargain and discard information when that information is already in the media limelight.

The judge and prosecutors working on the Lava-Jato case have made it abundantly clear that public attention to corruption (through media attention) is central to the efforts of combatting corruption (Albuquerque 2017, Dallagnol and Martelo 2016, Moro 2004). This proactive public relations strategy is close to the heart of the Lava-Jato task-force's strategy for maintaining pressure on the political system and legitimizing lengthy preventive imprisonment of public officials and businessmen. In interviews and opinion pieces, the prosecutors have repeatedly argued that the preventive arrests would seem unjust in the eye of the public if citizens were not informed of the political transgression. Leaks thus join legally publicized material as elements of a strategy for gaining sufficient legitimacy to enact extraordinary judicial measures. For these reasons, it makes sense that the judiciary and prosecuting actors have little interest in finding, investigating or punishing any internal sources of leaks. Furthermore, since many restrictions apply to the disclosure of pending legal actions, the instances where these restrictions are bypassed by individuals within the judiciary system are sure to generate interest among journalists. Therefore, a leak of information, merely in virtue of its extraordinary disclosure, generates an important thrust to get information past the initial gate. In particular, the moment and timing of disclosed evidence is of the utmost importance in the situations we will consider in the next section of this chapter.

The bottom line of all this is that in the publication of leaks, the sources and their motives are hidden from view, in contrast to either pre-packaged material or the "live" situations described above. In the Lava-Jato case, this meant that the insiders of the corruption cases (lawyers, prosecutors, and judges) have had the privilege of being able to decide whether they want to present information to the public (and how much). Because the mere connection to this scandal warranted front-page and prime-time attention, journalists were eager to reproduce scandalous allegations from investigations and testimonies. The tendency to uncritically reproduce denunciations thus circumvents gatekeeping and changes the dynamics of the source-journalist relation.

While in theory, leaks contribute in fostering accountability (Benkler 2014, Russell and Waisbord 2017), the occultation of sources shrouds the enunciation of the leak in necessary shadows, while the media coverage paradoxically is affirming the dangers of secrecy in public space. The transparency created by leaks is shallow and one-dimensional, because the leaking agent remains incognito (Wahl-Jørgensen 2014). The accountability of politicians to their constituencies and the general public is a democratic necessity, but the accountability of the sources of news is rarely under scrutiny. In other leak cases and leak organizations, such as WikiLeaks and Panama Papers, the various ways of protecting whistle-blowers and other sources are even built into the information distribution technology and the organization itself, which completely removes the sources from the limelight. The concealment of sources is in reality an inversion of the transparency supposedly created by leaks: While a sudden disclosure of information may force political actors to account for themselves, the lightning-strike that forces visibility upon the targets simultaneously blind the spectators. The visibility is only directed toward the objects of the leaks, and rarely shines a light upon the position of the enunciator.

Beyond the shrouding of sources, certain institutional actors of Brazil also gain a privileged position through leaks:

- Prosecutors and police agents (because these, at different times, apparently control the timing of at least some of the leaks, and control to whom they leak the information).
- Judiciary actors (gaining legitimacy relative to the political branch of government, because leaks cast suspicion upon the politicians while suppressing the question of political agency behind the leaky investigations and trials).
- Media conglomerates (because only the large mainstream media have resources to extract and process all the scoops, and the agenda-setting power attractive to the leaking agents).

Having established how information relating to corruption investigations is controlled and disclosed in general, I will now describe the specific sequence of major leaks that dominated the front-pages and newscasts in Brazil between 2014 and 2017.

Leaks of the Lava-Jato Case

In this section, I will present the chronology of the leaks in the form of a narrative that also outlines the immediate political impact of the leaks and the unfolding scandal. The sections that follow this one will provide the theoretical framework for exploring the effects of the leaks in depth.

The leaks of the Lava-Jato operation began a few months after the initial arrests, described in the introductory chapter. These early stages of the investigation targeted different departments and executive offices of the state oil company Petrobras, and although speculations abounded, few named politicians were implicated in the case until the presidential campaign of 2014 was well underway, in August and September 2014.

The first major leak, on October 23, 2014, happened just three days before the second round of presidential elections. In this election round, the incumbent Dilma Rousseff of PT was pitted against Aécio Neves, candidate for the liberal party PSDB. A leak of the testimony given by Youssef, the main money launderer of the case, was published by the tabloid magazine *Veja*, out of the normal publication schedule. The corruption in Petrobras and the losses to the state were denounced on the front page of this lightning-strike special issue, and, quoting from the leaked testimony, the headline, "They knew it all," was printed on top of the faces of Rousseff and her mentor, ex-president Lula, both looking pale and desperate against a black and foreboding background. The election resulted in a historically close race, with Rousseff barely securing a win.

Costa (the ex-director of Petrobras) and Youssef both negotiated plea bargains in order to reduce their sentences. This generated a snowballing chain of evidence, as these two plea bargains incriminated more CEOs, bosses from subcontractors, and clandestine financial operators. The testimony of another Petrobras manager was leaked to *Estado* on December 14, 2014, targeting João Vaccari Neto, the national treasurer of the president's party PT. Several others implicated in the case also pointed to the treasurer as the man collecting kickbacks, and the media picked up on various bits from these testimonies during January and February 2015. On February 5, the treasurer was forced to testify to the police, and Vaccari Neto was denounced on March 16, and arrested the following month.

In the first days of March, leaks about the Vaccari's role in the Petrobras graft were overshadowed by the rumors and leaks about the list being compiled by the prosecutor-general's office, awaiting approval of the Supreme Court. The prosecutor-general's list, and its many appendices detailing evidence, requested the authorization of criminal investigations into scores of parliamentarians. The information seeping from the prosecutor-general's office into *Folha* and then the other major newspapers formed the second major leak and forced both the president of the Senate and the president of the *Câmara dos Deputados* (the Lower

House of Congress) to take political action. The Senate leader, Renan Calheiros of PMDB, blocked the government's budget adjustment in retaliation for the leak, which he perceived to be politically motivated, while the president of the Câmara, Eduardo Cunha (also of PMDB), went on stand in a parliamentary investigative committee and denied his involvement in the case. Both reactions became emblematic, as the government struggled for the rest of the year in pushing the 2015 budget through Congress, and because those leaks ostensibly started the antagonism between Cunha and the government.

The third major leak, publicized in *O Globo* on July 15, 2015, also targeted Eduardo Cunha, and Cunha repeated his reaction by blaming the government for the leak, and augmented this by calling for his party PMDB to remove their support for the government. Splitting PMDB, the largest center party in the Congress, in two, would in effect create a sitting-duck president out of Dilma Rousseff through the lack of this party's votes. Half of the congressmen from PMDB followed Cunha's line, thus making it extremely difficult for Rousseff to pass legislation or even the state budget for the rest of 2015.

The top leader of Cunha's party, Vice-President of the Republic Michel Temer, was asked by the President to take on political responsibility, but their relationship, never friendly, soured considerably as the vice-president did little to contain the discontent of his party. Even after a cabinet reshuffle in October, giving more minister positions to the PMDB politicians, the government still had not managed to pass the year's budget. During these months, the Swiss prosecutor-general had publicized evidence, confirming that Cunha indeed had accounts in the country, and a disciplinary process against Cunha ensued. In November, Cunha tried to secure votes for filing away this process by promising to block impeachment charges against the President Rousseff. Her party members in the Ethics Commission of the Câmara did not yield to blackmail, in the end, and voted to start a process that would eventually lead to Cunha losing his mandate. A few hours after this vote in the Ethics Commission, on December 3, Cunha responded by using his prerogative as president of the Câmara to initiate impeachment proceedings. President Rousseff had gotten her state budget passed at the last minute, with an extraordinary deficit, but now faced a political-juridical process charging her with the ultimate responsibility for delayed transfers between the State Treasury and a number of public sector banks. Repaying the interest on those delayed transfers, in order to avoid impeachment charges for illegal obtainment of loans, increased the state budget deficit to 170 billion Brazilian *reais*.

A fortnight later, a week before Christmas, the federal police searched the offices and houses owned or associated with Cunha, confiscating documents and mobile phones. The text message material of these phones allowed the police to draw several new connections in their probe. The fourth major leak, publicized in *Estado* on January 7, 2016, comprised a vast amount of text messages extracted from the cell phone of the construction company boss Leo Pinheiro. Pinheiro, in messages to many politicians, including Cunha and several other PMDB and PT leaders, had negotiated economic support for election campaigns in various suspect ways. The chief of cabinet was also implicated and had to evade the media in the following weeks. Pinheiro's company, OAS, was one of the heavy-weight sub-contractors in the Petrobras case. OAS and Pinheiro in particular turned out to have connections to the ex-president Lula. This strengthened the original claim of *Veja* and the tabloid press, heralded back in 2014 (and even before the Petrobras case, see Damgaard 2015a), that Lula "knew all" about the corruption in PT and was behind it all.

This notion – that Lula somehow was behind it all – was also the main thrust of the fifth major leak comprising 400 pages of testimony from the imprisoned senator Delcídio do Amaral. The former PT leader and Petrobras director had tried to help one of the arrested Petrobras CEOs flee the country and had been caught red-handed. Following three months of preventive arrest, Amaral opted for a plea bargain, and between the many pages of information, first presented on March 3 by the tabloid *IstoÉ*, Lula and Rousseff's knowledge of corruption was denounced again. The senator had also denounced a number of other notable politicians, including the ex-president Cardoso and the 2014 presidential runner-up Neves. Notwithstanding this, pressure mounted on Rousseff, as PMDB threatened to follow Cunha by leaving the government altogether. In addition to this, the marketing boss of the PT was arrested on corruption charges linked to Petrobras.

The ties between Lula and the construction company OAS had been pursued by journalists of all the main media in January and February, gradually turning up pieces of documentary evidence, witness accounts and archive files that showed how OAS had worked on two real estate sites linked to Lula. None of this was leaked from investigations, but it turned up through investigative journalism. However, the federal police conducted parallel investigations, and since the real estate case had already been mentioned in *Folha* and *Veja* in 2015, it is reasonable to assume that the media interest is not merely coincidental with the police investigation. In any case, more evidence of relations between Lula and OAS accumulated; evidence that arguably needed to be linked to actual crimes, however. Lula was forced to testify on March 4, being escorted from his home in São Paulo at dawn. The Globo news team was ready with cameras at the ex-president's house before the police arrived, which suggests a leak in the local police force.

The leaks of Delcídio do Amaral and the much-covered testimony of Lula also provided the backdrop for huge protests in the capitals of Brazil on March 13. While many opposition leaders cast these protests as anti-PT, not many succeeded in gaining political capital from these protests, as many protesters were disenchanted with politics in general. A few opposition politicians were threatened violently as they made their appearance in protests in São Paulo.

The sixth major leak followed on March 16, where phone taps of Lula were publicized and heavily covered. The legality of the taps was in question, as was the publication. The federal judge presiding over the Lava-Jato case, Sérgio Moro, had made the recordings of Lula's conversations accessible to journalists working on the case, and one recording in particular was extraordinary: In this conversation, Lula's interlocutor was the president herself. Secretly taping the president and making the recording public was, no doubt, a radical move. The reason given by judge Moro, however, was to expose the implicit motivation for the conversation between President Rousseff and the ex-president. Rousseff said she wanted Lula to enter her straggling government, reinforcing her team with his considerable political capital. Moro and the prosecutors argued that this was only a decoy explanation, because a minister position would also give Lula the benefit of having his case judged before the Supreme Court, which was notoriously slow and lenient to politicians. In the recorded conversation, Rousseff suggests that Lula could use the official document that would effectively install him as minister "in case of necessity." This phrase became the object of much controversy in the following days. The recording was breaking news in all media, triggering spontaneous protests in front of the Presidential Palace, and the conversation was quoted ad verbatim on the newspaper front pages the following morning.

With the steadily mounting pressure of leaks and arrests, PT could not prevent allied parties from jumping ship. Cunha, in yet two more leaks, had been linked to corruption in the reconstruction of Rio de Janeiro sites prior to the Olympics, but he succeeded in slowing down the congressional disciplinary process against him. Still in command of the Câmara, he presided over the impeachment proceedings and scheduled the first vote for April 17. Scores of congressmen declared their support for impeachment of Rousseff, and several parties left the government and their minister seats (discussed in depth below). The vote resulted in a two-thirds majority for impeachment in the Câmara, and the impeachment proceeded to the Senate, who would act as a final jury in another vote.

In the midst of the turmoil of impeachment, the seventh major leak was mostly disregarded by the TV Globo, although it received some coverage in the rest of the mainstream media. Based on apprehended documents from the country's largest construction company, Odebrecht, no less than 25 different political parties and hundreds of politicians were suspected of taking bribes during campaigns. This included scores of the more important parliamentarians that had voted for impeaching Rousseff the week before. The bribe files of Odebrecht became the straw that bent the back of the heir to the Odebrecht dynasty, Marcelo Odebrecht, who had been arrested preventively and kept in prison since June 2015. Resisting up until this point, he finally admitted to corruption charges and opted for a plea bargain, drawing 76 managers of the many branches of the Odebrecht holding group with him into a monumental testimony. True to form, once finalized, this mega-plea bargain also had numerous parts leaked, but only after the political elite had finished ousting Dilma Rousseff from the presidency.

Suspended temporarily by the Senate on May 12, Rousseff left the Presidency to Vice-President Michel Temer. Having appointed an all-male, all-white cabinet, Temer had to let three ministers go within three weeks as new secret recordings were published by *Folha* in the eighth major leak. Most prominently, the minister of Planning and Budgets, Romero Jucá of the PMDB, had to take his leave after 12 days as minister. In the recorded conversations with Sérgio Machado (a state company director and potential target of the Lava-Jato probe), Jucá discussed how to stop the corruption probe from reaching himself and his allies. A number of PMDB bosses, including ex-President José Sarney, argued likewise in the conversations that were recorded. The conversations were taped by the state company director to be used as bargaining chip if he should be arrested and eventually wished to negotiate a plea bargain. The very same Jucá, upon stepping down, returned to his seat in the Senate, and participated in the Senate's final impeachment verdict against Rousseff on August 31, when Michel Temer was permanently proclaimed President.

A minor, but interesting leak was provided by the independent, leftist blog *Tijolaço*. The journalist Fernando Brito, who runs the blog, showed that the supposedly independent survey company DataFolha (part of the Folha group) had omitted crucial aspects of a publicized survey, providing *Folha* information about the new president's approval ratings. The information of the poll was erroneous if not downright manipulative. On July 17, *Folha* ran the results of the recent DataFolha survey as a graphical element on the front page, showing that 50 percent of the respondents would prefer Temer to Rousseff as president (Folha de S. Paulo 2016). The actual percentage of affirmative responses to the question of whether they wanted Temer to stay was only 3. However, the curiously restricted question, "If you had to choose between the return of Dilma Rousseff as president and Michel Temer staying in office, what would you prefer?" had 50 percent of respondents answering that they preferred Temer, with 32 percent preferring the return of Rousseff. Brito had discovered that DataFolha had produced a second version of the survey to support the front page of *Folha*, where questions implying hostility to Temer were omitted. The original survey was, however, still available and Brito quickly downloaded it, published it on his blog and had the American journalist Glenn Greenwald (of Snowden and WikiLeaks fame) mirror the manipulation on his site *The Intercept*. The situation was remarkable because the political influence was obvious (although not a unique situation for DataFolha; see Biroli et al. 2011), but the *Folha* editor Sérgio D'Avila denied this, even though his newspaper not many months before published the editorial, "Neither Rousseff nor Temer," indicating the editor's preference for calling new elections instead of inaugurating Temer as President.

In the latter half of 2016, the ninth major leak gradually dripped into various media (*Veja, O Globo* and *Folha* most prominently among these). The information derived from the plea bargain of the Odebrecht group, and it continued to rock the boat of the new PMDB-led government. More ministers stepped down, and the new president experienced a national record of all-time low, single-digit approval ratings during the second half of 2016. The plea bargain became known as the End-Of-The-World testimony (*Delação do Fim do Mundo* – a term that emerged in a column with that title in Folha, see Rossi 2016) and was heralded by the tabloid and quality press to be of "apocalyptic proportions." The Supreme Court judge authorizing the plea bargain unexpectedly died in an airplane crash in January 2017, but the Supreme Court president pushed the plea bargain through and initiated 76 investigations against congressmen and ministers, while redistributing 201 cases to other courts, including probes into 12 out of the federation's 27 state governors. A range of these cases had already been leaked to the press, so the information of the Odebrecht material constitutes the ninth major leak in the Lava-Jato case.

Many weeks before the Odebrecht material was actually distributed to the various Brazilian courts, on March 15, 2016, 16 politicians were named on the front pages of the newspapers, implicated in the corruption scheme. The names comprised the top of yet another swathe of inquiries, for which Prosecutor-General Rodrigo Janot requested authorization. All of the three main newspapers had gotten access to this list and featured that information prominently on their front pages, likening the situation to the first list of names, back in March 2015. *Folha* reported that five of Temer's ministers, plus Lula, Rousseff, Aécio Neves, José Serra, as well as the PMDB senators Renan Calheiros, Romero Jucá and Edison Lobão were all implicated in the testimonies of the Odebrecht bosses. Estado highlighted Lula and Roussef, along with the PT ex-ministers of Finance Antônio Palocci and Guido Mantega, then the PSDB senators José Serra and Aécio Neves, as well as the new presidents of Congress, Rodrigo Maia (DEM) and Eunício Oliveira (PMDB). Below these names (and faces), the same five ministers mentioned by *Folha* were shown. *O Globo*'s front page named Lula, Rousseff, Aécio, and Serra at the top, continuing with the same names as mentioned by the others – ministers, PMDB senators and ex-ministers of Finance from PT. This constituted the tenth major leak, an exceptional one because the source of the leak was revealed and discussed in the very same media the following days.

The obvious overlap of this information became the topic of an editorial penned by the journalistic ombudsman at *Folha*, Paula Cesarino Costa. She claimed that a strictly off-the-record press conference had been held by the prosecutor-general with a select circle of journalists, leaking exactly these 16 names (from a total of 320 requests for investigations). Furthermore, Cesarino Costa questioned the motives of the prosecutor-general for planting these names, omitting the many other names of allegedly corrupt politicians that surfaced the following days. These subsequent leaks, she argued, were channeled through the usual, one-on-one relationships between journalists and their sources. The collective off-the-record interview was suspect, to the ombudsman of *Folha*, however, because the journalists had simply submitted to the selection criteria of the leaking prosecutors. Cesarino Costa affirmed that the dependence of journalists upon their sources in the Lava-Jato case was becoming excessive (Cesarino Costa 2017a). The *Estado* columnist and political commentator Vera Magalhães argued that the overlap of the 16 names was simply due to the existing stock of leaks from Odebrecht, available in the public sphere to all journalists. Thus, Magalhães argued that the front pages were constructed from the news about the requests for inquiries and the existing knowledge of the journalists (Magalhães 2017). The prosecutor-general denied any leak, while the independent blog *O Antagonista* argued that federal prosecutors not working on the Lava-Jato case (pointing, in particular, to the ex-minister of the Rousseff administration,

Eugênio Aragão) were behind the leak. The *Folha* ombudsman reiterated the claim and stated that three independent sources had confirmed the existence of an off-the-record collective interview (Cesarino Costa 2017b).

The eleventh major leak almost resulted in the removal of Michel Temer. The *O Globo* journalist Lauro Jardim, usually in charge of editing a small column of minor political rumors, struck gold in April 2017. He got access to information from the prosecutor-general's office about a number of so-called "controlled actions," – covert operations involving secret surveillance, civil agents, and plea bargaining individuals of the Lava-Jato case. The operations inculpated both President Michel Temer and Aécio Neves. *O Globo*'s site finally published the leak on May 17, and the journalist stated in interviews afterwards that the timing was chosen to avoid damaging these investigative operations. That requires knowledge about the processes of prosecution and suggests that Jardim was told exactly when he was cleared to go public.

The contents of this leak shocked the political arena to the core. First off, the president was caught on tape agreeing that paying Eduardo Cunha to shut up and not negotiate a plea bargain was a good idea. This conversation had been taped by the owner of the meat production giant JBS, Joesley Batista, in the presidential palace. Furthermore, a close associate of Temer was caught with a carry-on luggage filled with money bills – half a million real in total. Aécio Neves, meanwhile, had been caught negotiating a R$2 million kickback with Batista on the phone, in order to pay his bills for lawyers – ironically, his defense lawyers in the Lava-Jato case. The money delivery was handled by Neves' relative, and delivered to an associate of Neves' fellow Minas Gerais senator, Zeze Perella (PMDB). While their close aides and Neves' sister went to prison, both Temer and Neves ended up escaping prosecution altogether in the second half of 2017, which is described in the next chapter.

On the basis of this narrative of 11 major leaks in the Lava-Jato case, I will develop theoretically the claim that leaks can have perverse effects that do not help democracy or provide transparency or accountability to the public. In the next section, I will prepare this argument by building a brief theoretical model for assessing the effects of leaks in different institutional settings.

Tracing Institutional Interactions Triggered by Leaks

In this section, I will go deeper into the ramifications of the many leaks in the Lava-Jato case. I will argue that leaks, as a subset of information flows in the public sphere, constitute an especially powerful and dramatic style of interaction between institutions and organizations of the judiciary system, political system and media. I use the term "interaction" in a broad sense here, to capture the various processes that emerge from these different arenas. Based on the leaks described above, as well as a range of legal and legislative processes (detailed in the next chapter), I have compiled a number of cases where the institutions interacted or clashed in response to the leaks. These cases are then examined with a simplified process-tracing methodology.

First, I will briefly explain this chapter's conception of institutions. The field of media organizations is viewed here as one market-driven, political institution (Hughes 2006: 47ff.), while the various branches of government are viewed as separate institutional fields. Scholars have argued that media organizations, because of their roles in democracies, should be viewed as parts of a single political institution (Cook 2006, Sparrow 1999). "[T]hese multi-layered news media institutions are, by and large, mutually consistent; they cohere into a single actor for most intents and purposes" (Sparrow 1999: 133). Cook pointed out several caveats of this viewpoint, emphasizing a transactional perspective and demonstrating the heterogeneity of media organizations. Since the media are not formally structured like political institutions, contain much diversity within them, and constantly communicate and transact with actors outside the institutional walls of media, media should not be considered an institution like Congress or a court (Cook 2006: 162). Keeping Cook's caveats in mind, later North European theories (e.g., Hjarvard 2013, Krotz 2014) have cast media as one institution within the broader social and organizational strand of theory dubbed new institutionalism (Thornton et al. 2012). In this second wave of institutional theory, a complex concept of institutions was proposed in order to grasp local agency and dynamics that led to change and conflict in institutions.

Following these authors, the interactions of media institutions and other institutions vary locally because particular institutional actors work strategically within the "socially constructed, historical patterns of material practices, assumptions, values, beliefs, and rules by which individuals produce and reproduce their material subsistence, organize time and space, and provide meaning to their social reality" (Thornton and Ocasio 2008: 101). Organizational action or reform might coalesce around one or multiple such "patterns" in a local context. This theoretical approach defines institution as one repertoire of logics, organizing principles, and vocabularies for articulating and enacting agency and subjectivity.

Because of the attention to variant patterns and logics, new institutionalism allows for further sub-distinctions between the institutions of democratic systems, such as the political institutions of parliaments and governments, the judiciary institutions of courts, prosecuting bodies and auditing bodies. The sub-distinctions among Brazil's accountability institutions are only discussed in the next chapter, however. Admittedly, the Brazilian judiciary is not a homogeneous actor but rather a many-headed hydra of hierarchy and multi-layered bureaucracy, just as the legislative branch of government is (in its representative or delegative nature) a multiple political body configured to contain within it conflicts of interest. Furthermore, the public prosecutors play a central role in the web of accountability institutions, but they are only one among many actors investigating and processing corruption. Congressional committees and hybrid budget tribunals also produce horizontal accountability and act as checks and balances, but they are partly controlled by legislative actors supporting the executive branch. However, for the purposes of this chapter, the sub-distinctions of institutional intersections and allegiances need not occupy us, because the leaks, as we saw above, mostly juxtapose the three branches of government (the executive, legislative, and judiciary) to each other, as well as to the media.

Having preliminarily (and deliberately in a simplified manner) outlined the actors, I will now turn to the situations of the Lava-Jato scandal where these institutional actors and spheres interact and react to each other in consequence of leaks. In the following analysis of institutional interactions emerging in the wake of leaks, I will use a simplified, case-centric variant of process-tracing (Beach and Brun Pedersen 2013) that merely aims at explaining the outcomes of a particular case. The idea here is neither to approach the case deductively, nor try to develop generalizable mechanisms of leaks, because a number of scope conditions (Falletti and Lynch 2009) are not generalizable. Scope conditions include the "relevant aspects of a setting (analytical, temporal, spatial, or institutional) in which a set of initial conditions leads ... to an outcome of a defined scope and meaning via a specified causal mechanism or set of causal mechanisms" (ibid.: 1152). The scope conditions of this case, such as the Brazilian media system, the Constitutional framework, and the legal jurisprudence, to name a few contingencies, are particular to this national context, and cannot easily be generalized to leaks and scandals in other contexts. However, the insights of the case-centric process-tracing may very well be helpful to comparative research into different settings, and to generate new questions.

The process-tracing methodology adopted here will simply point out the instances where a leak came to be a necessary, but not in itself sufficient, cause for an outcome. Trying to establish every necessary condition would be a huge undertaking, and not helpful to the research scope in this chapter. This section will instead approach the case more modestly by "crafting an explanation that accounts for a particular outcome" (Beach and Brun Pedersen 2013: 11). Here, I divide outcomes into two categories, depending on the institutional setting, and define these *post hoc* as changes in the state of the relevant system.

The terms "interaction" and "conflict" are defined, in turn, on the basis of such outcomes:

* Political outcome: In the political system, an outcome could be changes in coalition formation, the passing or rejection of a bill, or other movements with implications for democratic governance.
* Judicial outcome: In the legal system, an outcome could be changes in legal status, such as indictments, or pressing charges, or moving a case from one court to another.
* Institutional interaction will be defined here as an event where the outcome of one institutional setting or system impacts upon another (e.g., legal actions against parliamentarians, policy aimed at obstructing justice, the political appointment of a judge, etc.).
* Conflicts between institutions are more loosely defined here, as a subset of institutional interactions, usually involving public critique, protests, appeals, or contestation through either media or institutional measures.

The Leaks about Eduardo Cunha and Judiciary Intervention in the Legislative Branch

I will start out by illustrating one process, pertaining to the preventive arrest and indefinite imprisonment of Eduardo Cunha, former president of the Câmara, on corruption charges. This outcome was the final result of a protracted struggle in Congress to remove him from office and from his mandate, which would also result in Cunha losing the prerogative of trial before the Supreme Court. In this case, I will argue that a necessary, but not by itself sufficient, condition for this outcome was the leak that exposed Cunha's lie in the CPI of Petrobras.

As described, Cunha's name had cropped up in leaks in the early days of the Lava-Jato probe. As newly elected president of the Câmara, he went on stand on March 12, 2015, in an investigative commission he himself had recently opened to examine the Petrobras corruption. There, Cunha calmly denied a number of charges and openly claimed that he did not have any overseas bank accounts. Cunha's defense was covered as an event of redress and vindication, full of eulogies for Cunha from both opposition parties and the center-left parts of government (e.g., Mascarenhas and Talento 2015, in *Folha*). In the commission meeting, Cunha opened a flank of attack against the Prosecutor-General Rodrigo Janot, first claiming that the government had forced Janot to leak information in order to weaken him in Congress, and later arguing that Janot was persecuting him extra-officially. The same critique, not coincidentally, was used by Michel Temer's lawyers in 2017 as well as the Supreme Judge Gilmar Mendes.

However, the assertion that Cunha made about the bank accounts was belied by the facts uncovered by the MPF. On September 21, the lobbyist João Augusto Henriques was apprehended, and he admitted to having transferred more than R$1 million in kickback money to Cunha's account in the Swiss bank Julius Baer. This information spread from the MPF to the parties in Congress, and the small left-wing party PSOL, on October 1, demanded official access to that information from the prosecutor-general. Although not revealing the files themselves, the prosecutor responded in the affirmative to the question of whether Cunha had bank accounts in Switzerland. With that response, and the earlier denial of bank accounts in mind, PSOL filed a disciplinary action against Cunha in the Ethics Council of the Câmara on October 13. In the meantime, files documenting the bank account had been leaked to the press. Despite substantial pressure, because he was in control of the Câmara, Cunha managed to stall even the simple delivery of that action to the Council for a fortnight, and the opening of the process was delayed for a full month.

Fast-forwarding to mid-2016: Finally, after a tortuous eight-month process, the Ethics Council decided (in a very close vote) to approve a recommendation for the removal of Cunha. At that point, Cunha had already been removed from the presidency of the Câmara by the Supreme Judge Teori Zavascki. Cunha appealed, and the action moved to the Commission of Justice in the Câmara, but after one month, the appeal was rejected. His substitute at the head of the Câmara, Rodrigo Maia, then had to schedule a plenary vote for removal of his mandate, and on September 12, 354 days after the Swiss bank account was first detected, Cunha lost his mandate, 450 votes against 10. The next month, Cunha was arrested and imprisoned preventively in Curitiba at the order of the judge, Sérgio Moro, and was sentenced to 15 years in prison, in the first of several indictments in March 2017.

Cunha's sentence was the upshot of the leak, in the sense that the other parliamentarian (Senator and ex-President Fernando Mello de Collor) indicted by the prosecutor-general on similar charges in the same month as Cunha (August 2015) remains in Parliament and was only charged before the Supreme Court in August 2017; but Collor has neither been removed from office nor convicted. Thus, the processes of the Supreme Court delay the sentencing substantially. Without the removal of his mandate in Congress, Cunha would have preserved the prerogative called *foro privilegiado*, escaping the jurisdiction of the Curitiba court handling the Petrobras case. (The *foro* prerogative means that congressmen and ministers automatically move to the top of the Brazilian three-tier system of courts.) Thus, Sérgio Moro would not have been able to order his arrest, and eventually sentence Cunha. The lie in the investigative commission in response to leaks, and the leak of documents providing the disciplinary process with crucial evidence constituted the necessary conditions for the outcome of his imprisonment and sentence.

The political outcome of the case was brought about with the intervention of the judiciary into the legislative branch, and the leaks (probably coming from public prosecutors) that provided PSOL with the means to initiate a disciplinary process was the triggering cause of this intervention. The imprisonment of Cunha was the first time an (ex-)president of the Câmara was imprisoned (but repeated six months later, in 2017, with the arrest of his ally Henrique Eduardo Alves, also of PDMB). Cunha's removal from office in May 2016, ordered by the Supreme Court, was likewise a historically unique intervention in the federal legislative body by the judiciary, albeit not connected causally to any leak. The Supreme Court was compelled to consider the prosecutor-general's request for removal with urgency as it became clear that Dilma Rousseff would be ousted, making Cunha the de facto vice-president according to the law of presidential succession in the Brazilian presidential system. This situation is analyzed in the next chapter.

Protecting Supreme Justice by Cancelling a Plea Bargain

Leaks also influenced outcomes within the Brazilian judiciary. A leaked testimony from the plea bargain of Leo Pinheiro, the president of the OAS construction company, resulted in the exceptional cancellation of the plea bargain negotiations by order from the Prosecutor-General. In edition #2492 (August 2016), *Veja* published leaked material of the testimony, in which Leo Pinheiro had described how he and his company had helped the Supreme Justice Dias Toffoli installing security measures in his house. Pinheiro had directed Toffoli to a security company of Brasília. The bill, according to *Veja*, was paid by Toffoli, however (a fact that was omitted in other media's accounts of the testimony). But the mere inclusion of the name of a supreme justice in a testimony about criminal and corrupt activity grabbed the attention of the media.

The next day, August 22, Prosecutor-General Janot denied that the leak came from his office, or that this part of the testimony had ever entered his office. Janot went on to cancel the negotiation of the plea bargain entirely, claiming that this leaked information seemed to be an attempt at baiting the agents of the investigation. Pinheiro had already been sentenced to 17 years of prison by Sérgio Moro at that point, so he had a weighty incentive to negotiate a plea bargain in order to reduce the sentence. Janot claimed that OAS, or Pinheiro's lawyers, had leaked the testimony to *Veja* because the public interest in the matter would force the prosecutor's hand in the negotiation. One political commentator, Luis Nassif, speculated that the Lava-Jato task force had leaked this as payback against Toffoli, who had cancelled a preventive arrest of a former PT minister in one of the investigation's many phases (Nassif 2016), and this was also argued by the Supreme Judge Gilmar Mendes, who over the course of the Lava-Jato investigations began to critique the methods of the probe. Like Toffoli, Mendes would go on to release arrested individuals in the Lava-Jato case, contrary to the pattern established in Curitiba.

The immediate cancellation of the plea bargain negotiation sent a strong signal to other individuals implicated in the Lava-Jato case: The Supreme Court Judges should not be mentioned. Naturally, much speculation ensued about other secret motives for cancelling the plea bargain, given the fact that a number of plea bargains had leaked without any requests for cancellation. The commentator Nassif, for instance, speculated that annulling the plea bargain of Leo Pinheiro would also mean protecting the PSDB parliamentarians implicated in this testimony (ibid.). The same could be said, on the other hand, for Lula, who supposedly had been in contact with Pinheiro on many occasions and allegedly benefitted personally from various services provided by his company OAS. In any case, the debate demonstrated that lawyers in plea bargain negotiations seem to assume that public attention will help defendants – or, at least, that the federal prosecutors claim that lawyers leak with this motive.

The Phone Tap Case and the Suspension of Lula's Nomination as Minister

The leak case with the most far-reaching consequences during the Lava-Jato investigation was, arguably, the leak of recorded phone conversations between President Rousseff and the ex-President Lula. To recapitulate: Sérgio Moro had ordered phone taps of Lula in the days preceding his testimony. This was only suspended on March 16, and the audio files were – according to the Curitiba court – by human error publicized to the journalists following the case. In reality, this meant that every journalist with access to the public parts of the investigations received a push notification in their inbox reporting that new material had been added to the case. That afternoon, word spread rapidly from newsroom to newsroom and the audio files, despite being taken down from the site of the Curitiba court, kept circulating.

A number of conversations featuring Lula were of interest to the press, but the central object of the leak was the conversation where Rousseff mentions his nomination, and that Lula could use the official document that would effectively install him as minister "in case of necessity." Because this could be interpreted as one way of ensuring the *foro privilegiado* for Lula, removing his case from the jurisdiction of Sérgio Moro and relocating the case to the Supreme Court, it would also effectively mean that the president and the ex-president had worked toward obstructing justice. If this was the case, the leak was – arguably – justified. If not, Moro had been out of bounds by not only ordering the recording of the president (which is the exclusive jurisdiction of the Supreme Court, but only if he or she is officially investigated), but also by publicizing this in relation to a criminal case without authorization. Compounding the problems of jurisdictional competency and the legality of publicity was the fact that this particular conversation, in contrast to the rest of the recordings, had occurred after the order for ending the phone taps had been issued by Moro. Thus, as evidence in a trial, it would not even be legal on formal grounds.

Nevertheless, the argument for obstruction of justice became the centerpiece of a number of petitions, filed by diverse independent individuals (lawyers and parliamentarians among these), requesting various Brazilian courts for a suspension of Lula's appointment as minister. Because of the national character of a minister, all federal courts could actually effect such a suspension. As the day wore on, rulings came from several courts, decreeing such a preliminary suspension of Lula's position as minister, and a few rulings from other courts annulled those suspensions. Confusion mounted as to the legality of the petitions, as well as the status of Lula in relation to a hypothetical arrest order issued by Moro. For the duration of those minutes in which Lula was minister, he held the prerogative of the *foro privilegiado*, and responded to the Supreme Court. As an ordinary citizen without holding public office, he was in the jurisdiction of Moro insofar as his case related to the Petrobras case. In total, 50 petitions were considered by Brazilian courts, and 13 of these were filed in the Supreme Court, with 9 of these being allocated to the Supreme Judge Gilmar Mendes.

While protests were gathering in front of the Palacio de Planalto that afternoon, journalists were working frantically to check out all the material of the leaked audio files. That night, the *Jornal Nacional* started by introducing the leaks as the height of the crisis of the Lava-Jato scandal: The first words of the anchor William Bonner were "A crise no governo Dilma Rousseff atinge o ponto mais alto" ("the crisis of the Dilma Rousseff government peaks"). The peaking crisis was then related to the nomination of Lula for the cabinet, without mentioning at this point why a nomination by itself could constitute a crisis. The implicit justification was given in the third sentence of the newscast, where Bonner repeated the suspicion of the Lava-Jato task force and the judge of Curitiba: The nomination would let Lula escape the reach of Sergio Moro and the Lava-Jato investigations. Thus, the crisis presented in the opening sentence was predicated on the nomination having this subversive intention. The newscast went on to report live, on site, concerning the protests in the federal capital. More protests ignited the same night and continued the following day in the larger cities of Brazil.

The following morning, the conversation was quoted ad verbatim on the newspaper front pages. By midday, Rousseff swore Lula in as minister in a ceremony in the Palácio do Planalto, but shadows of doubt and attrition were showing on the face of Lula. During the ceremony, Rousseff pointed out that his appointment as minister (*termos de posse*) had not been signed in advance by her – and that this declaration, therefore, would have been null and void as a legal shield for Lula if Moro had ordered his arrest. Rousseff asserted that the phone taps were illegal, and the two PT leaders signed the document and exited the palace soon afterwards.

Two days after the leak, on the 18th, Supreme Judge Gilmar Mendes ended the controversy between the different courts and judges of diverse jurisdictions by suspending Lula's nomination as minister. Historically affiliated with the main opposition party PSDB (and nominated for the STF during the last PSDB government), it came as no surprise that Mendes ratified the suspensions doled out by other judges. In his verdict, Mendes affirmed the malevolent intentions of Rousseff:

The goal of the lie is clear: Avoiding compliance with an arrest order from the first-level judge. A kind of amnesty, issued by the President of the Republic. That is, the issuing demonstrates not only the objective elements of deviant finality, but also the intent of fraud.

(Mendes 2016: 33, translation mine)

As it turned out, no arrest order would come from Sérgio Moro, but the STF anyway filed away the remaining counter-petitions in Lula's favor. As the impeachment process removed Rousseff from the presidency, all ministers were discharged, and the judicial proceedings on the matter ground to a halt.

The case was emblematic, because the leaking actor was clearly identified, and because it clearly demonstrated the power of leaks combined with judicial measures. A government powerless to nominate ministers[1] is, arguably, hardly a government. The level of judicial interference in a matter of the executive branch was extraordinary, based on evidence with only dubious legality. These leaks – or rather the mediatized spectacle, sparking protests and spates of speculation – discredited Lula and Rousseff in the eyes of their opponents, and crucially demonstrated that the government was fighting an uphill battle, not just against political opponents, but also actors of the judiciary. In the following chapter, several aspects of this case are discussed further.

Leaks Against Ex-Presidents

Rousseff and Lula would not be the only ex-presidents to feel the power of leaks, however. In fact, all of the elected Brazilian presidents since the return to democracy (that is, all but Itamar Franco) have been implicated by leaks of the Lava-Jato probe. But these leaks have provoked a varied range of reactions and responses in the legal arena, from the complete absence of inquiries to a historical sentence: The first civilian president, José Sarney (who was only indirectly elected vice-president by the Colégio Eleitoral in January 1985, and took the mantle from the dying president-elect Tancredo Neves at the moment of his inauguration) was caught on tape in a leak in May 2016. In the series of secret recordings of conversations made by the Transpetro director Sergio Machado, Sarney was caught discussing how he could help Machado avoid being arrested by the Lava-Jato probe. The recordings were leaked to *Folha* immediately after Temer took power, and in June 2016, the prosecutor-general requested the immediate imprisonment of Sarney along with the other interlocutors of Machado. The STF denied the request. Sarney has not been known to be the object of the Lava-Jato investigations, even though he had retired from the Senate in 2015, and therefore was not protected by the *foro privilegiado* nor in the jurisdiction of the STF.

Another former president, Fernando Collor de Mello (who served in 1990–1992 as the first democratically elected president after the dictatorship, and who became the first Brazilian president to be removed through impeachment) was also indicted several times by the prosecutor-general based on evidence from the Lava-Jato investigations, and Collor is facing charges in the Supreme Court in one of these cases at the time of writing. The evidence against Collor emerged from the very first plea bargains of the case. Along with Eduardo Cunha, he was among the first politicians to be denounced in the Lava-Jato case, and he is the third senator who is facing a trial in the Supreme Court case.

The arrested senator Delcídio do Amaral, ex-PSDB, ex-PT and ex-Petrobras manager, testified in prison and implicated the next elected president, Fernando Henrique Cardoso (1995–2002). Amaral's testimony depicted corruption as a generalized model of management in Petrobras in the 1990s, and documents found in his house suggested that Cardoso was well aware of the fact.

As described in the overview of the leaks, as well as in the section above, both Lula and Temer were implicated in the Lava-Jato case by leaks at several points. Temer was, as vice-president and president, shielded from denunciations of corruption in periods outside of his current mandate, just as Dilma Rousseff was during her presidency. After the so-called "controlled actions" of the Lava-Jato investigation in 2017, however, the prosecutor-general filed two indictments, to be ratified by Congress before the corruption charges against Temer could be sent to the STF. This was legal because the evidence collected in those phases of investigations indicated criminal activity while Temer was functioning as president. On August 2, 2017, the Congress voted against the first indictment, 263 to 267 votes, protecting the executive from this interference, and on October 25, 251 congressmen voted against and 233 for the indictment. Meanwhile, Lula, as we saw above, did not gain any such protection despite his historical influence. Five different corruption cases (resulting in nine trials) were brought to bear on the ex-president, and on July 12, 2017, Lula became the first convicted ex-president ever in Brazilian history. Sérgio Moro sentenced him to nine years and six months in the case of the beachside apartment refurbished by the construction company OAS, and the federal appeal court augmented the sentence to 12 years and 1 month. Lula was incarcerated in Curitiba on April 7, 2018.

Media Outlets under Attack

Latin American governments in the last decade have been highly critical of the region's media (Kitzberger 2014), and Brazil is increasingly conforming to that pattern. The attention given to the Lava-Jato scandals has pushed Lula, Rousseff, Temer, as well as many other politicians into aggressive stances vis-à-vis the Brazilian media outlets. Throughout the three years of the Lava-Jato case, politicians implicated in the case have repeatedly denounced the Brazilian media for being biased, printing slander, manipulating, lying and actively interfering in political matters related to publication of leaks. In Chapter 5, the reader may observe the exact level of bias of attention in three Brazilian media outlets, while the following example is merely an illustration. It serves to illustrate that almost no matter what they do to prevent it, political actors perceive that they are at the mercy of the media.

The first major leak in the Lava-Jato case, publicized by the weekly magazine *Veja*, initiated a two-year period of intense dispute between the press and the presidency. At the final debate between the two presidential candidates left in the race, the incumbent Rousseff lashed out against *Veja*:

I cannot keep silent facing this act of election terrorism, articulated by *Veja* and its secret partners. It is a shameful attitude for the press and it damages our democratic tradition. Without providing any concrete evidence, and yet again based on supposed declarations made by persons from the criminal underworld, this magazine tries to involve me and President Lula in the Petrobras situation under legal investigation. All of the voters know about the systematic campaign this magazine has been waging for years against Lula and me, but this time, *Veja* trespassed all boundaries.

(Dilma Rousseff, cited in Chaia 2016: 50, translation mine)

At this point, PT, Lula, and Rousseff initiated a range of lawsuits and libel suits against *Veja* for calumny. In total, nine different lawsuits were initiated, but the freedom of expression clause of the Constitution protected *Veja* in each of these cases. The same pattern has been true of other weekly magazines and Globo.

The openly confrontational stance of Rousseff (and, in 2016, Lula) toward specific media outlets (see Almeida 2016) aligns Brazil with many of the leftist governments in neighboring countries, most notably Argentina in the Kirchner period (Kitzberger 2014). However, while Lula in his second mandate launched a public broadcasting policy (Matos 2012: 161ff.), Rousseff never got around to challenging mainstream media through reform. In the legal arena, the PT leaders had to accept that their constitutionally protected right to respond to media coverage only got them into the very last paragraphs of articles. Other examples of libel suits have involved Eduardo Cunha, Aécio Neves, and a range of other prominent politicians, but the conflict initiated by leaks has not – in the Lava-Jato case, anyway – resulted in substantial changes in the way these media outlets cover corruption.

The Effect of Leaks upon Coalition Formation

The political scientist Manuel Balán has convincingly showed how that corruption denunciations have been used strategically in Latin American democracies during the last decades (Balán 2011, 2014). Denunciations are useful in two different strategic moves: Either as a convenient way of leaving a government coalition (which Balán calls "to jump ship") or as a way of increasing power within government at the expense of other coalition partners (which is termed "leap-frog"). Thus, the public denunciation, or leak to one or more media organization, provides a pretext for challenging and renegotiating power relations between parties, but also between Congress and the presidency. In some cases, Balán notes (2011: 462), governments are not under much pressure from a weak or fragmented opposition in Congress, in which case corruption leaks are more useful for leap-frogging than for jumping ship. With a strong opposition, there are more constraints for the leap-frog strategy, while jumping ship becomes viable if (but only if) there is space in the opposition coalition for another party.

As seen in the case of Eduardo Cunha's break with the government (the third major leak of the case, described above), the leaks and subsequent denunciations of corruption in Brazil provided exactly that: A pretext for jumping ship. Eventually, the jump-ship strategy of PMDB was wildly successful, giving the party control of the presidency and remaining in control of the Senate. In the following, I will describe how the leaks fed this jump-ship strategy and gradually undermined the coalition formation of the Rousseff government. I will heuristically use cabinet positions as a proxy for the distribution of coalition goods (Raile et al. 2011), as the ideological coherence of Brazilian parties is often weak. This means that the use of roll-call votes as a proxy for government coalition yields an unstable picture, while the cabinet positions are more stable over time.

At the start of her second mandate, Dilma Rousseff counted upon the following ten parties to govern: PT, PMDB, PSD, PP, PR, PRB, PDT, PTB, Pros, and PCdoB, which tallied up to 329 members of the Câmara's 513 seats (distributed in the following way: PT 70, PMDB 66, PSD 37, PP 36, PR 34, PTB 25, PRB 21, PDT 19, Pros 11, and PCdoB 10). In the Senate, the coalition numbered 57 parliamentarians out of 81 seats (distributed in the following way: PMDB 18, PT 14, PDT 8, PP 5, PR 4, PSD 3, PTB 3, PCdoB 1, Pros 1) (D'Agostino 2014). In both houses of Congress, the coalition numbered around three-fifths of the congressmen – enough to pass constitutional amendments, if need be.

However, these numbers covered the fact that a large number of the coalition parties had elected conservative politicians for their seats. This created a center-right majority in Congress that throughout 2015 succeeded in passing an unusually high number of bills authored by the legislators, rather than the executive branch. The frenetic pace of legislative activity was directed by the PMDB leaders Eduardo Cunha and Renan Calheiros, occupying the positions as presidents of the two houses of Congress.

The cabinet positions of the coalition were distributed with a heavy emphasis on PT leaders (nine slots) and experts from civil society, leaving six minister slots for PMDB (most of them heavy-weight ministries such as Agriculture and Energy), while one slot was distributed to each of the minor coalition partners: Pros, initially, had Cid Gomes as minister of Education, PSD's Gilberto Kassab headed the Ministry of Cities, PCdoB's Aldo Rebelo was in charge of the Defence Ministry, PRB's George Hilton headed the Ministry of Sports, PP had Gilberto Occhi in the Ministry of National Integration, PR was represented by Antônio Carlos Rodrigues as Minister of Transports and Manoel Dias of PDT as Labour Minister. The PMDB politician and former president of the Câmara, Henrique Eduardo Alves entered the cabinet in April, after a minor reshuffle.

As Eduardo Cunha became the center of attention with the leak implicating him in the Lava-Jato case, he urged his party PMDB to break with the government. In response, president Rousseff decided to offer more cabinet positions to PMDB and closed the deal on October 2, 2015. The number of ministries was reduced from 39 to 31, but PMDB gained a cabinet position, going from six to seven ministers.[2] However, the government still struggled to find support in Congress, and the final approval of the year's fiscal goal was only passed on December 2.

The minister of Civil Aviation, Eliseu Padilha of PMDB, left the cabinet on December 4, just after the impeachment petition had been accepted by his party colleague Cunha. That became the first sign that the government coalition was ripping at the seams. Over the Christmas holidays, and the Carnival season in February, political negotiations slowed, but in early March 2016, a number of events transpired that undermined Rousseff and PT. Two major leaks (numbers 4 and 5, in the overview of leaks above) rocked the Rousseff administration, Lula was forced to testify, and protests dominated the streets of the state capitals on the weekends. From then on, the parties of the coalition began withdrawing support: On March 16, the PRB announced that it would leave the government. "This crisis cannot be endured, or be allowed to continue. The Brazilians are suffering," said the PRB president Marcos Pereira, referencing the wave of protests (on March 13) and the negative news about the PT (especially the leak of the imprisoned Senator Delcídio do Amaral the week before). The party also announced that its minister of Sports, George Hilton, would leave the position. In response, Hilton left PRB, announced his affiliation with Pros, and remained minister of Sports until the impeachment of Rousseff. The then-president of PTB, Cristiane Brasil, likewise, announced that she would vote for the impeachment of Rousseff, on March 18, although the party only officially recommended impeachment on April 13.

PMDB had been deliberating internally when to leave ever since Cunha urged the party to leave the year before. During the parliamentary recess and the internal elections for party president, the discussions had demonstrated increasing hostility toward Rousseff, and a party convention was called shortly after the 2016 carnival. The agenda was simple: A vote whether or not to leave the government. Henrique Eduardo Alves left his minister position on the eve of the convention, on March 28. The following day, PMDB pulled off the shortest party convention ever seen in Brazil, as the sole point on the agenda was resolved in three minutes. After a symbolic vote, the senator Romero Jucá, who would become minister for a fortnight before resigning after a new leak, announced that the motion for withdrawing from government was approved. Next to Jucá stood Eduardo Cunha, and the event ended with the 100 delegates shouting "Brasil pra Frente, Temer Presidente" ("Go Brazil, Temer for President"). Nonetheless, the ministers Celso Pansera, Marcelo Castro, and Katia Abreu remained ministers in the Rousseff administration until she was ousted.

Sensing that a new majority was about to form, the strategy of jumping ship suddenly became attractive to the rest of the coalition parties, and the exit of PMDB therefore started a wave of defections: On April 12, PP announced their decision to abandon government, support impeachment, and Occhi left the Ministry of National Integration the following day. The same day, April 13, the PSD group leader in the Congress, Rogerio Rosso, declared that there was a broad consensus about supporting impeachment, and that the minister of the party, Kassab, was known to respect the will of the parliamentary group. Kassab resigned two days later, despite stating that he "was convinced of the President's personal integrity." The parliamentarians of PR never decided upon an official party line and ended up mostly voting for impeachment (with the votes 26 for and 10 against), but the PR minister Rodrigues continued in the cabinet until the final removal of Rousseff.

The process of coalition breakdown (and subsequent formation) in 2015–2016 was a two-step process, triggered by leaks: First, in July 2015, the initial conflict between the legislative and executive branches, or rather between Cunha and Rousseff, and then, the leaks targeting Lula and PT in March 2016, which influenced and boosted the large-scale protests in the streets of the capitals on March 13 and 16.

Most of the parties jumping ship went on to adhere to the line of PMDB and the new president throughout 2016, essentially replacing PT with PMDB in charge. The new government was thus based on center-party votes, just like the Rousseff government, but crucially augmented by the votes of the former opposition-leading party PSDB.

The strategy of jumping ship, however, later came to be used against PMDB and Michel Temer as the JBS leak turned public. The large coalition partner PSDB became divided, had one minister (Bruno Araújo) state that he would leave the cabinet and two smaller coalition parties also left (PTN and PPS, with the minister Roberto Freire). Araujo only left the cabinet six months after the scandal, however, as PSDB was preparing to leave the government *en bloc*. The rupture of the Temer government coalition resulted in further delays to the reform bills in Congress in 2017.

Preliminary Conclusion

I will sum up the preceding sections by highlighting several interesting aspects of leaks from these cases. Media leaks about corruption provide political actors with opportunities for shifting political allegiances, and leaks also provide the conditions for a range of exceptional judicial interventions into politics and even conditions for political interference in accountability processes. This means that leaks may be harnessed for political effect through four mechanisms. First, leaks may rapidly bypass normal gatekeeping and dominate the media agenda, and this will be discussed further in Chapter 5. Second, by virtue of their extraordinariness, leaks absorb attention and this also means eclipsing other information on certain actors; in other words, the leaks work as a distraction-spin, by removing emphasis from political attempts at active agenda setting. Third, this locates specific politicians in defensive or reactive positions in media narratives, as news on leaks frequently assesses the political capital of denounced and implicated actors, ultimately signaling potential outcomes of political and judicial processes and the relative probabilities of these outcomes. Fourth, leaks are crucial for setting the media agenda at timely moments before previously scheduled public protests and manifestations, thereby mobilizing and supporting the goals of these protests. Leaks thus provide legitimation for planned or spontaneous protests, but they may also legitimate legal actions on the horizon, such as upcoming trials or expected arrests.

The timing of leaks is also crucial. The visibility conferred by leaks to certain bits of scandalous information worked at key moments of the political events that eventually resulted in the impeachment of the president. With this, I claim that the political effect of these leaks went beyond the mere sequence of scapegoating and scandalizing parties in the mainstream media: At critical moments, the leaks shed light on certain elements in the public sphere (evidence, connections, and allegations) and what they made visible in this light, then, was a certain knowledge – knowledge of the moral comportment of politicians, as well as knowledge of positions of denunciation and defense. This is further elaborated in the final discussions of this chapter.

Leaks and the Question of Truth, Knowledge, and Visibility in Public Spheres

In this section, I will move the problem of leaks into more philosophical territory and explore how leaks relate to knowledge in public spheres. I will make a general argument about the desire for transparency in contemporary democracies, and then show that this produces a particular kind of visibility in the Brazilian mainstream media. First, however, I will consider how information becomes knowledge and how knowledge can be known as truthful in public spheres.

When particular news items reporting on the Lava-Jato investigations and leaks are closely examined, it becomes apparent that such texts at times play hard and fast with the truth – or at least work in a gray area of conjecture and conflicting truth claims. Grammatically, many news items exhibit far more sentences in the conditional and subjunctive than usually seen in the news. There are many reasons for journalists to produce news with speculative content, having to do with the availability and quality of information in leaks, especially leaks of testimonies. Specifically, information gathered by journalists might be incomplete, based on not verified (or not verifiable) witness accounts, and it may often come from obviously biased sources, or in other ways be of debatable credibility. This leads reporting to revolve around speculation and inference, and, in order to stay within (mainstream) journalistic ethical bounds, it requires the journalists to emphasize that statements of facts are merely possibly true.

News texts describing leaked information, like other forms of speech events, organize information in more or less coherent story arcs through intertextuality (Wortham and Rhodes 2012). One news text, by association, connects to earlier news texts dealing with the same case or related corruption. Therefore, if an earlier story about the corruption of an actor is well-known, then the new text will work as confirmation ("actor A is corrupt") or continuation ("he was corrupt then and still is") at the level of reception. For each new piece of evidence, denunciation, or testimony, the suspicions of political transgression are reinforced. This reinforcement works through the ongoing link of news media texts, accumulating on top of earlier texts in the chain of scandals and leaked testimonies, by suspending the ambiguity or implied uncertainty embedded in each individual text. This suspension is effected by weight of numbers and through blunt repetition. In other words, repeated news items about corruption will seemingly demonstrate that the denunciations are factual, bringing to mind the old idiom "where there is smoke, there's fire."

Furthermore, news texts do not merely talk about the past. In scandal news texts, it is especially apparent that the question of consequences is also of great interest, and such texts will usually include one or more sentences about the reactions (demands for justice, for instance) and the likely scenarios triggered by the revelations. Thus, through these intertextual connections and speculative predictions, story arcs emerge, projecting certain futures for the implicated actors. Thus, grammatically, as well as conceptually, revelations and corruption stories branch into the fictional territory, and therefore, when written coherently, scandalous information turns into "a story" (Bird 1997), in both the journalistic sense (Tuchman 1978) and the narrative sense.

No matter the grammatical ambiguity and hedging, the information presented in news items then turns into public knowledge about corruption. This knowledge (of stories and actors) spins a web of facticity (ibid.: 82), constructed and mutually legitimized by various media institutions (Kristensen and Mortensen 2013). Repeatedly recycled information from leaks winds up as truth because the watchdog role of the media carries expectations of truth: Audiences (or at least audiences before the age of post-factual politics) expect media to check facts, to investigate, and to correct their coverage if new information comes to light. So, a continuous chain of news texts about a parliamentarian's corruption will normally be considered a tell-tale sign that he is *in fact* corrupt – even if each text included many conditional clauses and textual hedges. Audiences presume some kernel of truth despite ambiguity, qualifying clauses, and conjecture in the grammatical content of the news reports. This is one aspect of the regime of truth (Foucault 1980) governing modern mediatized societies: News media coverage represents truth, and that assumption has only lately been called into question with the increased attention to fake news and post-truth politics.

Truth and knowledge is always constructed, however. One of the seminal philosophers of social sciences, Michel Foucault, argued that truth was produced by institutions, politics, and social practices. He suggested that we can think of society as constituted in part by certain regimes of truth, defining and thereby creating what normally passes for accepted truth:

> Each society has its regime of truth, its "general politics" of truth: that is, the types of discourse which it accepts and makes function as true; the mechanisms and instances which enable one to distinguish true and false statements, the means by which each is sanctioned; the techniques and pro-cedures accorded value in the acquisition of truth; the status of those who are charged with saying what counts as true.
>
> (Ibid.: 131)

Among other things, Foucault worked with the installment of truth through mental institutions, medical professions and techniques. The practices surround-ing these defined (and continues to define) what it means to be sane and insane, thus partly defining truth and erecting the boundaries for the accepted experience of the world. Media organizations, meanwhile, install truths about the leaders and decision-makers of our world. The regime of knowledge relevant to leaks is that which John Thompson has termed "the new visibility" – a unidirectional, mediated *episteme* (or horizon of knowledge), structured by a global framework of media technologies, experiential and cultural forms, peculiar to the age of television and internet. In Thompson's words, the emerging visibility regime of the modern (if not the post-modern) sphere of media creates "a society in which it was possible and, indeed, increasingly common for political leaders and other individuals to appear before distant audiences and lay bare some aspect of their self or their personal life" (Thompson 2005: 38). Thus, politics across the globe are in part governed by the techniques and practices that allow our leaders to appear before us – which is, needless to say, media techniques and practices. The disclosure of the personal back-region (ibid.: 44, Goffmann 1956) has become the norm of politics – and a willful manipulation of that disclosure, though perhaps always present and always expected, is the centerpiece of many scandals in the late twentieth and early twenty-first century.

The mediated visibility that Thompson speaks of enables the public to "know" their leaders, and audiences generally suppose that media render politics and political personalities visible. Leaks shed a new light on this knowledge in the public sphere at critical moments with disclosure of evidence, connections, and allegations. What leaks make visible in this light, then, is a more specific kind of case-based knowledge – a knowledge of the moral comportment of politicians, as well as knowledge of rhetorical positions of denunciation and defense. This shows that audiences are also aware that sometimes, leaders deceitfully provide disinformation or misinformation (see Chapter 5 concerning this distinction). Tellingly, TV viewership in Brazil is negatively correlated with support for political actors such as government, Congress, and parties (Mesquita 2014: 24). The possibility of deceit by media personalities is always present, and leaks either confirm suspicions of deceit and disinformation, or, if the allegation is proven wrong, underscore the truth of the leaks' possible impact upon a specific political career. In sum, when performing the role of society's watchdog (Waisbord 2000), media organizations act in the role of an arbiter of truth in the public sphere at the same time, and the power inherent in this role is tremendous.

A politician in public office is assumed to promote the collective will of his or her constituency – that is the justification for electoral and representative democracy. However, there is also the background assumption that the public office should not be used for personal gain at the expense of that collective goal. In ordinary politics, that assumption goes largely unnoticed, but it becomes very visible with leaks. Indeed, leaks are interesting to the public because they present a rupture in that assumption. Leaks thus perform a double check on the visibility maxim already in place: Did this politician present a truthful picture of herself? Did he or she show the true backstage persona on the screen, in the radio or in text, or at least a representation in which the supporters could believe? Thompson points out that this check is a crucial test for politics at large in these conditions of mediatized visibility:

> People become more concerned with the character of the individuals who are (or might become) their leaders and more concerned about their trustworthiness, because increasingly these become the principal means of guaranteeing that political promises will be kept and that difficult decisions in the face of complexity and uncertainty will be made on the basis of sound judgement. The politics of trust becomes increasingly important, not because politicians are inherently less trustworthy today than they were in the past, but because the social conditions that had previously underwritten their credibility have been eroded.
>
> (Thompson 2005: 46)

The kind of public-political individual groomed in our mediatized world is a subject formed by the virtual subjugation to the regime of visibility. Thus, the threat of a leak works like a spectral Panopticon – always looming, always monitoring, but to an unknowable extent. Public officeholders are punishable in consequence of their visibility, and in consequence of the traces their actions produce in various public domains, be it bank accounts, investments, tax information, or entertainment preferences. The public individual must internalize this visibility in order to present a clean backstage persona to media and (through media) to supporters and voters. The emergence of a scandal represents a failed test of accountability to supporters, constituencies, and the public at large: Trust has been invested (say, by a constituency) but the trustee has failed to live up to this trust (Boltanski and Thevenot 2006: 133ff.).

What is at stake in a scandal is not merely the trust in one individual, however. The scandal is also a process that draws boundaries in social space, that is, a process that allocates (negative) value to certain kinds of behavior performed by the representative bodies of the State. With a scandalizing leak, the news items and commentary will valorize and laud some actions (the disclosure and distribution of the leaked information, for the sake of the public), while the disclosed political or economic actions (embezzling, bribing, money laundering, etc.) are condemned.

In the journalistic discourse on the disclosure of such actions through leaks, boundaries of the social space are drawn, and certain sets of knowledge about the society are constituted, and media thereby provides "publicly available and politically vital spaces for imagining communities" (Damgaard 2015: 419ff.). The imagined political communities, however, might be imagined as corrupted (Gupta 1995). The mediatized space for imagining the State, or a nation, is also contested, as is the knowledge within these spaces. More insidiously, they are eroded in the sense that the arbiters of the space are not journalists and editors with public profiles, ethical standards, and explicit agendas subject to scrutiny. Instead, the space created by leaks emerges from a vault of information controlled by unknowable leaking actors, through channels that are inaccessible to the public.

Summing up, scandals provide knowledge about specific individuals, their actions, and their trustworthiness, but at the same time, scandals negotiate meaning concerning the values that govern public life in general. One of the values of political life that is increasingly becoming important is transparency, and the next section will discuss the relationship between transparency, knowledge, and leaks.

Media, Leaks, and the Transparency Creep

The mechanism of leaks in public spheres taps into a larger ideological current that has been emerging at least since the early 1990s. This current has consisted in the promotion of transparency and a number of associated concepts (due diligence, compliance, and to some extent corporate social responsibility) and was catapulted unto the international scene of governance when former World Bank employees founded the NGO Transparency International. This section explores how leaks play into the discourse and practices of transparency in the global media ecology. First, I will define the contours of transparency discourse, and then point out how leaks (especially leaks about corruption) fit into the mold provided by this discourse.

Although the contemporary discourse concerning transparency is of a recent vintage, it is a societal value with deep roots. It is the selective application of a more general moral principle inherited from the Enlightenment:

As a moral principle, however, transparency, stretched farther than calls for self-repair of oversight systems. It proposes an overall "antiseptic treatment" of visibility for the society. Its canonical roots also date back to Enlightenment political imaginaries, deriving from Jeremy Bentham's utilitarianism, which claims that maximum transparency contributes to maximal happiness ... A diluted version of this legacy is embedded in professional journalism, as the notions of the Fourth Estate and watchdog function of journalists suggest.

(Heikkilä and Kunelius 2017)

Heikkilä and Kunelius highlight that watchdog journalism and the political imaginary of transparency are linked. This is particularly evident now, in this precise historical moment, where leaks enter the scene: A combination of particular forms of data handling, information distribution, and oaths and technologies of secrecy, with journalistic collaboration across national borders and an at times uneasy commitment to traditional news values. In this way, leaks provide journalists with the raw material of the scandals of the twenty-first century, quite different in its incipient form from the pattern of Watergate (two dedicated journalists digging after facts for several years). The outcome – for instance, media pressure and popular protests against corrupt leaders – might still be the same, but the raw material and the labor of the scandal looks much different now, because of the whole gamut of server technology, hacker communities, social media, and popular post-Watergate mythology.

It is not just media technologies and their viral potential that make leaks fit exceedingly well with transparency discourse, however. A keyword in transparency discourse is accountability, and this is another cross-over between scandals and transparency efforts. As Michael Power and other British scholars have argued (Power 1997, 2000, Strathern 2000), a transparency creep has been globally visible for decades, so that audits and accountability are invasive concepts in many social and institutional settings: "The concept of audit in turn has broken loose from its moorings in finance and accounting; its own expanded presence gives it the power of a descriptor seemingly applicable to all kinds of reckonings, evaluations and measurements" (Strathern 2000: 2). Expanding this argument, a decade later, Hansen and Flyverbom note that

the project of exposing the hidden is important in many contexts, ranging from business and politics to science, but when put into practice it often ends up concealing more than is revealed, such as when an account of something in the past simplifies so much that it eliminates important, contextual information. In this way, transparency can easily become part of the problem it was intended to solve, producing concerns with distortion, concealment and collusion. Similarly, we need to consider whether highly touted phenomena like "big data" will make it possible to uncover the unknown while remaining sensitive to contextual dynamics ... or rather lead to new types of opacity. More generally, the project of transparency elicits a particular stance towards what counts as truth and certainty. When transparency is "rolled out" programmatically in organizations or societies, typically with a view to correcting failures or empowering employees and citizens, it is understood narrowly as a superior mode of knowledge, a cultural signifier of unmediated objective information.

(Hansen and Flyverbom 2014: 2)

Leaks are, in an interesting way, connected to the transparency culture and the desire for ever more disclosure. The technological organization of WikiLeaks, for instance, is based in the alternative democratic and informational ideals of hacker communities, where the disclosure of any and all information is good in principle and practice. Nick Davies, a journalist at the *Guardian*, working with WikiLeaks, described the ideology of the WikiLeaks founder: "The problem is [that Julian Assange is] basically a computer hacker. He comes from a simplistic ideology, or at that stage he did, that all information has to be published, that all information is good" (quoted in Leigh and Harding 2011: Ch. 8, para. 24). In this ideology lies a tension with principles of news value (Chadwick 2013), and moreover, as seen above, a tension with the gatekeeping role of journalism – and the position of the journalists as disclosing agents in public spheres.

The ideology of leaks, furthermore, is interesting in relation to the question of knowledge. As Hansen and Flyverbom argue above, when information is exposed, even if it distorts or conceals, it is positioned as unmediated and objective because of its disclosure. This is logically flawed, of course, but it works at a symbolic level: Leaks create a new terrain of knowledge which has been less contested than many other scandals, because leaks are imagined as rooted in data and facts.

Scandals were, to be sure, always a potential setup – the Dreyfus affair of France at the turn of the last century being the most prominent, classic case. Leaks, in contrast, ostensibly enter the public sphere as ready and transparent information. The information of leaks is apparently spawned as truth but may not be indicative of any criminal acts or moral wrongdoings. In the Lava-Jato case, the leaks at times seemed to be quite true but tedious and non-transgressive, and the power/knowledge relation they enacted was, instead, that of generally tarnishing the image of an individual politician. By leaking pieces of information cast as evidence in a trial (although no trial existed at that time), anything could be made to indicate something heinous and a secret motive.

Scholars (such as Allern and Pollack 2012, Thompson 2000, Tumber and Waisbord 2004) have thought of scandals as a dramatization of political or moral conflict, an occasion for deliberating the limits of public behavior, for judging transgressive behavior, and expelling, catharsis-style, offensive moral phenomena from the body politic. Media are ubiquitous in these processes of fertilizing the ground for scandalous denunciations and then reaping the rewards of attention through quasi-public processes of sense-making and extra-judicial trial. And media scandals have always been contested and objects of critique – media hunts are perceived to be sensationalizing, dramatizing, and individualizing, or just plain wrong. But with leaks, informational content is being pushed into public spheres in a qualitatively new way, in a manner that is rarely questioned on epistemological grounds. This innovation reflects the wider cultural and socio-political developments: The episteme and imaginaries of visibility of modern media worlds (Krotz 2014: 84ff., Thompson 2005) have evolved since Watergate, and leaks are now forcing political practices into the limelight, promising transparency and accountability. When they do so with vested political interests, leaks may circumvent both journalistic pretensions to un-biased or objective truth, judicial pretensions to fair trials, and societal pretensions to citizenship under a rule of law. This targeted transparency can have perverse effects, however; some of these effects have been demonstrated in this chapter. The ultimate consequences of media disclosure of corruption for the Brazilian democracy is a thread that runs through the following chapters and is treated in detail in the final chapter.

Notes

1 The Rousseff administration had, earlier in March, nominated Wellington César Lima for Minister of Justice, but his nomination was also overturned, because Lima was employed as prosecutor in the MPF, and this overlap is not permitted under the Constitution.
2 The second cabinet of 2015 was announced on October 2 by Dilma Rousseff. The reshuffle reduced the number of ministries from 39 to 31, and retained most of the minor coalition partners' ministers, but installed several new ministers from the ranks of PMDB: Kátia Abreu, Leonardo Picciani, Eliseu Padilha, Eduardo Braga, Helder Barbalho, Marcelo Castro, Henrique Eduardo Alves, and Celso Pansera represented PMDB in the cabinet. PT had nine slots, and the cabinet included eight ministers not affiliated politically. The other coalition partners with ministerial positions were PDT (André Figueiredo), PSD (Gilberto Kassab), PTB (Armando Monteiro), PCdoB (Aldo Rebelo), PRB (George Hilton), PP (Gilberto Occhi), and PR (Antônio Carlos Rodrigues).

References

Albuquerque, A.L. (2017) "Sem exposição, é impossível avançar contra poderosos, afirma Dallagnol" *Folha de S. Paulo*, p. A4, November 24. Retrieved from www1. folha.uol.com.br/poder/2017/11/1937812-sem-exposicao-e-impossivel-avancar-contra-poderosos-afirma-dallagnol.shtml.
Allern, S. and Pollack, E. (eds.) (2012) *Scandalous! The Mediated Construction of Political Scandals in Four Nordic Countries*. Göteborg: Nordicom.
Almeida, R. de (2016) *A Sombra do Poder. Os Bastidores da Crise Que Derrubou Dilma Rousseff*. Rio de Janeiro: Editora LeYa.
Arantes, R. (2002) *Ministério Público e Política no Brasil*. São Paulo: Sumaré/Fabesp.
Arantes, R. (2011) "The Federal Police and the Ministério Público." In T. Power and M. Taylor (eds.), *Corruption and Democracy in Brazil* (184–217). South Bend, IN: University of Notre Dame Press.
Balán, M. (2011) "Competition by Denunciation: The Political Dynamics of Corruption Scandals in Argentina and Chile" *Comparative Politics*, vol. 43(4), 459–478.

Balán, M. (2014) "Surviving Corruption in Brazil: Lula's and Dilma's Success Despite Corruption Allegations, and Its Consequences" *Journal of Politics in Latin America*, vol. 6(3), 67–93.

Beach, D. and Pedersen, R.B. (2013) *Process-Tracing Methods: Foundations and Guidelines*. Ann Arbor: University of Michigan Press.

Benkler, Y. (2014) "A Public Accountability Defense for National Security Leakers and Whistleblowers" *Harvard Law and Policy Review*, vol. 8, 281–326.

Bird, E. (1997) "What a Story! Understanding the Audience for Scandal." In J. Lull and S. Hinerman (eds.), *Media Scandals: Morality and Desire in the Popular Culture Marketplace* (99–121). New York: Columbia University Press.

Biroli, F., Miguel, L.F., and Mota, F. (2011) "Mídia, eleições e pesquisa de opinião no Brasil (1989–2010): um mapeamento da presença das pesquisas na cobertura eleitoral" *Revista Compolítica*, vol. 1(1), 67–89.

Boltanski, L. and Thévenot, L. (2006) *On Justification. Economies of Worth*. (C. Porter, Trans.). Princeton, NJ: Princeton University Press.

Cabra, M. and Kissane, E. (2016) "The People and the Tech Behind the Panama Papers" *The Source*, April 11. Retrieved from https://source.opennews.org/en-US/articles/people-and-tech-behind-panama-papers/.

Cesarino Costa, P. (2017a) "Um jato de água fria" *Folha de S. Paulo*, March 19. Retrieved from www1.folha.uol.com.br/colunas/paula-cesarino-costa-ombudsman/2017/03/1867852-um-jato-de-agua-fria.shtml.

Cesarino Costa, P. (2017b) "Pela transparência e a boa prática jornalística" *Folha de S. Paulo*, March 26. Retrieved from www1.folha.uol.com.br/colunas/paula-cesarino-costa-ombudsman/2017/03/1869768-pela-transparencia-e-a-boa-pratica-jornalistica.shtml.

Chadwick, A. (2013) *The Hybrid Media System: Politics and Power*. Oxford: Oxford University Press.

Chaia, V. (2016) "O Impeachment da president Dilma Rousseff?????" *Em Debate*, vol. 8(2), 47–54.

Chaia, V. and Teixeira, M. (2000) "Máfia dos Fiscais e as estrelas de cidadania" *Observatório da imprensa, ed. 63, Mídia e política*, 31–37. Retrieved from http://observatoriodaimprensa.com.br/primeiras-edicoes/mfia-dos-fiscais-eas-estrelas-da-cidadania/.

Coleman, G. (2014) *Hacker, Hoaxer, Whistleblower, Spy: The Many Faces of Anonymous*. London: Verso.

Cook, T. (2006) "The News Media as a Political Institution: Looking Backward and Looking Forward" *Political Communication*, vol. 23(2), 159–171.

D'Agostino, R. (2014) "PT e PMDB encolhem, mas mantêm maiores bancadas; PSDB cresce" *G1 Eleição em Números*, special section of G1 website, published October 6, 2014. Retrieved from http://g1.globo.com/politica/eleicoes/2014/blog/eleicao-em-numeros/post/pt-e-pmdb-encolhem-mas-mantem-maiores-bancadas-no-congresso-psdb-cresce-na-camara.html.

Dallagnol, D. and Martelo, O. (2016) "Lava Jato, de onde veio e para onde vamos" *Folha de S. Paulo*, October 30. Retrieved from www1.folha.uol.com.br/opiniao/2016/10/1827555-lava-jato-de-onde-veio-e-para-onde-vamos.shtml.

Damgaard, M. (2015) "Multiple Margins and Mediatized Transgression" *Ephemera –Theory and Politics in Organization*, vol. 15(2), 411–434.

Delli Carpini, M. and Williams, B. (2001) "Let Us Infotain You: Politics in the New Media Age." In W.L. Bennett and R. Entman (eds.), *Mediated Politics: Communication in the Future of Democracy* (160–181). Cambridge: Cambridge University Press.

Drezner, D.W. (2016) "Nothing to See Here, Just the Biggest Global Corruption Scandal in History," *Washington Post*. Retrieved from www.washingtonpost.com/postevery thing/wp/2016/04/04/nothing-to-see-here-just-the-biggest-global-corruption-scandal-in-history/?utm_term=.97e0725c5542.

Falleti, T.G. and Lynch, J.F. (2009) "Context and Causal Mechanisms in Political Analysis" *Comparative Political Studies*, vol. 42, 1143–1166.

Folha de S. Paulo (2016) "Cresce otimismo com a economia, diz Datafolha" *Folha de S. Paulo*, front page, July 17, 2016.

Foucault, M. (1980) *Power/Knowledge: Selected Interviews and Other Writings 1972–1977*. New York: Pantheon.

Fuchs, C. (2011) "WikiLeaks: Power 2.0? Surveillance 2.0? Criticism 2.0? Alternative Media 2.0? A Political-Economic Analysis" *Global Media Journal* (Australian Edition), 5(1), 1–17.

Galtung, J. and Ruge, M. (1965) "The Structure of Foreign News" *Journal of Peace Research*, vol. 2(1), 64–91.

Goffmann, E. (1956) *The Presentation of Self in Everyday Life*. Edinburgh: University of Edinburgh.

Gupta, A. (1995) "Blurred Boundaries: The Discourse of Corruption" *American Ethnologist*, vol. 22(2), 375–402.

Hansen, H.K. and Flyverbom, M. (2014) "The Politics of Transparency and the Calibration of Knowledge in the Digital Age" *Organization*, vol. 22(6), 872–889.

Heikkilä, H. and Kunelius, R. (2017) "Surveillance and the Structural Transformation of Privacy. Mapping the Conceptual Landscape of Journalism in the Post-Snowden Era" *Digital Journalism Studies*, vol. 5 (3), 262–276.

Hirschl, R. (2008) "The Judicialization of Mega-Politics and the Rise of Political Courts" *Annual Review of Political Science*, vol. 11(1), 93–118.

Hjarvard, S. (2013) *The Mediatization of Culture and Society*. London: Routledge.

Hughes, S. (2006) *Newsrooms in Conflict: Journalism and the Democratization of Mexico*. Pittsburgh, PA: University of Pittsburgh Press.

Hutchby, I. (2001) *Conversation and Technology: From the Telephone to the Internet*. Cambridge: Polity.

International Consortium of Investigative Journalists (2016) *Panama Papers*. Retrieved from https://panamapapers.icij.org/.

Kitzberger, P. (2014) "Demands for Media Democratisation and the Latin American 'New Left'." Hamburg: GIGA German Institute of Global and Area Studies.

Kristensen, N.N. and Mortensen, M. (2015) "Amateur Sources Breaking the News, Meta-sources Authorizing the News of Gaddafi's Death: New Patterns of Journalistic Information Gathering and Dissemination in the Digital Age" *Digital Journalism*, vol. 1(3), 352–367.

Krotz, F. (2014) "Media, Mediatization and Mediatized Worlds: A Discussion of the Basic Concepts." In A. Hepp and F. Krotz (eds.), *Mediatized Worlds* (72–87). London: Palgrave Macmillan.

Landerer, N. (2013) "Rethinking the Logics: A Conceptual Framework for the Mediatization of Politics" *Communication Theory*, vol. 23, 239–258.

Leigh, D. and Harding, L. (2011) *WikiLeaks: Inside Julian Assange's War on Secrecy*. London: Guardian Books.

Llanos, M. and Marsteintredet, L. (eds.) (2010) *Presidential Breakdowns in Latin America: Causes and Outcomes of Executive Instability in Developing Democracies*. London: Palgrave Macmillan.

Magalhães, V. (2017) "Castelo de Areia 2?" *Estado de S. Paulo*, March 22. Retrieved from http://politica.estadao.com.br/noticias/geral,castelo-de-areia-2,70001709012.

Maier, J. (2011) "The Impact of Political Scandals on Political Support: An Experimental Test of Two Theories" *International Political Science* 32(3), 283–302.

Matos, C. (2012) *Media and Politics in Latin America. Globalization, Democracy and Identity.* London: I.B. Tauris.

Mendes, G. (2016) *DJE nº 54. Decisão monocrática.* Brasília: Supremo Tribunal Federal. Published on March 22, 2016. Retrieved from http://portal.stf.jus.br/processos/down loadPeca.asp?id=308995628&ext=.pdf.

Mesquita, N.C. (2014) "Media and the Quality of Democracy: The Different Impacts of the Media on Regime Support in Brazil." In R. Figueiras, P. Espírito Santo, and I.F. Cunha (eds.), *Democracy at Work: Pressure and Propaganda in Portugal and Brazil* (13–38). Coimbra: University of Coimbra Press.

Miguel, L.F. (2003) "A Eleição Visível: A Rede Globo Descobre a Política em 2002" *Dados*, vol. 46(2), 289–310.

Moro, S. (2004) "Considerações sobre a Operação Mani Pulite" *Revista CEJ*, vol. 8(26), 56–62.

Munro, I. (2016) "Whistle-Blowing and the Politics of Truth: Mobilizing 'Truth Games' in the WikiLeaks Case" *Human Relations*, 69(1), 1–25.

Nassif, L. (2016) "A vingança torpe da Lava Jato contra Dias Toffoli" *JornalGGN*, published August 20, 2016. Retrieved from https://jornalggn.com.br/noticia/a-vinganca-torpe-da-lava-jato-contra-dias-toffoli.

Pérez-Liñán, A. and Rodríguez-Raga, J.C. (2009) "Veto Players in Presidential Regimes: Institutional Variables and Policy Change" *Revista de Ciencia Política*, vol. 29(3), 693–720.

Porto, M. (2011) "The Media and Political Accountability." In T. Power and M. Taylor (eds.), *Corruption and Democracy in Brazil* (103–126). South Bend, IN: University of Notre Dame Press.

Power, M. (1997) *Audit Society: Rituals of Verification.* Oxford: Oxford University Press.

Power, M. (2000) "The Audit Society – Second Thoughts" *International Journal of Auditing*, vol. 4, 111–119.

Raile, E., Pereira, C., and Power, T. (2011) "The Executive Toolbox: Building Legislative Support in a Multiparty Presidential Regime" *Political Research Quarterly* vol. 64(2), 323–364.

Rossi, C. (2016) "A Delação do Fim do Mundo" in Folha de S. Paulo, published on March 23, 2016. Retrieved from www1.folha.uol.com.br/poder/2016/03/1753135-a-delacao-do-fim-do-mundo.shtml.

Russell, A. and Waisbord, S. (2017) "The Snowden Revelations and the Networked Fourth Estate" *International Journal of Communication*, vol. 11, 858–878.

Seligson, M. (2002) "The Impact of Corruption on Regime Legitimacy: A Comparative Study of Four Latin American Countries" *The Journal of Politics*, vol. 64(2), 408–433.

Shoemaker, P. and Vos, T. (2009) *Gatekeeping Theory.* New York: Routledge.

Strathern, M. (2000) *Audit Cultures: Anthropological Studies in Accountability, Ethics, and the Academy.* London: Routledge.

Sparrow, B. (1999) *Uncertain Guardians: The News Media as a Political Institution.* Baltimore, MD: Johns Hopkins University Press.

Tate, N. and Vallinder, T. (1995) *The Global Expansion of Judicial Power.* New York: New York University Press.

Thompson, J.P. (2000) *Political Scandal: Power and Visibility in the Media Age*. Cambridge: Polity Press.

Thompson, J.P. (2005) "The New Visibility" *Theory, Culture & Society*, vol. 22(6), 31–51.

Thornton, P. and Ocasio, W. (2008) "Institutional Logics." In R. Greenwood, C. Oliver, K. Sahlin, and R. Suddaby (eds.), *The SAGE Handbook of Organizational Institutionalism* (99–129). Los Angeles, CA: Sage.

Thornton, P., Ocasio, W., and Lounsbury, M. (2012) *The Institutional Logics Perspective. A New Approach to Culture, Structure and Process*. Oxford: Oxford University Press.

Tuchman, G. (1978) *Making News. A Study in the Construction of Reality*. New York: The Free Press.

Tumber, H. and Waisbord, S. (2004) "Introduction" *American Behavioral Scientist*, vol. 47, 1143–1152.

Wahl-Jørgensen, K. (2014) "Is WikiLeaks Challenging the Paradigm of Journalism? Boundary Work and Beyond" *International Journal of Communication*, vol. 8, 2581–2592.

Waisbord, S. (2000) *Watchdog Journalism in South America. News, Accountability, and Democracy*. New York: Columbia University Press.

White, D.M. (1950) "The 'Gate Keeper': A Case Study in the Selection of News" *Journalism Quarterly*, vol. 27, 383–391.

Wortham, S. and Rhodes, C.R. (2012) "Narratives Across Speech Events." In A. De Fina and A. Georgakopoulou (eds.), *The Handbook of Narrative Analysis* (160–177). Malden, MA: Wiley-Blackwell.

4 Lawfare and the Judiciary-Political Relations during the Lava-Jato Corruption Scandal

In Brazil, holding corrupt politicians accountable has proven to be notoriously difficult (Power and Taylor 2011). The Lava-Jato investigations have been heralded as an exception to that rule, although in reality, very few of the many investigated politicians have been sentenced or charged thus far. In this chapter, I will explore the various ways that the legal actions triggered by the Lava-Jato probe have produced or failed to produce accountability, as well as the perverse effects of judicial intervention in the political system of Brazil. The chapter provides sections on each of the relevant accountability institutions and brief case studies of the most important legal actions and trials – distinct or entangled, depending on the case – that together constituted the core of Lava-Jato scandal. Together with the analysis of leaks in the previous chapter, these case studies explain the trajectory of the scandal. Several of these legal actions generated sustained media coverage, which contributed to a second stage of the informational cascade, wherein the same signal of political corruption was recycled. The question I will answer in this chapter is how judicial processes work in contemporary Brazilian politics, and how weak accountability mechanisms, despite their shortcomings, may nevertheless become potent political weapons when combined with leaks and cascades of disclosure.

I will start the chapter by introducing the main actors in the accountability and audit institutions of the Brazilian system, describing their various institutional traits, and discuss their general role in accountability processes in the political arena. Readers eager to learn about the specific cases can skip ahead to the subsequent sections, where I will consider the interplay of political actors, prosecuting authorities, and judicial institutions. First up is the curious process in the Supreme Electoral Court, which, based in the Lava-Jato investigations, detected fraud in the 2014 presidential campaign in the amount of R$112 million. The trial, however, ended up acquitting the defendants, Dilma Rousseff and Michel Temer. Second, I will show how accountability mechanisms targeting corruption in the Câmara dos Deputados are incapacitated in the current configuration of the Congress, with the exception of the former president of the Câmara, Eduardo Cunha. Third, Cunha's case had consequences for the two cases described next, in which individual judges of the STF tried (but failed) to remove two of the most important Brazilian Senators, Renan Calheiros and

Aécio Neves. Fourth, I turn to the processes against the ex-president Lula and his family, observing how the timing of the investigations, denunciations, and sentencing was ultimately crucial to his chances of running for president in 2018.

Throughout the analysis, I will show that the outcomes of accountability processes are rarely the punishment of political transgression, and that the Lava-Jato case was not simply a case of lost political capital for those in public office. This finding has resonance with extant research, but the chapter contributes to research on Brazilian accountability institutions by showing that several macro-level changes and various side-effects surfaced in the political arena due to legal processes spawned during the Lava-Jato investigations. In discussing the outcomes of the legal processes, I will argue that political actors use legal action and corruption denunciations strategically to wage political war through the institutions of law and the repressive power of the state, which has been termed "lawfare" (Zanin Martins et al. 2017, drawing on Comaroff and Comaroff 2006). The term has already been the object of much debate in Brazil, since the lawyers of the ex-president Lula began to use the term when criticizing the Lava-Jato investigations. Seen from the opposite perspective, the lawfare waged in Brazilian courts is one tactic within the quest to combat corruption, advance justice and remedy the (perceived) lack of electoral accountability.

Theoretically, I contend that despite the imprecision in relation to the original concept, it can be fruitful to import the concept of lawfare into the context of contemporary media spheres and, especially, mediatized politics (Lima 2004, 2009). In the Latin American historical experience of many presidential and democratic breakdowns (Llanos and Marsteintredet 2010), such a concept gives researchers purchase on the mediatized relationship between legal actions, political agency, and contested constitutions.

Accountability Institutions in the Political Arena

Judicial interventions in politics are common in Brazil at many levels, and the inclination toward settling political disputes through law has been termed judicialization (Avritzer and Marona 2014, Werneck Vianna et al. 1999). International scholars have conceived of "judicialization of politics" as either the kind of macro-change observed when legal concepts and practices spread through political discourse and political organizations, or "the reliance on courts and judicial means for addressing core moral predicaments, public policy questions, and political controversies" (Hirschl 2008: 94). Such increasing reliance on judicial means results in increasing judicial power in the political arena, which also leads to gradual structural and communicative changes. Thus, the term judicialization may also simultaneously encompass the contemporary transformations of judicial institutions and the structural shifts seen in judiciary communication (Couso et al. 2010, Peruzzotti and Smulovitz 2006: 19, Tate and Vallinder 1995).

The concept of judicialization may only be relevant here at first glance, however. In response to scandals, increasing attention to legal frameworks and judicialization is one political strategy used to signal accountability and maintain organizational legitimacy. It is therefore to be expected that courts and accountability institutions enter political arenas in a political system rife with allegations of corruption. It is also well established that such allegations may trigger horizontal accountability mechanisms and subsequently become elements within intra-elite power struggles (e.g., Peruzzotti 2006). As most literature on judicialization deals with judicial interventions and policy review of areas that are not commonly the object of legal processes, I will not draw on the literature on this subject in the following. Rather, the questions at stake in this chapter will aim to focus more on the dimensions and mechanisms of this accountability.

The importance of horizontal accountability in the web of Brazilian accountability institutions is linked with weak electoral accountability. Because of this weakness, the horizontal accountability institutions and the media institutions are typically the main accountability actors when corruption is disclosed in Brazil. Despite the fact that the activation of either accountability or media institutions in a scandal should entail reputational costs for the politicians involved, those suspected of corruption (as well as those who have been indicted or charged) frequently manage to get re-elected. Several arguments have been advanced to explain this:

- There is a lack of information regarding corruption in the media at a local level, often because of illegal overlap between owners of the media and the political elite, or due to other protections negotiated through clientelistic networks (Abramo 2007, Lima 2004). Despite the fact that voters prefer not to elect politicians they know to be corrupt, corrupt politicians often manage re-election because their constituencies are not sufficiently aware of the corruption (Winters and Weitz-Shapiro 2013).
- Another argument, contrary to the above, is that there is plenty of information available regarding corruption among the political elite, and precisely because of this, ideological preferences become more important determinants of votes. In the 2006 presidential elections, Rennó showed that "[p]erception of corruption matters only when it comes to choices between candidates on the same side of the ideological spectrum" (Rennó 2011: 71). The rationale thus being: "If they are all corrupt, I might as well vote for the politician who, albeit corrupt, is closest to my ideological viewpoint." Comparing the re-election frequency of congressmen in the 2006 elections, Pereira et al. (2011: 94) found that parliamentarians involved in the Mensalão scandal that sought reelection were not at a statistical disadvantage relative to fellow congressmen. Furthermore, at the local level, voters' clientelistic rationales and expectations of pork-barrel politics may also play into the choice of voting for corrupt politicians: In 184 municipal campaigns for the position of mayor in the state of Pernambuco, Pereira and Melo (2015) found that incumbent mayors could mitigate the negative impact of corruption denunciations and special audits upon their re-election chances by increasing public spending.

• It has been argued that Brazilian voters are tolerant of corruption, as long as the politician in office is also perceived to be efficient. The adage "rouba mas faz" ("he steals, but gets things done") famously described the São Paulo governor Adhemar de Barros (Cotta 2008). This argument also explains why politicians such as Paulo Maluf remained in office for decades (until December 2017), despite being internationally convicted, wanted by Interpol, and targeted by 572 suits in Brazil since the 1980s (Arantes 2011: 199). The hypothesis of "rouba mas faz" has been tested and explored in various studies (e.g., Ferraz and Finan 2008, Pereira and Melo 2015, Pereira, Melo, and Figueiredo 2009; Rennó 2011, and Winters and Weitz-Shapiro 2013).

Several initiatives have been implemented over the past two decades in order to remedy this weak electoral accountability. Most importantly, the law of the Clean Slate (*Lei da Ficha Limpa*, see Koerner 2013, Michener and Pereira 2016: 500, Presidência da República 2010, Taylor 2011: 170) was passed in 2010. The law prevents individuals from running for public office if they are sentenced for corruption, administrative improbity, and common crimes. It has been applied in thousands of candidatures since it was enacted, and during the 2016 municipal elections, around 1,600 candidates were impeded from either running or taking office (Pontes 2016).

Despite the Ficha Limpa law coming into force in 2010, the current national Legislative Assembly still consists of numerous parliamentarians facing trials: 48 out of 81 senators are under investigation or charged before the Supreme Court, as is roughly a third of the Câmara at the time of writing (Macedo 2017a, 2017b, Taylor 2011: 164). The accountability mechanisms are not as effective as one could hope, and some of the mechanisms can even be rigged for political effect. While the Ficha Limpa law remedies this somewhat, a potential perverse side-effect has arisen from the combination of the Lava-Jato trials and the Ficha Limpa law. This side-effect would play an important role in the general elections of 2018.

The prohibition of candidature warranted by the Ficha Limpa law requires either an admission of guilt, or that the politician in question is found guilty of corruption or political maladministration and sentenced twice – by an ordinary court as well an appeals court, or in the Supreme Court. This ratification clause of the Ficha Limpa law makes the timing and sequence of investigations, trials, and eventual appeals of the Lava-Jato cases very important. Since the trials against parliamentarians were not concluded (indeed, many had barely moved to the initial stage) before the candidate deadline in August 2018, the Ficha Limpa law did not apply to politicians in office, allowing them to run for re-election. In the case of Lula, who expected to run for the presidency in 2018, the sentence of 9.5 years in prison on corruption charges (on June 12, 2017) would not by itself stop him from running, but the decision of the appeals court of the Fourth Federal Region in Porto Alegre, on January 24, 2018, however, disqualified him from running due to the Ficha Limpa law. At the time of writing, further appeals to the Supreme Court and the supreme electoral court were expected.

The Ficha Limpa law thus floated, like a Damocles sword, above each of the political actors that once seemed most likely to run for president after Dilma Rousseff's second term. Like Lula, senators Aécio Neves and José Serra (of PSDB), both previous presidential runner-ups, are currently the subject of investigations by the Supreme Court and sentencing here will render them ineligible for public office. Unlike Lula (and other Brazilians without a federal mandate), Neves and other politicians in office however benefit from the so-called law of privileged right (*foro especial por prerrogativa de função*, or in normal parlance *foro privilegiado*). The *foro* is a legal reminiscence of colonial times, automatically relocating to the Supreme Court all cases involving federal representatives. The prerogative means that congressmen and ministers automatically move to the top of the Brazilian three-tier system of courts. Similarly, state governors can only be tried before the Supreme Tribunal of Justice (Arantes 2002). In 2017, 38,431 individuals could claim the *foro* on the basis of the federal constitution, while 16,559 individuals had similar rights under the state constitutions (Barroso 2017, Bulla and Moura 2017). Upon losing or renouncing a mandate (or failing to obtain re-election), a case involving a politician is then redistributed to a local court. If obtaining a new mandate, for example in a State Assembly, the case is then relocated once more. This provides denounced parliamentarians with opportunities for manipulating this mechanism of the legal system, stalling processes, etc.

Beyond the Ficha Limpa law, several other legal instruments threatened the politicians suspected of corruption. Preventative arrests, for extended periods of time, constituted another means of legal intervention by the public prosecutors, and this was the subject of much debate during the Lava-Jato investigations. Based on the evidence turning up in the probe, the Supreme Electoral Court also came close to annulling the result of the 2014 presidential elections. Each accountability institution intervenes with different instruments, so in order to analyze the complexities of the horizontal accountability interventions executed during the Lava-Jato probe, I need to clarify several important distinctions between the accountability institutions. Apart from their differing institutional relations, the courts, the police, and the prosecutors are also divided by their professional goals and modus operandi. In the following, each of the relevant judicial and prosecuting bodies and their institutional configurations are described.

The State Prosecutors and the Ministério Público Federal

The first accountability institution described here is the Ministério Público Federal (henceforth MPF). The MPF is the federal public prosecutorial body of Brazil, tasked with defending societal collective rights, protecting civil society, the environment, and public heritage, as well as curbing corruption in public administration. Each state has a local Ministério Público, and in total there are 10,000 state MP and MPF members distributed across the nation (Arantes 2011: 187).

The prosecutor-general of the Republic (henceforth PGR) holds office heading the MPF for periods of two years. The PGR in charge during the Lava-Jato case was Rodrigo Janot, who held two consecutive mandates. The incumbent Raquel Dodge (appointed in September 2017), is the first woman to hold this office. The national association of Brazilian prosecutors nominates three candidates for the position of PGR, with one of these candidates continuing to be selected for the position by the president of the Republic. The candidate will be questioned before taking office by the Senate's Commission of Justice and Constitutionality, and the candidacy will be put to a vote in the plenary of the Senate.[1]

In investigations into corruption, the members of the MPF work closely together with state or federal police forces to obtain evidence. The decision to initiate an investigation lies with the state MP or the MPF, however prosecutors must request authorization from the relevant local court with jurisdiction in order to obtain legal evidence pertaining to the crime scene(s). In the case of Lava-Jato, the initial investigations of money laundering and smuggling happened in the southern state of Paraná, close to the borders of Argentina and Paraguay. The investigation has remained in the capital city Curitiba, where a small team of MPF prosecutors originally obtained authorization to expand the scope of their probe from judge Sergio Moro. Since then, several state MPs (of São Paulo and Rio de Janeiro) have been handed material for local investigation by the task-force in Curitiba.

The prosecutors of Brazil work as a corporation in the sense that the institution has a distinct organizational goal, a hierarchy of status and a career ladder, a bureaucratic structure, and strong inwards loyalty. Arantes highlights that the MPF of Brazil is "motivated by a strong ideological component of … 'political volun-tarism'" (2011: 187), with members of this institution viewing society as weak, representative political institutions as corrupt, and the MP as the "preferred repre-sentative of a weak society, especially in contrast to inept bureaucracies that fail to enforce the law" (ibid.: 188). The strong professional identity of the MP members is also externally recognized: The MPF is, in Brazilian administrative circles, referred to as a "corporation," and during the Lava-Jato case, many have accused the MPF of "corporatism," with reference to the historical experience of the Portu-guese corporatist state and the corporatist ideology espoused by Brazilian Presi-dent Getúlio Vargas, inspired by Salazar's Portugal (Wiarda 2004). At times in the current debate, the concept of corporatism often simply denotes the class-interest of a particular group within the state (e.g., Araujo et al. 2016: 112), acting to defend privileges vis-à-vis other actors. The MPF has frequently been criticized for enacting such "corporativismo," but this sort of critique is variously directed at the judiciary, teachers in the public schools, the police, public servants in general, and parliamentarians.

Whether or not this critique rings true in the case of the prosecutors, it is beyond doubt that the MPF has gained much autonomy and independent dis-cretion since the days of Geraldo Brindeiro, the PGR of the 1990s who became known as the filing clerk of the Republic. Autonomy and independence are pre-requisites for the anti-corruption activities of the MPF, however independence may also pose a problem when considered from alternate perspectives. It has been pointed out that the corporatist thinking of the MPF has harmed the national economy (by crippling major construction firms), the legitimacy of democratic institutions (by repeatedly and loudly scandalizing the Congress), as well as the legitimacy of the judiciary.[2] Several situations that led to these accusations are detailed in this chapter. The legitimacy of investigations is frequently defended by prosecutors from the Lava-Jato task force (e.g., Dallagnol and Martelo 2016), many of whom are active speakers at conferences and public events, on social media, and even religious ceremonies. In contrast, PGR Janot was less outspoken, as he was already criticized for appearing in the media following the initial inquiries in March 2015 (Netto 2016: 145).

The Federal Police

The federal police force (henceforth PF) of Brazil is, in its current configuration, quite new. The PF has its historical roots in the nineteenth-century court of the King Dom João VI, while the name goes back to a new organization of the police force instituted at the end of the Estado Novo period in 1944. The following year, a unit of this organization gained national responsibilities; however, neither the Estado Novo federal police nor the nineteenth-century unit ever grew to become particularly effective (Arantes 2011: 190). During the earlier, less centralized regimes, the states of the federation displayed little interest in constructing a national police force, and later, during periods of greater centralization and more authoritarian regimes, the military displayed no interest in yielding either power or jurisdiction to civilian forces. Thus, only with the first Lula administration in the 2000s did the federal police become a significant force for combatting corruption and increasing accountability in the political realm (ibid.: 194). The scope and number of operations has grown from 18 operations in 2003, to 187 in 2007, and to 550 in 2016 (Polícia Federal 2017). The PF had 3,471 positions for detectives and 11,381 for agents, clerks, and analysts in 2015 (Ministério de Planejamento, Orçamento e Gestão 2015: 5). Due to budget cuts in 2016 and 2017, the number of positions is now decreasing.

Because of the rising number of operations, the PF has become a more visible entity. Arantes notes that the press "has been filled with cleverly named police operations," and the catchy names engage public and media attention, giving "a sense of the result and the likely responsibility of those being implicated" (Arantes 2011: 201). This symbolic naming of operations provides simultaneously an informational shortcut, a hashtag-like function for digital and cognitive retrieval, and a discursive node organizing public debate. The media strategy of the PF is distinct from that of the MPF (see above), and agents rarely appear in interviews and columns. This is probably due to the organizational subordination of the PF to the Ministry of Justice.

In investigative operations, the MPF works in tandem with the PF, while the state MPs work with state police agents. The police agents and the MPF are legally interlinked:

although the Polícia Federal is subordinate to the executive branch (and its activities can thus be curtailed or directed by the Justice Ministry), its main tools for investigating and addressing crimes require the agreement of independent judges and take place under the oversight of the MPF.

(Ibid.: 192)

However, neither judges nor MPF direct the police investigations, and thus legal processes shift between these institutions throughout the phases of an investigation.

In addition to its subordination to the executive branch of government, federal police work is less prestigious than judgeship or prosecutorial positions (and also less well-remunerated than private lawyer work – although better than other federal civil servants), meaning that the PF has a weaker institutional identity and sense of independence than the corporation of the MPF (ibid.).

The federal police force consists of various specialized units for specific tasks. In cases such as Lava-Jato, a local or regional police director may select police agents from diverse units to form a task-force with resources dedicated to a specific investigation. Across Brazil, a range of similar groups work on other political corruption cases and depending on the context these groups may incorporate members from other accountability institutions such as the Federal Tax authorities and financial audit bodies. Regardless of composition, they depend on judges for authorization to use force in their investigations (for incidents such as detaining individuals, forcing them to testify, or breaking the secrecy of bank or telephone accounts).

The Lava-Jato task-force of the Curitiba-based PF was constructed in April 2014 from police agents and prosecutors. The PGR installed a national team of prosecutors on the case in January 2015, while the state prosecutors of Rio de Janeiro and São Paulo picked out task-forces in June 2016 and July 2017, respectively. The PF's relationship of dependence or independence vis-à-vis the MPF was contested on numerous occasions during the Lava-Jato case. In particular, the right to negotiate and agree to plea bargains has been a cause for strife between the MPF and the PF during recent years. While both institutions work to obtain evidence when negotiating a plea bargain, differences in (political) scope and intention may emerge between the two. Such differences arise principally because the PF is organized under the Ministry of Justice, while the state MPs and the MPF are formally independent.

After the impeachment of Dilma Rousseff, several circumstances have reduced the efficiency of the PF investigations of the Lava-Jato case. Beyond the general situation of budget cuts in the federal police forces of Curitiba and Paraná (budget cuts from R$29.1 million in 2016 to R$20.5 million in 2017), the number of agents managing the case was reduced in May 2017 from nine to six. In November 2017, a new director of the PF was appointed by Michel Temer, and with a new director and a new prosecutor-general, the political control of the Lava-Jato probe is rumored to have increased. Former PGR Rodrigo Janot publicly voiced his suspicions in the matter via Reuters news agency (Brooks 2017).

Leaving the investigative and executive branches of the Brazilian account-ability institutions, I now turn to the four courts embroiled in the trials of 2014–2017, starting with an example contrasting the practices and organizational ideals of the prosecutors and police to that of the judges and courts.

The Courts of Brazil

This section describes four courts of Brazil: The Supreme Court (STF), the Tribunal of Accounts (TCU), and the electoral court (TSE), as well as the 13th Vara of Curitiba where judge Sérgio Moro has been conducting the trials in the Lava-Jato case. Initially, I will contrast the institutional perspective of the courts to that of the prosecutors through the example of preventive arrests. The debate on preventive arrests may elucidate how accountability is perceived and enacted in different ways in two governmental institutions, and how the belief systems and logics of these institutions provide governmental actors different ways to inter-pret specific interventions.

As already mentioned, the Brazilian courts contribute to accountability in different ways than prosecuting and investigating bodies. The production of accountability is one sub-goal of the courts, among a range of other organiza-tional and institutional goals and conceptualizations, dealing with civil and cor-porate rights, due process, legality, the fairness of the legal order, and compliance (Edelman 2016). The goal of producing political accountability, it must be emphasized, has become a very important topic in the Brazilian dis-course about justice – not least because of the Lava-Jato case and its many rami-fications. To clerks and judges of the courts, this goal may only be one among many. Although the MPF and PF are intertwined with courts in corruption probes, the primary actors of courts, that is, the judges, may still consider them-selves distinct from these accountability bodies on account of their professional identity and distinct work ethos. The judges of the Brazilian courts form a pro-fessionalized bureaucracy in the Weberian sense, valuing professional reputa-tion, network, and individual expertise, grounded in the professional knowledge base and language. That public prosecutors and the judges have distinct profes-sional ideals are apparent in many aspects of the Lava-Jato investigations, but especially so in the case of preventive arrests.

The rationale of preventive arrests, in the institutional logic of prosecutors and police agents, is to secure evidence and avoid the obstruction of further investigations. During the unravelling of the criminal network behind the Petro-bras graft, the MPF has requested and succeeded in obtaining authorization for preventive arrests on numerous occasions. Such authorizations are issued by courts. This kind of arrest is ostensibly used to impede any attempts at destroy-ing evidence or fleeing the country (Taylor 2011: 171). However, because the Lava-Jato investigations have continuously been revealing new layers of corrupt networks, many arrested individuals have been kept incarcerated for extended periods of time on the assumption that they would obstruct not just their own case, but also the next tier of involved persons.

Extended preventive arrests did not used to be standard practice in Brazilian courts, however. From the professional perspective of Brazilian courts and the judges, preventive arrests interfere with several principles of justice, especially individual freedom rights and the assumption of innocence until culpability is proven. The courts are historically fond of *habeas corpus* injunctions for the political elite, commonly letting a high proportion of defendants enjoy their liberty during trials and appeal processes (ibid.). The logic here is different from that of the prosecuting body because judges are concerned with the constitutional right of freedom, to the possible detriment of the quality of investigations. The predilection of the courts for maintaining (upper-class) defendants and convicted individuals in freedom has created a sense of impunity for crimes of political corruption (Arantes 2011: 195). Meanwhile, Brazil's courts are less lenient in cases of petty crimes among poorer segments of the population.

The preventive arrests of the Lava-Jato case have been interpreted as an exception to the assumption of innocence. The topic has drawn headlines, because leading businessmen and ex-ministers such as José Dirceu (PT), Antônio Palocci (PT), and Henrique Eduardo Alves (PMDB) have been incarcerated between 6 and 12 months before being tried, while Lula was, as described in the previous chapter, essentially denied the possibility of taking office as minister in the Rousseff administration with the argument that his nomination was really a step to avoid a preventive arrest.

The use of preventive arrest remains a hot topic in the public sphere and between the local courts of the Lava-Jato case (Rio and Curitiba) and individual STF judges. The diverging interpretations subsequently made it into the commentary, op-ed pieces, and opinion columns of the Brazilian news media, recycling the news of corruption disclosure with new layers of legal discourse and debate on top. The debate can be boiled down to this: At what point should political actors under suspicion of corruption be held accountable and arrested? Should it be when suspicion first arises, or with denunciation, or after evidence has been collected, or after one or multiple sentences have been declared? Regardless of the correct answer here, I will merely point out that the agitated debate concerning preventive arrests reflects an important distinction to be made between the institutional logics of courts and the judiciary on one hand, and the prosecuting bodies of the State on the other. The two organizational fields, in general, do not view transgression of laws and individual or political rights in the same way, nor do they use the same channels for intervention and sanction.

In sum, the different roles of police and prosecutors compared to judges have led these two groups to interpret preventive arrests quite differently. This illustrates that although accountability institutions are organizationally embedded in the State, the roles and functions of these different bodies are distinct from each other but are not, however, entirely subsumed under the democratic ideals of modern state constitutions and checks and balances. The different institutions belong to separate "macro-level belief systems that shape cognitions and influence decision-making processes in organizational fields" (McPherson and Sauder

2013: 167). Concordantly, the timing of the application of sanctions and methods of intervention differ.

The daily routines and working logic deployed by prosecutors or police agents in corruption investigations are not dependent upon a democratic mandate. Like the courts, these agents are ideally independent actors working to ensure the effective enforcement of laws passed in other sectors of the State – the executive, legislative, and judiciary branches of government. The goal of prosecutors and police agents is to obtain weighty and legal evidence and minimize the harm done to society by actors perceived as perpetrators. Courts on the other hand are oriented toward another goal: judging, in an equilibrated manner, the evidence produced in investigations and then applying the "field-level manifestation of the logic of the state ... in the legal realm ... [which] extols the virtues of just incarceration and formal social control, the markers of traditional punitive legal enforcement strategies" (ibid.: 172). None of these institutional logics (Thornton and Ocasio 2008, Thornton et al. 2012) are necessarily based in the participatory ideals of the democratic state, but despite the formal, practical-discursive, and professional independence of the courts, they still form a part of the government, and are in some contexts very attuned to the political atmosphere. However, the degree to which Brazilian courts are sensitive to political influence can vary. The Supreme Court, to which I first turn, is the court most frequently interacting with the political branches of government, and thus the most central piece in the accountability mechanism of corruption scandals such as Lava-Jato.

The Supreme Court of Brazil

The Supreme Court of Brazil (STF) is in principle a constitutional court, although it also holds extended powers for policy revision. STF is frequently the ultimate appellate court, and acts in criminal cases related to individuals in public office at the federal level, that is, senators, state representatives, as well as ministers and presidents.

The STF has been and remains extremely overloaded with cases: While 77,304 verdicts have been handed down in the decade 2007 to 2017, 8,904 of these made by the court plenary (Mariani et al. 2017), but in recent years, the court has been receiving up to 70,000 new cases per year (Falcão et al. 2016: 66). The US Supreme Court, by comparison, only decides around 80 cases each year (Boydstun 2013: 11). Despite only assessing a fraction of this plethora of processes, Brazil's STF has occasionally been protagonist in the political field. During the last decade the STF has exhibited a growing independency (Avritzer and Marona 2014: 83) and judged the constitutionality of a range of (sometimes unpopular but still important) cases and causes.[3]

The politically sensitive corruption cases of the Lava-Jato investigations, not to mention the impeachment process, have resulted in extraordinary public and media attention directed at the work of the STF. As the case studies of this chapter demonstrate, the court and the individual judges of the court have been decisive in the political outcomes characterizing Brazilian politics in 2014 till 2017. The court has increasingly had "an important rule-making effect on how the accountability game plays out in the rest of the political system" (Taylor 2011: 177). Judges Zavascki and Fachin, in the function of their role as *judge rapporteurs* of the Lava-Jato cases, have been particularly important, as have the judges Mendes and Mello, who have publicly adopted critical postures to the investigation and the work of the MPF.

The STF consists of 11 presidentially appointed judges who may occupy the bench until the mandatory retirement age of 70. These 11 judges are divided into two teams (*turmas*) of 5 while the president of the court remains outside of these teams, instead managing the agenda and various other coordination tasks. In a plenary decision, the president of the court acts as tiebreaker when votes are tied. The presidency of the STF rotates every two years to the judge with the longest career in the STF who has not yet presided over the court. Three of the STF judges also serve in the TSE (see below).

The make-up of the court (at the time of writing) is a mixture of judges chosen by Lula (three), one for each of the presidents before him (save Itamar Franco), four chosen by Dilma Rousseff, and one chosen by Michel Temer. The court is currently presided by Cármen Lúcia (nominated as judge by Lula in 2006, having assumed the presidency in 2016).

First team (*Primeira Turma*)

• Rosa Weber (nominated by Dilma Rousseff in 2011)
• Luis Fux (nominated by Dilma Rousseff in 2011)
• Luís Roberto Barroso (nominated by Dilma Rousseff in 2013)
• Marco Aurélio Mello (nominated by Fernando Collor in 1990)
• Alexander de Moraes (nominated by Michel Temer in 2017)

Second team (*Segunda Turma*)

• Dias Toffoli (nominated by Lula in 2009)
• Edson Fachin (nominated by Dilma Rousseff in 2015)
• Gilmar Mendes (nominated by Fernando Henrique Cardoso in 2002)
• Celso de Mello (nominated by José Sarney in 1989)
• Ricardo Lewandowski (nominated by Lula in 2006)

The judges are, in principle, able to rule on their own (monocratically) or collectively in the *turmas* as well as the plenary of the court. The decision to bring a case to either collective is taken by individual ministers, or the court president can schedule cases for the plenary. In collective processes in the court, one minister is designated to lead the case as *judge rapporteur* and suggest a ruling (this position is called the *ministro relator*), while another acts as overseeing or auditing judge (the *ministro revisor*). Monocratic decisions can also be audited and revised by other STF judges, but this measure is usually, though not always, avoided.

The case distribution system of STF is digitized, sealed off from other systems as well as from the judges themselves. It randomly distributes cases according to types and is supposedly designed to equilibrate the workload of processes between the judges. In the national political corruption cases, individual judges normally take the case to either the team or to the plenary, but the vast majority of other cases in the STF docket are decided by the judge designated *relator*. The exact distribution algorithm is therefore of interest in a court consisting of politically appointed judges.

The Lava-Jato case was originally headed by the judge Teori Zavascki, because the very first Lava-Jato inquiries into politicians with *foro privilegiado* were distributed to him by the algorithm. From 2014 to 2017 Zavascki managed the increasing caseload, authorizing and sometimes denying inquiries, as well as investigative measures such as the preventive arrests. However, the Dilma Rousseff-appointed judge died in an airplane crash off the coast of Paraty in the state of Rio de Janeiro. This happened precisely at the moment in January 2017 where Zavascki was about to authorize the plea bargains of 77 Odebrecht executives, who had admitted to large-scale corruption. When Zavascki suddenly died, the topic of redistribution of the Lava-Jato cases became politically very sensitive. The STF denies public access to the source code of the algorithm, so the decision-making inherent in the code is completely opaque to the public, for now. Without Zavascki, STF president Cármen Lúcia then authorized the testimonies of the Odebrecht company as evidence, and the Lava-Jato case was randomly redistributed to judge Fachin. Having obtained the legalization of the evidence, the PGR requested and was granted approval for the opening of further inquiries into more than 200 parliamentarians and governors.

As already mentioned, the politicians elected for federal public office (federal representatives, senators, ministers, and presidents) will automatically have criminal cases judged before the STF because of the *foro privilegiado*. In general, cases linger in the STF docket for years on end; the case type with the longest delay in the STF are the penal cases – and the penal cases against parliamentarians are the most common penal cases in the STF (Falcão et al. 2014: 56–57). One example of the tardiness of the system was the corruption case in the state administration of Minas Gerais in 1998. The trial in the STF against Eduardo Azeredo, former national president of PSDB and ex-governor of Minas Gerais, finally commenced 11 years after the events. The verdict was handed down in 2015, 17 years later, but even then, the sentence of a 20-year prison term was appealed. The appellate court of Minas Gerais upheld the verdict for Eduardo Azeredo in 2017. Azeredo maintained another appeal option, and by 2018, his penalty might be reduced or even suspended entirely because of his age.

What is interesting about corruption cases is not the fact that such cases are often massively delayed, as exemplified in the case of the 18-year process of the ex-governor of Minas Gerais. The crucial question of corruption cases, especially after the Ficha Limpa law, is the timing in the STF. As exemplified above, cases of politicians with *foro privilegiado* usually take much longer than corruption cases at a local or regional level, with the official explanation for this being that the STF is geared to judge constitutional law rather than criminal law. The first stage, between investigation and indictment, can take years. The processes of penal cases, which normally move between PF and the MPF, are slowed down in the STF because auxiliary judges are required to check constitutional legality of many steps in the processes. Since the start of the Lava-Jato case, most of the STF investigations targeting politicians with the *foro* have lasted 2.5 years. The first probes were authorized in March 2015 (47 politicians were included), and most of the indictments were presented during the final days of Rodrigo Janot's mandate as PGR, in September 2017. The first indictments (against Cunha and Collor, among others) were presented in August 2015, and while Cunha's case went to trial in March 2016, Collor's case went to trial in August 2017. This second stage, between indictment by the PGR and the charges being accepted or dismissed in the STF, has only been sped up in one case apart from Cunha's: The PT president, senator Gleisi Hoffmann, was denounced in May 2016 and was charged before the STF after five months.

If the main body of indictments and trials follow this pattern, the cases against PT, PMDB, and PP leaders (denounced in 2016 and 2017) will most likely result in charges in 2018, however their cases will most likely not be tried before the STF in 2019; that is, after the general elections. Thus, the *foro privilegiado* and the process delays are partly to blame for refilling the Congress with politicians accused (albeit not yet convicted) of corruption. Verdicts are handed down with even less celerity: If the process of investigation and pre-process (from indictment to trial) under the auspices of STF seems slow, the trial processes appear comparatively glacial. On average, the penal processes last five and a half years in the STF (Falcão et al. 2014: 57), often because one judge asks for more time to review the cases, and these review delays have indefinite durations. After verdicts, the appeal processes last, on average, 2.2 years (ibid.: 81).

In February 2016 however, the STF ruled that prison terms should be served immediately after a sentence has been confirmed by an appellate court. This change in the principle of assumption of innocence, producing the so-called *princípio de prisão em segunda instância*, represented an innovation of jurisprudence, since in most non-lethal cases (such as ordinary political corruption), the assumption of innocence was preserved all the way through multiple appeal trials and eventual changes of jurisdictional competency. Until then, the established jurisprudence gave politicians the option of appealing numerous times while maintaining their freedom. The result, in nearly all cases of grand political corruption, has been massive delays in sanctions and a sense of impunity (Arantes 2011, Macaulay 2011: 229, Taylor 2011: 170ff.). Furthermore, by switching to other public offices (such as state government or state assemblies, or to municipal politics), cases could be virtually restarted due to their *foro privilegiado* rights changing (ibid.: 182).

There have been several notable exceptions to this general sense of impunity, which have been important in maintaining the legitimacy of the STF. The watershed case according to Brazilian media was the Mensalão case (described in the introductory chapter). This case demonstrated that political corruption would not always be treated with impunity – although this milestone verdict required that the STF introduced and completely reinterpreted the German legal principle of *Herrschaftsprinzip* as basis of the verdict for the defendants from the political system (Greco and Leite 2014). Despite the latest changes to legal interpretation that might mitigate the infinite delays between sentence and prison terms, debates on STF's interventions into politics continue to rage in the media, as well as in the court itself.

Amid the climate of political crisis surrounding the Lava-Jato scandal, the internal accountability mechanisms of Congress have stopped working (as described below). The STF is therefore the only real obstacle to having corrupt politicians in public office. The timing of trials relative to the fixed dates of the parliamentary elections is at the center of this problem, because a final verdict in the STF will render those politicians sentenced ineligible for office as a consequence to the Ficha Limpa law. Furthermore, PT has criticized a perceived inequality in the deliberation time required to reach these verdicts, depending on the political party of the defendant. As seen in the examples from the Senate above, the PT leader Gleisi Hoffmann seems to have a case moving more rapidly in the STF than other indicted senators, making hers the only Senate candidacy likely to be barred in 2018. This critique of the priorities and processing speeds of the STF parallels the discussion on Lula's eventual 2018 candidacy (described below). In cases that drag on without a verdict, politicians can run for office and continue to exercise power from within the legislative body, and the STF has been extremely reluctant to remove politicians in office, despite the potential abuse of political power for hampering investigations (with two important exceptions described later in this chapter).

In the period 2015–2016, the majority of the STF judges, with notable and controversial exceptions, have taken some care to present the court as actively working toward ending the law of impunity and protecting the Lava-Jato investigations. Whether that representation, in the end, will turn out to be justified, remains to be seen. In the final weeks of 2017, many indictments against politicians were dismissed by the STF's *Segunda Turma*, and judge Gilmar Mendes liberated a number of individuals preventively arrested in the case. So far, no politician in office has been tried and convicted before the STF in the Lava-Jato case, and only a few of the scores of the investigated politicians have been charged before the court at the time of writing.[4] The politicians without *foro privilegiado*, like the businessmen involved in the Lava-Jato case, have been sentenced in the common court of Curitiba, to which I now turn.

The Federal Regional Courts and the 13th Vara in Curitiba

Criminal cases are normally brought before common courts (or the first judicial instance, *primeira instância*). The common courts are divided into topical and geographical jurisdictions, or *varas*. Different judges thus specialize in different areas of law. Specializing in crimes of corruption, embezzlement, and money-laundering, judge Sérgio Moro presides one of these *varas* in Curitiba. Moro, a federal judge since the mid-1990s, previously served as auxiliary-judge in the STF during the Mensalão case and judged the Banestado case. This case investigated tax evasion and massive financial movements from Brazilian corporations via a bank in Paraná to overseas accounts, amounting to at least US$20 billion and possibly as much as US$124 billion. Like later cases (such as the Mensalão and Lava-Jato cases), the Banestado case involved elite businessmen, politicians, and even Henrique Meirelles, then-director of the Central Bank, currently the minister of Finances. The Banestado case was ultimately unsuccessful in producing accountability for the political elite, as both the trials and the parliamentary investigative committee sparked by the scandal ended mostly in impunity (Cardoso and di Fatima 2013). Ninety-seven petty criminals and money launderers were sentenced in these trials conducted by Moro (Netto 2016: 30).

Moro continued to specialize in money laundering and corruption cases and became the judge of all Lava-Jato inquiries by virtue of the principle of the "natural judge." This principle fixes jurisdiction of derived criminal cases to the judge presiding the originating case. Since the first money launderer caught in the Lava-Jato investigation was the *doleiro* Alberto Youssef, working out of Paraná, cases deriving from Youssef's corrupt activities would automatically pertain to the jurisdiction of Moro. Likewise, all appeals in the Lava-Jato case are sent to the regional appeals court of Porto Alegre. Appeals courts are the second level of the court system (pt. *segunda instância*), and these courts are organized at the federal level, but are divided into five regions, approximating the geographical regions of Brazil, yielding a center/northern court located in Brasília, one in Rio de Janeiro, one in São Paulo which also covers the state of Mato Grosso do Sul, a court in Recife covering the northeastern states, and the southern regional court (abbreviated TRF-4), located in Porto Alegre, covering the states of Paraná, Rio Grande do Sul, and Santa Catarina.

Unlike many other Brazilian courts, the appeal court (TRF-4) linked to the Lava-Jato cases ratify Moro's sentences relatively quickly, yielding average trial durations of eight months in the 13th Vara, plus 13,5 months in the TRF-4 (Campos 2017). This is rapid for Brazilian courts in politicized cases, and since TRF-4 rarely overturns Moro's sentences, instead preferring to augment them (ibid.), the Lava-Jato trials have been hailed as an example to follow for other courts.

The much-publicized results of the Lava-Jato case have also propelled Sérgio Moro to the front of the public imaginary surrounding the corruption probe. Moro has become the national poster boy of the combat against corruption, featuring on the front page of numerous editions of the popular weekly magazines *IstoÉ*, *Época*, and *Veja* since 2014. Nationally, Moro has received various awards and been the topic of several books, and internationally, he has been named one of the 100 most influential people in the world by *Time Magazine*. Without having a political profile or ever expressing an interest in running for office, the name Sérgio Moro appears regularly alongside political actors in popularity surveys conducted by the large Brazilian poll institutes (e.g., Datafolha 2017). Moro became an icon – literally – in the protests of 2015 and 2016: Inflatable dolls of the judge, dressed up as a Brazilian Superman, and cardboard masks and banners proclaiming "we are all Sérgio Moro" were commonplace artefacts during the street protests. Standing in for the Lava-Jato investigations, the task-force, or the "combat against corruption," Moro's iconicity may also have glossed over essential differences between the branches of government and motivated other judges to attempt a more assertive style of political intervention.

The public support (whether truly "popular" or not) for the judiciary was, in a way, an ambition that Moro himself formulated explicitly in a paper published in 2008, titled "Considerations about the operation Clean Hands." This paper deals with the successes of the Italian combat against corruption during the 1990s scandal known as Tangentopolis, although the paper also warns of a paradoxical outcome in that combat: Silvio Berlusconi ascended to power in the aftermath of the successful operation and collapse of the existing political system in Italy. In the paper, Moro stated that public attention to corruption cases is necessary to get to the root of the problem:

> Perhaps the most important lesson of the whole episode is that legal action against corruption is only effective with the support of democracy. This defines the limits and the possibilities of legal action. With the support of public opinion, the conditions for progress and good results exist. Without it, trials can hardly succeed. Also, to get a favorable public opinion, trials must also reach good results ... It is the enlightened public opinion that can, by its own institutional means, attack the structural causes of corruption. Furthermore, the judicial punishment of corruption is always difficult ... In this perspective, public opinion can be a healthy substitute, being able to impose some punishment of corrupt public officials, by condemning them to ostracism.
>
> (Moro 2004: 61, translation mine)

The quote, and Moro himself, became the target of much critique, essentially because this Western-centric ideal of accountability through public opinion is not necessarily true in Brazil. Critics emphasized that the spectacle of public opinion, especially knowing the vested or explicit interests of Brazilian media, was not conducive to the Rule of Law (e.g., Guimarães 2016). During the Lava-Jato trials, Moro has largely avoided the media, only sporadically allowing journalists direct quotes. This contrasts to the practice of the Lava-Jato task-force, from which several prosecutors frequently appear in the media (e.g., Dallagnol and Martelo 2016) and as speakers at public events.

The Supreme Electoral Court

As with the legal areas of labor rights and military law, the area of elections is ultimately governed and overseen by a specific court – the Supreme Electoral Court (Tribunal Superior Eleitoral, henceforth TSE). The tasks of the TSE include overseeing elections and candidatures, regulating and auditing campaign expenditure during elections, processing and publicizing election results, and other tasks of an administrative and regulative nature related to elections. In the

1990s, the court was responsible for implementing electronic voting machines across the country in an effort to put an end to accusations of vote fraud. The TSE also, in cooperation and sometimes conflict with the STF (Marchetti 2008, Taylor 2011: 177), determines certain questions of political nature, including rules for party representation thresholds (and the minimum number of votes parties must obtain to obtain seats), the vertical integration of coalitions across state and federal levels (the rules for *coligações*, i.e., electoral alliances), and party loyalty in Congress.

Historically, the TSE has been known as an institution with a high degree of legitimacy, which gave it special status during the transition to democracy in the 1980s (ibid.: 166). Since then, the TSE has been relatively efficient (compared to the STF) in producing accountability in high-level cases, removing several governors from their mandates (in Tocantins, Maranhão, Roraima, Paraíba, Piauí, and, in 2017, Amazonas). In February 2017, the governor of Rio de Janeiro, Luiz Fernando Pezão, lost his mandate in a verdict by the Regional Electoral Court of Rio de Janeiro, but the process has been appealed to TSE and has since stalled. This is one of the most prominent contemporary cases of the lower-level federal electoral courts producing accountability. Each state has a permanent lower-level court (abbreviated TRE) overseeing state elections, and at the municipal level, the temporary accountability institution, which is set up for each election, is called electoral juntas (Marchetti 2008: 40).

Overall, the electoral court system has limited resources and too few personnel to ensure fair elections for all citizens across such an extensive territory. Furthermore, a two-year renewal of the mandate of TSE judge was once problematic for producing consistent jurisprudence in the court (Taylor 2011: 165ff.). This timeframe of two-year terms has resulted in a constant reshuffling of the court's composition. The court's bench is designed to contain a mixture of judges and respected lawyers: Two slots are filled by lawyers of public renown, each chosen by the president on the basis of a list of three names nominated by the STF, which has selected these names from a list of six names nominated by the national bar association (OAB). The remaining five seats are allocated to three STF judges and two STJ judges[5] (and each of these judges must be nominated for a slot by consensus in their respective courts of origin).

Members are permitted to sit for up to two terms of two years. The STJ judges normally sit on the TSE bench for a single term, while two terms have become the norm for the other members (Marchetti 2008: 885). This principle of rotation proved to be of the utmost importance during the trial aiming at the cancellation of the presidential elections of 2014, described below.

Since the TSE is presided over by one of the STF judges, the two courts normally act in a concerted way. Some of the high-profiled rulings of TSE have been challenged on constitutional grounds and thus become the topic of deliberation in the STF, but the TSE rulings have generally been ratified there (Taylor 2011: 170). In effect, the STF has delegated competency of legal interpretation in the electoral area to TSE and avoids direct interference, although the overlap of STF and TSE judges aligns the courts somewhat. The STF ratifications grant a shroud of legitimacy to the audits of party and candidate campaign spending, although it is well known that the auditors of TSE are unable to scratch the surface of the vast budgets commanded by the Brazilian parties (ibid.). Special audit procedures can be initiated by the TSE when whistle-blowers emerge, or, as we shall see, when political actors eye opportunities to denounce their opponents.

The Tribunal for the Accounts of the Union

A number of governmental audit bodies exist in parallel in Brazil. The executive branch appoints a comptroller-general (Controladoria Geral da União), the Ministério Público has offices called Ministério Público de Contas at both federal and state levels, while the audit organization of the legislative branch of government is the Tribunal das Contas da União (henceforth TCU). In this auditing body, routine accounting, state budget auditing, and special case-by-case investigations are conducted. The TCU reports on budget irregularities in large-scale government projects and produces a yearly independent audit of the state finances. TCU normally only acts as advisor to Congress, but can also (since 2001, when the state budget regulation was revised) request that the parliamentary budget committee block fund transfers when severe irregularities are encountered in projects.

The TCU court is headed by nine so-called ministers, titled like the Supreme Court judges, despite the fact that TCU judges are not part of the judiciary, nor necessarily trained in law. Six of the TCU judges are nominated by the Congress, and three are nominated by the president. Two of the latter must be career public servants with a background in the TCU. The ministers are appointed for life but must retire at the age of 70. This means that "politicians are frequently nominated to join the TCU at the height or the end of their political career, in what is sometimes seen as a kind of early retirement" (Speck 2011: 155). The leadership of this accounting body thus, to a certain extent, reflects the composition and leading coalition of the Congress. The nomination for a seat in the TCU "comes with strings attached, since the government with its majority in Congress does not expect any trouble from its former allies once they are transferred to the TCU" (ibid.). TCU auditors are, for that reason, rarely called to testify about audit findings in the committees and hearings of Congress (ibid.: 147).

Despite not being part of the judiciary branch, the TCU has some powers to sanction and issue fines to government actors found guilty of misconduct. In practice, the implementation of sanctions and fines is often delayed, because the TCU verdicts can and normally will be questioned in the state and federal courts. This fact, according to Speck, is the weakest link of the accountability mechanisms of the TCU (ibid.: 144).

The political network and dependency of TCU ministers is probably an even weaker link, however. During 2015–2016, three TCU ministers underwent investigation during the Lava-Jato scandal. According to various testimonies of the case, the ministers Aroldo Cedraz, Vital do Rego, and Raimundo Carreira have received bribes, possibly to entice them to actively obstruct audits in the TCU, or as kickbacks related to when they were still in political office. Moreover, Cedraz's son, the lawyer Tiago Cedraz, was subpoenaed by the police in 2017 on the suspicion that he had negotiated contracts between Petrobras and an American company and received US$20 million in kickbacks. In one of the plea bargain testimonies of the Lava-Jato case, the expelled PP ex-parliamentarian Pedro Corrêa claimed that Cedraz was actually selected for the TCU as a part of a political bargain struck in the wake of the Mensalão scandal. Cedraz was appointed as payment for votes to save the mandate of the PP leader José Janene, according to the testimony. Moreover, the minister Augusto Nardes is investigated in the operation named Zelotes.

The TCU, in conclusion, is perhaps the most politically aligned accountability institution, at least insofar as concerns the leaders of the organization. It is also the body least likely to react to large-scale budget problems at the federal level: Only in 1937 did TCU refuse to accept the state accounts (in a situation where then-President Vargas had threatened the independence of the governmental branches with a new constitution). The string of 77 consecutive approvals of the state accounts came to an end in 2015, however, when a TCU report on fiscal delays in the State Treasury was interpreted as a grave infraction of the Law of Fiscal Responsibility by Augusto Nardes, conducting the yearly audit of state accounts. His recommendation of rejection of the state finances was unanimously supported in TCU, and the rejection precipitated the impeachment proceedings, described in more detail in the final chapter. This outcome was the most obvious example of the ways in which accountability mechanisms and legal actions were deployed in the wake of the Lava-Jato scandal – although the TCU report on fiscal delays had nothing to do with the Petrobras corruption.

Judicial Consequences of Corruption Cases

The following sections consist in five case studies drawn from the vast range of judicial processes that have interfered in the struggles of the Brazilian political arena. Two of these cases emerged outside of the criminal actions of the Lava-Jato probe but had their roots in this investigation of corruption. The case study of the impeachment process is saved for the final chapter, and so the empirical cases analyzed here are:

- The TSE process for cancellation of the 2014 presidential elections
- Eduardo Cunha's disciplinary process in the parliamentary *Conselho de Ética*
- Two cases of suspension of senatorial mandates (Senators Calheiros and Neves)
- The nine legal actions against ex-President Lula

From these cases, I have abstracted a range of direct and indirect outcomes specific to the Brazilian system of accountability institutions and checks and balances in their current configuration. These outcomes include overturning and rigging elections, removing politicians from public office, changing the valorization of political capital and the informal rules for coalition formation. The outcomes are discussed as a conclusion to the following brief case studies. Each of the cases had a great impact on the media agenda. The cases of Cunha and Lula are centerpieces of the informational cascade described in the next chapter, and for the sake of clarity the quantitative media content analysis concerning these cases is also located there. Like these cases, the TSE process and the cases pertaining to Senators' mandates were dominant elements of national news for many weeks, but these cases lie outside of the sample period of the quantitative study.

The TSE Process for Cancellation of the 2014 Presidential Elections

The case with the most explosive potential of all started with a petition for cancelling the result of the 2014 presidential elections. The case was initially comprised of four different petitions, due to the losing opposition party, PSDB, having filed a range of different actions in TSE. The following overview of these cases is based on the comprehensive log of legal documents available at the TSE website (Tribunal Superior Eleitoral 2017).

• On the 2nd of October 2014, PSDB and the coalition behind the candidacy of Aécio Neves filed a petition for investigation (*investigação judicial eleitoral*) into the incumbent president's abuse of public mechanisms, such as illegal distribution of pamphlets via the state postal service and abuse of ministerial positions for campaigning (AIJE 154781).
• On the 30th of October 2014, PSDB announced it would file a petition for impugnation (*ação de impugnação de mandato eletivo*), calling for an audit of the votes cast during the elections (AIME 761). One argument for this court action was the use of funds obtained from corruption in Petrobras during the campaign, based on testimonies made by Paulo Roberto da Costa, Ricardo Pessoa, Alberto Youssef, and Pedro Barusco. It was submitted to the TSE on January 2.
• On the 18th of December 2014, PSDB filed another petition for investigation (*investigação judicial eleitoral*) into the president's use of public ceremonies and events to perform political, and thus non-public, campaigning activities (AIJE 194358).
• In October 2014, PSDB also announced it would file a *representação* (RP 846), technically another kind of petition, also claiming that the state postal service (*Correios*) had obstructed Neves' election mail campaign. It was submitted to the TSE on January 2. Like the AIJE 154781, this action also targeted the postal service director Walter Pinheiro.

The allegation that kickbacks from the corruption in Petrobras helped Rousseff fund her campaign was included in both the second and third petitions, however it was in the second petition that the denunciation of corruption was highlighted. Both petitions referenced the media leaks from the Lava-Jato case. In the following, I will describe the interactions between the investigative bodies, judicial actors and the political system. Based on this, I will venture an answer to the question of how a large amount of evidence of corruption could end up being completely disregarded, focusing on two types of interaction and the key role played by the TSE president (and STF judge) Gilmar Mendes.

The eventual consequence of the actions in the electoral court could have been the removal of the winning president and vice-president from office, leaving Brazil with a third president in the space of one year. Jurisprudence as to whether this would result in new elections or the inauguration of the losing presidential candidate was not clear, however, as different Brazilian courts had solved similar situations differently in the past. At the time of the initial petitions, commentators assumed that the cancellation of the 2014 election result would have positioned PSDB favorably. This assumption was due to the increasing negative focus and coverage of the PT and the Petrobras scandal, but the timing of the electoral court actions eventually put PSDB in an unexpectedly vulnerable position. The process was characterized by many delays, fits and starts.

Initially, the petition AIME 761 was rejected by TSE Justice Maria Thereza de Assis Moura in February 2015. The rejection was appealed in March by PSDB and then sent to the TSE plenary, where judge Gilmar Mendes delayed the process through an extension of the deadline for review. In August 2015, the *ministro relator* João Otávio Noronha of the petition AIJE 154781 asked the STF to share material from the Petrobras case, and synchronously the judge Luis Fux suggested combining all PSDB petitions while Gilmar Mendes and two other judges voted to continue the investigations. Fux's idea of combining the petitions was debated in the plenary, but would only be realized the following year. The AIME 761 was reopened by then-president of TSE, Dias Toffoli, on October 6, 2015. On December 17, the representation RP 846 was rejected, but PSDB appealed with the argument that new evidence had come to light. That argument came to be the Achilles' heel of the case 18 months later.

On top of the four petitions for cancellation of the election of Rousseff, PSDB also petitioned the prosecutor-general of elections (PGE) to discard PT from further elections, as a consequence of the denunciation made by the ex-director of Petrobras, Nestor Cerveró. In a testimony, Cerveró claimed that PT received laundered money from Angolan funds through the actions of the ex-President Lula, in violation of the law prohibiting foreign influence upon Brazilian elections. This separate petition has lingered in the TSE docket since.

In February 2016, the four initial PSDB petitions were integrated into one aggregate suit, maintaining the file name AIJE 194358 under the auspices of the auditor-general of TSE (a position rotating biennially between the TSE judges). At that point, the cases were to be judged by Maria Thereza de Assis Moura, and she restarted the process of collecting evidence of fraud in the campaign, despite the fact that one year earlier, she had recommended the case be rejected by the

TSE. Various appeals from PT were then denied in the TSE plenary, ruling that the excessive use of formal appeals (*agravos*) was slowing the process down. Events overtook the TSE process in any case, as Rousseff was impeached, which led to a new situation for the defense lawyers of Rousseff and Temer. Formerly united as defendants, the newly inaugurated President Michel Temer now tried to advance the argument in TSE that the campaign accounts of Rousseff and Temer were distinct in principle and practice, and that the eventual annulment of Rousseff's bid wouldn't apply to his mandate, as he was without blame. Several cross-payments from the PT campaign to PMDB weakened this argument, however.

In August 2016, TSE audits of printing companies contracted by PT demonstrated that three of these companies – Focal, Red Seg, and Grafica VPTB – could not prove the capability to produce large amounts of printed material, nor that they in fact had produced all of the material paid for during the 2014 campaign. This was taken to be an indication that the companies were in fact used to produce fraudulent contracts. It was not clear then who benefitted from this money laundering, since the money was, in fact, spent by the PT. The mismatch of contracts and products led the electoral prosecutor, Nicolao Dino, to believe that campaign funds had financed other areas than the printed material, since the occultation of transfers could indicate the presence of illegal financing. The printing company audits became the cornerstone of the inquiry led by the new TSE Auditor-General Herman Benjamin. Taking over from judge Moura who rotated out of TSE on September 2, Herman called a number of individuals imprisoned or sentenced by the Lava-Jato investigations to testify to the TSE, including the *doleiro* Alberto Youssef, the ex-senator Delcídio do Amaral and a number of construction company CEOs.

On October 13, 2016, judge Benjamin called for an investigation of the printing companies' bank accounts, and in December, police agents entered the premises of the printing companies on Benjamin's request. Further testimonies were solicited, and Benjamin set up a task-force dealing with the investigation. Furthermore, Benjamin's case now included evidence from the Lava-Jato investigations phase dubbed Acarajé; evidence that linked the Odebrecht group to certain offshore companies and the marketing expert of PT, João Santana. Santana had admitted to being paid by Odebrecht for services delivered to PT as kickback for the advantages the construction company received in federal procurement and public tenders.

Seventy-seven Odebrecht executives had agreed to a plea bargains in the Lava-Jato case, and key testimonies of this process were included in the TSE process. The top executives of the company's so-called "department of bribes" appeared before the court, along with the incarcerated heir to the Odebrecht dynasty, Marcelo Odebrecht, in February and early March 2017. The inclusion of these testimonies was both a blessing and a curse for Michel Temer because they posed a greater risk of a cancelled election. On the other hand, each court session with new testimonies[6] moved the court closer to the rotation deadline of two judges. This was, in a nutshell, the most important interaction between the political and the judicial system: Extending the testimony process gave Temer an opportunity to pack the bench of the TSE.

This type of interaction has been studied in other Latin American contexts of presidential and democratic crises, and based on comparative studies of such cases, Helmke concludes that "judges are clearly capable of altering the various parameters that affect presidential instability" (Helmke 2017: 128). Court-packing is one strategy a president may pursue to secure stability, and this was exactly what swayed the vote, in the end, in Temer's favor. As TSE judges Henrique Neves and Luciana Lóssio left their positions (in April and May, respectively), Temer could appoint two new judges to the bench, and he called in Admar Gonzaga and Tarcísio Vieira, both of them shortlisted by judges of the STF.

The two new judges on the bench meant that a new majority formed among the judges. The judge overseeing the process, Herman Benjamin, had declared in the press that the court would provide a historical ruling, and it was believed that two out of the three STF judges serving on the TSE bench (Luis Fux and Rosa Weber) would vote with Benjamin for cancelling the 2014 presidential elections. This would, indeed, have been a historical moment, since no presidential election had ever been overturned by the TSE. However, as the process of hearing the testimonies extended over March and April, Judge Luciana Lóssio's mandate ended. Lóssio was expected to vote for cancelling the election (e.g., Mattoso et al. 2017). With Lóssio now gone, what had previously been a majority of TSE judges inclining toward cancellation, became a minority on the bench.

The final days of the trial in the TSE plenary, on June 7, 8, and 9, were dominated by discussion on the original scope of the petitions, and whether the trial could expand this scope to any and all corruption relating to parties of the president and the vice-president. The inclusion of testimonies of the expelled senator Delcídio do Amaral, the Odebrecht executives, and the marketing expert Santana, did not strongly support the initial accusations (that had referenced leaked plea bargains from Paulo Roberto Costa and Alberto Youssef), as these testimonies dealt with other situations of graft and corruption. The report of the electoral prosecutor affirmed the narrative of Petrobras contracts leading to kickbacks to the government parties, but not directly to the election campaign.

The judge in charge of the process, Benjamin, initiated the procedure of the verdict, unsurprisingly recommending that the election of Rousseff and Temer should be annulled (Benjamin 2017). The first judge to vote after Benjamin was Napoleão Nunes, who insisted that the trial could not take into consideration elements that were not present in the original petition – such as the Odebrecht testimonies. Nunes therefore recommended denying the petitions. Judge Luis Fux in turn contradicted Nunes, as Fux affirmed that rejecting the use of Odebrecht testimonies would mean ignoring evidence. TSE president Gilmar Mendes scorned this stance during the debate, calling it "moralist."

The two judges appointed by Temer in 2017 supported Judge Nunes, while the two judges from STF (Luis Fux and Rosa Weber) followed the recommendation of Benjamin. The dissent in the court meant that Judge Mendes had the decisive vote, and he ultimately denied the petition, stating that the instability of the country was in question, and that presidents should not be removed every other day. Both Rousseff and Temer thus ended up acquitted in the final verdict. PSDB's lawyers had, in their final allegation prior to the verdict, highlighted that only Dilma Rousseff and the PT was to blame for illicit campaign funds, but with the tie-breaking vote of Mendes, the Rousseff-Temer ticket as a whole was acquitted as the majority of TSE voted not to separate the candidatures.

Another type of political-judicial interaction of interest here is the relation between the plaintiff's petition and the scope of investigation possible under the current legislation concerning the TSE. While PSDB had, from the very beginning, accused PT of abuse of public office and illegal funds for campaigning, throughout the two-year process TSE maintained that an eventual cancellation would remove both president and vice-president. However, the ultimate decision to restrict the scope of the verdict to the original allegation ran contrary to the process of collecting evidence for the court. In October 2016, the court had gathered a task-force from PF, tax authorities, and the Central Bank to determine the character of transfers to the companies printing campaign pamphlets for Rousseff and Temer in 2014. Soon after, the PGR had recommended including testimonies from the Odebrecht investigations, and the TSE obliged. In spite of this, the final verdict, the evidence produced had "expanded the object of the case" and had to be discarded.

The judicial decision to include and exclude material, in the end, made all the difference to whether Brazilian voters had the opportunity to democratically elect a new president. Instead, the country was stuck with a president tarnished by the very corruption scandal that had undermined the previous president. Meanwhile, both PSDB and the coalition that had originally backed Aécio Neves obtained several cabinet positions and no longer had any interest in the legal action they had started, nor any consensual candidate beyond Temer to put forth for the presidency.

In his final statement, Gilmar Mendes made ironic comments concerning the inclusion of any and all allegations floating in the press, and how this would delay the trial indefinitely. That observation in itself shows that Mendes and other judges were acutely aware that the timing of the trial in relation to Lava-Jato was of the utmost importance. Expecting (or perhaps knowing) more evidence of corruption and illicit campaign funding could turn up, Gilmar Mendes intervened in order to shut down the TSE trial and the threat of instability to Temer's presidency.

In sum, court-packing, the deliberate timing of the judicial action, and the reduction of scope in the investigations prevented TSE from producing accountability, despite the evidence collected by the court's task-force. Benjamin, commenting upon his colleagues' stances, stated that TSE seemed to invert the historical goal of the court by seeking only to adjudicate matters concerning official donations, denying the validity of evidence of unofficial transfers. The historical sentence that Benjamin foresaw early in 2017 ended up being historical only in the sense that it reflected the sense of impunity toward political corruption. Likewise, two parallel investigations that were opened by Judge Moura before leaving the TSE also stalled. These cases investigated the suspicions of PMDB and PP for campaign fraud in 2014. The electoral court case illustrates how accountability institutions, despite the best interests of many in the organization, may still be subjugated to the goals of other institutions, defeating the whole idea of checks and balances.

Eduardo Cunha's Disciplinary Process in the Parliamentary Conselho de Ética

One accountability institution not mentioned in the overview above is the internal disciplinary committees of the legislative branch of government: The *Conselhos da Ética* in the Senate and the Câmara. In this section, I will discuss the intricacies of this accountability mechanism, exemplified through the case in which Eduardo Cunha's mandate in the Congress was revoked. With this example, I will show how accountability institutions and processes can also turn out to be bargaining chips in complex political power struggles. I will highlight the entanglement of the political and the judicial fields in this legislative body, which is quite different from the investigations and court trials described previously, and is also perhaps much more crucial to the functioning of the political landscape in Brazil.

The reason why the two Conselhos da Ética of Congress were left out in the above discussion of accountability institutions is both conceptual and practical: Conceptually, these disciplinary committees do not pertain to the Judiciary, but are governed by the legislative bodies. Moreover, in practice they have only been used recently in minor internal disciplinary cases and not for producing accountability to the electorate. Though these disciplinary committees in principle treat all kinds of lapses of ethical comportment and hold the power to recommend the cancellation of mandates, they have only very rarely been activated in the corruption cases engulfing the Brazilian Legislative in the last three years.

One reason for this surprising state of affairs is the number of investigations, denunciations, and trials hovering over the legislative assemblies in the STF. With roughly half of parliament accused, and to a large extent investigated, there is little incentive for the parliamentarians to set up internal institutional investigations. Not only would accompanying disciplinary processes in every case of denunciation take up much time in parliament, it would certainly also sour relations between the many fragmented parties in Congress. In a certain sense, both Conselhos have effectively limited their reach to events occurring inside Congress and between congressmen, rather than taking a more inclusive view of the moral code of public office holders.

The Conselhos of Congress are complemented by another internal accountability mechanism: For more than a decade, the legislative modus operandi in corruption cases has been to set up parliamentary investigating committees (called CPIs) looking into political corruption – but seldom with great consequences for the accused (Power and Taylor 2011: 19). The prerogative to install and appoint a CPI lies with the president of the Senate or the Câmara, respectively (and joint commissions between the two Houses of Congress can also be constructed from time to time). For obvious reasons, the presidents of the Houses can easily avoid being investigated in the context of a CPI. So, despite the fact that the PMDB leader in the Câmara, Eduardo Cunha, was connected to the Petrobras graft in leaks in December 2014, he could still construct a CPI looking into the case when he was elected president of the Câmara in early 2015.

As mentioned in the previous chapter, Cunha went on the stand on March 12, 2015, calmly denying the accusations in the investigative commission he himself had opened to examine the Petrobras corruption. Furthermore, Cunha claimed that he did not have any overseas bank accounts. This claim became the basis of a process for annulling Cunha's mandate. It was a complex and excruciating process, and the only disciplinary process in the Conselho da Ética in the 2015–2017 period targeting a politician for being involved in the Lava-Jato case. The senators have, meanwhile, simply avoided to activate the Senate's Conselho, preferring to keep up the appearances of a harmonious Upper House.

When evidence of Swiss bank accounts, in Cunha's name, was leaked soon after the first indictment of the PGR targeting Cunha (in August 2015), the minor left-wing party PSOL filed for a disciplinary action in the Câmara. PSOL argued that since Cunha had specifically denied, in the CPI regarding Petrobras, having overseas accounts, he had lied to his peers. Lying in a CPI to his peers constituted a clear breach of decorum, enough to revoke the mandate of a congressman (in theory, but not in practice, a corruption scandal should also suffice). On October 1, 2015, PSOL and the party Rede Sustentabilidade requested documentation from the PGR in September, and on October 13, the two parties and half of the PT congressmen filed a petition urging the Conselho da Ética to open a case against Cunha. As president of the Câmara, Cunha maintained the rights to manage and to command the Board of the Câmara and the institutional resources before the process began, and even as the process got underway – despite being obviously partial in the resulting disciplinary process.

Cunha exploited various procedural loopholes and thus postponed the disciplinary process during October. First of all, the Board of the Câmara, which is formally responsible for all document handling and administrative tasks of the Lower House, simply waited the maximum number of days to hand over the process to the Conselho. This meant that the president of the Conselho, José Carlos Araújo, could not formally open the case, given the rules of the Câmara, and only on November 4 did he get to appoint a speaker (*relator*) to conduct the disciplinary process. During November, the speaker Fausto Pinato (then of the party PRB) tried to present his preliminary recommendation for opening a process. However, half of the 20 congressmen constituting the Conselho, known in the daily press as Cunha's "shock troop," repeatedly delayed the preliminary recommendation by extending discussions of formalities. The tactic of delaying (in the vein of the US tradition known as a *filibuster*) worked successfully throughout November. Furthermore, as the sub-committees of the Congress are prohibited from assembling in the time slots when the plenary assembles, Cunha could schedule the Câmara's activities, and this allowed him to simply call for a plenary vote in the Câmara whenever the Conselho was about to vote, automatically ending meetings of the sub-commission. With these tactics, Pinato was hindered in even reading his recommendation until December.

Toward the end of November, as Cunha's repertoire of delay tactics was slowly exhausted, it became clear that the speaker, the Council president and a small majority in the Council would not dismiss the case. The day of voting for opening the case was set for December 1. In the week leading up to the session, deliberations within the PT were reported by the press. The three PT members of the Ethics Council could, in principle, add their votes to the Cunha's so-called shock troops, letting him off the hook. Implicitly or explicitly, depending on the point of view, that would start a truce between Rousseff and Cunha, protecting the president of the Câmara from disciplinary action and the president of the Republic from impeachment. In effect, once the Conselho reached the point of voting for the preliminary assessment of Pinato, the three votes of PT in the Conselho became a bargaining chip for Cunha, since he held the prerogative to initiate impeachment proceedings against the PT president Dilma Rousseff.

The truce, or back-stage deal, between Cunha and PT leaders, never materialized, however. The Conselho, in the session on December 1, did not get around to vote. The members of PT looked hesitant and deliberated in hushed voices, while following the debate of the commission. As the meeting dragged on, the national president of PT tweeted (and media promptly reported) that PT had demanded the deputies to vote for opening a case against Cunha. The meeting ended, and the vote was postponed to the following day. Finally, under cross-pressure from nearly all of Congress and the divided allegiance to a party line, on one hand, and the best interests of their president on the other, the PT members of the Conselho finally decided how to vote. One of them, Zé Geraldo, outright declared the supposed truce negotiation to be blackmail, "a knife to the throat," and that he and his two colleagues in the Ethics Council were less than happy holding the trigger for the impeachment (Almeida 2016: 106).

The following day, with the votes of the PT representatives, the commission formed a majority in favor of Pinato's recommendation for opening the disciplinary process against Cunha. The meeting in the Conselho at the moment of the vote was highly agitated, featuring everything from verbal abuse to physical infighting. The feared retaliation arrived the same afternoon, as Cunha declared that impeachment proceedings would be initiated then, confirming PT's earlier suspicions of blackmail. These events became one of the cornerstones of the counter-narrative of a coup d'état deployed by PT.

Shortly before Christmas, the PGR filed for the removal of Cunha from office in the STF, with the argument that his position in Congress allowed him to systematically abuse his prerogatives and protect him from investigation. The same week, the soundness of that argument was amply demonstrated: Pinato's recommendation became overturned on formal grounds by the vice-president of the Câmara, Waldir Maranhão (PP). He ruled, on behalf of the Board of the Câmara, that since Pinato's party PRB was formally allied to the governing block, and thus to PMDB, Pinato could not be speaker of the case. In the ruling, Maranhão stated that a politician could not be the speaker of a disciplinary case against a colleague participating in the same parliamentary coalition. The ruling ran counter to logic, since Cunha had long ago given every possible signal that he wanted a new government coalition, declared his break with government, and since Pinato had actually recommended revoking Cunha's mandate, thus eliminating any suspicions of exchanging favors.

Nonetheless, the president of the Conselho was forced to appoint a new speaker on the case, this time from the opposition which Cunha was courting. That move gave Cunha another shot at delaying the case and possibly getting it filed away. Cunha's oppositional stance notwithstanding, the new speaker, Marcos Rogério of the then-opposition party Democratas, recommended revoking Cunha's mandate on December 15, but his report on the case was annulled, again by Maranhão, the vice-president of the Câmara. The argument brought up by Cunha-allied members of the Conselho consisted in a formal complaint that they had not been given time to process Rogério's recommendation. The process then returned to the starting point.

As usual in the Brazilian legislature, all processes ground to a halt in January and half of February. Synchronously, a window of opportunity for switching parties was opened in the Câmara, and as many as 14 percent of the Congressmen (71 in total) in the Câmara changed parties. This meant that the composition of the parliamentary blocks had changed, and in consequence, that the distribution of representation and substitute representatives in the Conselho was re-examined and changed accordingly. In the party-switching frenzy, Cunha had not managed to install a majority in his favor in the Conselho, however. Rogério's recommendation for opening the disciplinary process was to be voted on March 3, five months after the petition was filed.

One member of the Conselho, Vinícius Gurgel, who was planning to vote in Cunha's favor, could not participate in the vote, however, and his substitute was expected to vote against Cunha. The Board of the Câmara received a document where Gurgel resigned from his position in the Conselho (albeit with a falsified signature), and this allowed Gurgel's party leader to appoint another Congressman to the position and support Cunha's attempt to close down the disciplinary process. The maneuver ended to no avail with the late-night vote on March 3, when Rogerio's recommendation was passed, 11 votes to 10. Cunha then avoided being served by the legislative clerks, further delaying the process for one week.

At this moment, Cunha also faced corruption charges before the STF – as the first politician involved in the Lava-Jato scandal. That did not prevent him from conducting the impeachment proceedings of the Câmara in April, however. The STF only responded to the PGR's request for removal of Cunha from office in May 2016, based on a ruling that charged politicians cannot be in the line of succession to the presidency (which, with the eventual impeachment of Rousseff, would locate Cunha as the de facto vice-president). Using this clause, the STF abstained from creating a jurisprudence for removing politicians from office who were suspected of using their position to meddle in their investigations. This legal interpretation was what the PGR requested when filing for Cunha's removal, but the STF denied it.

With the turmoil of the advancing impeachment and the removal of Cunha on May 5, the presidency of the Câmara was left to Waldir Maranhão – also under investigation at that point – who had aligned with Cunha before. Maranhão, who had twice annulled votes in Cunha's case, surprisingly also tried to annul the impeachment vote of the Câmara, but after less than 24 hours of internal pressure proceeded to annul his own annulment. The former opposition negotiated a new governing coalition, and once the increasingly isolated Cunha renounced his presidency on July 7, party leaders decided to elect a new leader for the Câmara – one less associated with Cunha and less easily subdued to the cross-pressures of Congress.

Rodrigo Maia of the party Democratas was elected new president of the Câmara, and he scheduled a plenary vote for the recommendation of the Conselho da Ética for revoking Cunha's mandate. This vote occurred in September 2016, 11 months after the initial petition. The vote resulted in a massive majority backing the revocation of Cunha's mandate, 450 to 10, demonstrating that he had become a political pariah at that point. With his mandate revoked, Cunha's seven pending corruption cases were relocated to the regional court of Curitiba running the Lava-Jato investigations. True to the pattern, judge Sérgio Moro quickly authorized the preventive arrest of Cunha, apprehending him on October 19.

Despite being the first Lava-Jato investigated politician to be charged before the STF, Cunha thus never got to have a complete trial before that court. During the first months of the Lava-Jato probe, in 2014, the PT member André Vargas was the only other congressman to have his mandate revoked by the Câmara. In other words, aside from Vargas and Cunha, not even the politicians who were charged before the STF were made accountable to their peers through the mechanism of the Conselho, nor did the parties move to expel them based on corruption charges.

The case of Cunha's removal was emblematic of the problems inherent to Congress' internal accountability processes when Congress is faced with multiple corruption allegations. At each turn of the process in Conselho, the votes for the various reports were almost a tie, which indicates that this body of representatives will bow to the political pressures of their peers to the detriment of the voters. Furthermore, the quasi-legal framework used in disciplinary processes turned out to be so fragile that the process could very well have ended up acquitting Cunha. The tactics used to delay Cunha's removal from office were legally valid, although (literally) violently contested, which shows the democratic deficit of disciplinary procedures in the Câmara – procedures that have not been challenged although they are clearly malleable. His removal by the STF, however, provided some legal jurisprudence to the following cases, where the STF also intervened in the legislative branch of government.

The Case of Renan Calheiros and the Constitutional Mini-Crisis

A parallel to Eduardo Cunha's case removed Senate President Renan Calhei-ros, albeit briefly, from office. The verdict, in the case of Cunha, was that no parliamentarian charged before the STF could preside over any public office that would place him or her in the presidential line of succession. Tradition-ally, presidents are replaced by vice-presidents, and when both are absent, the vice-president of the Câmara acts as head of state. The next in line is the presi-dent of the Senate and the president of the STF. The STF, on November 3, 2016, initiated a plenary discussion of whether or not the Cunha case should turn into legal precedence, but postponed the decision indefinitely. At the point of postponement, the majority of judges in the STF plenary had already declared their votes, which meant that the court had a virtual, but not enacted, ruling on the matter.

Like Cunha, Senate President Renan Calheiros was targeted by the Lava-Jato investigations in March 2015, being perhaps the most prominent name on the PGR's list. In addition to that investigation, Calheiros became the target of 11 successive investigations for fraud, corruption and embezzlement. Of these cases, ten derived from the Lava-Jato probe, and on top of these Calheiros was investigated in a separate inquiry of the Zelotes case, mentioned below, as well as in a much older case from 2007 that, back then, almost cost him his career.

The oldest case, filed away in the STF for years, in which Calheiros became indicted and charged, dealt with the monthly payments to his former lover and mother to one of his children. The money allegedly came from the construction company Mendes Junior, in return for political support for legislation that bene-fitted the company. Together with a scandal of indirectly controlling media outlets in his home state Alagoas (which is prohibited for persons in public office), these cases brought Calheiros' first mandate as president of the Senate to an end in December 2007, when he resigned after months of pressure. However, he remained in the Senate and returned to the presidency of the Senate in February 2013.

The 2007 case of exchanging political support for clandestine payments to a mistress was put on the agenda of the STF on December 1, 2016, with the court accepting some of the elements of the PGR's indictment, meaning Calheiros now faced charges. The fact that Calheiros had been charged by the STF placed his position as president of the Senate at odds with the STF verdict in Cunha's case, which ruled that no charged individuals could remain in the line of succes-sion to the presidency. Four days later, STF judge Marco Aurélio de Mello received a petition, from the party Rede, for removing Calheiros from the posi-tion of president of the Senate. The very same day, Mello gave a preliminary ruling and suspended Calheiros from office. At first, Calheiros evaded the civil servant that was dispatched to notify him, and upon receiving the suspension, he simply ignored it – with the support of the Senate. The vice-president of the Senate, Jorge Viana (of the PT), and the Board of the Senate chose to wait out the impasse, expecting an eventual confirmation of the preliminary ruling by the

STF plenary. The failure to comply with a STF ruling, in theory, could mean that Renan Calheiros was now in danger of being apprehended by the police.

The conflict arose as the Senate was about to go on holiday break in December. This moment coincided with the very last days of Calheiros' mandate as president of the Senate. For two days, the sense of constitutional conflict filled the headlines, but on December 7, the STF plenary overturned Mello's ruling. Six of the nine judges present in the court argued that since Calheiros was not immediately next in the line of succession, there was no urgency to remove him at the very end of his mandate, and that the court should avoid ruptures of the "harmony between the branches of Government" (Mello 2016). So, in the end, Calheiros managed to weather the storm and left office as planned, handing the seat of the presidency in the Senate over to fellow PMDB senator Eunício Oliveira in February 2017. Oliveira also came under investigation in several inquiries of the Lava-Jato case. Following the Calheiros impasse, the principal parties of Congress deliberated over a constitutional amendment shielding presidents of both Houses from this kind of judicial intervention. Calheiros, moreover, called for reforms to reduce the salaries of judges and spoke in favor of harsher punishments for judges who abused their authority.

The Case of Aécio Neves and the Second Constitutional Crisis

The conflict between the Senate and the STF resurfaced in May 2017. The same basic question was at stake: The First Turma of the STF had, after repeated requests from the PGR, ruled that Aécio Neves be removed from his mandate, although the judges preferred not to rule that Neves be arrested. While in the cases of removing Cunha and Calheiros, the legal argument concerned the presidential line of succession, the STF had less jurisprudence on which to build the Neves case. Neves, like Michel Temer, had been caught on tape in conversation with the meat magnate Joesley Batista. In a meeting which was secretly recorded, Neves had asked Batista for bribes of R$2 million to pay for defense lawyers in the Lava-Jato case. Neves designated his cousin to receive the money, who, upon receiving it, hid the bags of cash with an aide of Neves' fellow senator from Minas Gerais, Zeze Perrella.[7] Since the deliveries of cash made by Neves' cousin were monitored by the PF, there was little doubt that Neves had been caught red-handed, but at the time the STF did not act in a consistent manner: As the information turned public, judge Fachin first decreed Neves be suspended from mandate and denied him the rights to leave the country or talk to others under investigation in the Lava-Jato case. Neves appealed and continued to appear in the Senate, talking to other politicians including other senators under investigation. The Senate clerks did not even remove Neves from the voting roll-call list.

As the limelight during this week in May was mostly directed at President Temer and his attempts to salvage his own credibility, Neves remained in Congress, ignoring the ruling. The corruption probe before the STF into Joesley Batista was separated from other Lava-Jato investigations, and because of this a new judge rapporteur was required. The case was redistributed to Judge Marco

Aurélio de Mello, who two months later reversed the ruling. Even though the PGR appealed Mello's ruling, Aécio Neves had now had time to ignore the scandal and consolidate the coalition of Michel Temer at a critical moment, just after the Batista leaks had shaken the government to its core. Neves' party, the PSDB, wound up divided in half over the question of supporting Temer and whether or not to suspend Neves permanently from presiding over the party.

Only in September 2017, four months after the tapes became public, did the STF deliberate on the matter of Aécio Neves again. This time, the case was taken up by the five ministers of the Primeira Turma, who decided, three votes to two, that they would reinstate the initial measures of judge Fachin by restricting both Neves' personal liberty (through a nightly curfew and prohibition of travels abroad) and his political rights by suspension of his mandate. Had they decided upon the arrest of Neves (as the PGR had requested), this decision would have had to have been ratified by the Senate – and nobody expected this to happen since Neves, runner-up in the 2014 presidential election, was central to the political games unfolding in the Senate and the government coalition.

Therefore, to avoid this situation, three of the five judges in the Primeira Turma decided not to order the arrest, instead restricting Neves' freedom and political rights – measures not hitherto seen. The earlier cases in the Lava-Jato scandal had exhibited some similarities, and also some differences: The arrest of the senator Delcídio do Amaral was ordered in a clear-cut *in flagrante* situation, while removing Cunha from his mandate was an exceptional measure without constitutional grounds. In both cases, the two parliamentarians had already lost their political support as the evidence mounted. In the case of Cunha, the presidential succession was included in the legal argument. This became the single point of jurisprudence for the (temporary and unsuccessful) removal of Calheiros. According to the Constitution, however, removing parliamentarians from mandate is the prerogative of the respective legislative bodies and arrest of parliamentarians in office requires ratification from the peers in Congress. Arguing for the restriction of Neves' liberty, Judges Fux and Barroso referred to the Brazilian criminal code which lists the restrictions analogous to prison – and these analogous restrictions are not mentioned in the Constitution's clauses on checks and balances which made the judges argue that these measures can be imposed on senators without ratification from the Senate plenary.

The Neves case was then put on the plenary agenda in the STF, resulting in another reversal on October 11. The small majority in the Primeira Turma in favor of restricting Neves' rights during the investigation was matched by a small majority of three judges in the Segunda Turma, voting against the intervention: Judges Fachin and Fux, Barroso, Weber and Celso de Mello preferred to avoid an outcome where Neves obstructed investigations and affronted the public sense of justice. The other five judges did not want to infringe upon the checks and balances laid down in the Constitution, preferring to leave it to the Senate to decide. STF president Cármen Lúcia ended up voting with the latter group, although she stated that she did agree with Judge Fachin's view (Supremo Tribunal Federal 2017). The following week, the Senate overruled the restrictions imposed by the Primeira

Turma (with the votes 44 for and 26 against), and two weeks later, the Conselho da Ética of the Senate also absolved Neves by filing away the disciplinary case against him.

Besides the recorded conversation with Batista, Aécio Neves had been the target of various other lines of inquiry in the Lava-Jato probe. Neves was simultaneously implicated by Odebrecht executives, by imprisoned politicians (Delcídio do Amaral and Pedro Corrêa), and by the *doleiros* Alberto Youssef and Carlos "Ceará" de Souza Rocha, leading to nine different inquiries.[8] None of these caught the attention of the media to the same degree as the case described in this section.

Neves' corruption cases, which led to discontent in the party and to his temporary stepping down from the party's presidency, became emblematic for the general image of the leading PSDB politicians. The party has been the ideological leader of the Brazilian right for two decades, and the only right-wing party to have fielded presidential candidates in the second round of voting since 1994. The established leaders of the party (apart from Neves, the São Paulo governor Geraldo Alckmin, presidential runner-up against Lula in 2006, and ex-minister José Serra, runner-up against Lula in 2002 and Dilma Rousseff in 2010) were also investigated in the Lava-Jato probe, implicated by the Odebrecht testimonies. With the constitutional crisis and the near-rupture of the party provoked by Neves case, PSDB was pressed for time to find a consensual presidential candidate.

The Nine Legal Actions Against Ex-President Lula

While PSDB suffered in the polls in 2016 and 2017, Lula's support among electors was not hampered much in the polls by corruption accusations. Comparing the cases of Neves and Lula, it becomes apparent that voters may indeed prefer not to switch political allegiances in the face of corruption denunciations, because the opponents, or the alternatives, look just as corrupt. The situation preceding the 2018 elections underscored Rennó's observation of Brazilian electoral accountability very clearly: "[p]erception of corruption matters only when it comes to choices between candidates on the same side of the ideological spectrum" (Rennó 2011: 71). Unlike the right wing, which had a number of virtual contenders for the 2018 presidential campaign, the left side of Brazilian politics could provide no obvious alternatives to Lula. With little incentive to switch sides, Lula's public support remained high throughout 2016 and 2017. However, when asked about which candidates they would never vote for in 2018, the group of voters rejecting Lula also grew, while his trials in various Brazilian courts progressed (Datafolha 2017: 5). In the following, I will describe these investigations and trials in greater detail.

The Triplex Case

In April 2015, almost one year before the MPF indicted Lula for corruption, the weekly magazine *Veja* denounced Lula and Léo Pinheiro, the president of the large Brazilian construction company OAS (Coura and Marques 2015). Pinheiro had been arrested and imprisoned preventively in November 2014, in the seventh phase of the Lava-Jato probe. The front page and a feature article of *Veja* (edition #2423, April 2015) revealed how OAS had built a few select beachside apartments in a larger construction project originally planned by a bank employee association named Bancoop. The real estate project, located in Guarujá, São Paulo, was co-owned by the shareholders of Bancoop, with the imprisoned PT treasurer João Vaccari Neto also having a share – as well as a commanding position in Bancoop.

According to the article, the beachside apartment complex was allegedly constructed at Lula's request. In fact, according to *Veja*'s interpretation of the OAS director's testimony, Bancoop had been used as a façade to funnel money into PT campaigns, and when Bancoop went bankrupt in 2009, the company never completed construction of the apartments it was supposed to provide for the associates. This information, however, was merely a repeat of an *O Globo* article from December 2014 (Oliveira 2014), detailing how Lula's wife had acquired a share in the association and the rights to an apartment. After the bankruptcy of Bancoop, OAS executed the construction of some of the buildings, in the end only providing apartments to 5,000 of the 8,000 shareholders, Lula's wife among them. The apartment (known as a *triplex*) allegedly intended for Lula's wife, moreover, had an elevator fitted, separate from the rest of the building.

The case of the Bancoop bankruptcy and its alleged role as façade for PT and Lula was brought before the prosecutors of São Paulo state in August 2015. *Veja* continued to publish on the case and reported that Lula had been seen at the apartment several times. Footage of this only surfaced in March the following year, however. The sale of the apartment was never finalized, as Lula and his wife declined to buy it in November 2015. That they never did get to enjoy the alleged fruits of this corruption did not hinder the prosecutor of the São Paulo state Cassio Conserino from affirming, during an interview in *Veja* (edition #2462) in January, that the ex-presidential couple were to be indicted. According to Conserino, Lula had concealed his ownership of the apartment in order to hide the spurious relationship to the construction company OAS.

The media storm following this interview was sustained into the following week, when federal police agents of the Lava-Jato investigation paid a visit to the beachside building in Guarujá on January 27. The agents investigated the imprisoned PT treasurer Vaccari Neto and a lawyer named Nelci Warken, who eventually would be found to have connections to the Mossack Fonseca company, of Panama Papers fame. The investigation did not target Lula specifically then, and the São Paulo prosecutors were still yet to denounce Lula. In fact, following the advance announcement of the denunciation in *Veja*, Lula's defense lawyers succeeded in challenging the competency of the São Paulo prosecutors. In a political climate becoming more polarized by the day, the São Paulo prosecutors originally looking into the Bancoop case called for a press conference on March 10. Here, the prosecutors Conserino, Blat, and Araújo presented a denunciation of Lula, his wife, and their oldest son Fábio Luis, and requested authorization of the judge to arrest Lula along with Vaccari Neto and two OAS employees. The request for his arrest had a favorable timing in relation to the protest marches scheduled in the major capitals of Brazil three days hence.

The request for Lula's arrest was first filed with the São Paulo judge initially allocated to the case, Maria Priscilla Oliveira. However, in a series of legal skirmishes, the right to not only indict but also to adjudicate the case of the beachside apartment was pushed back and forth between different courts during March and April 2016. Staying out of the media limelight, Oliveira abstained from the case by affirming that the triplex case derived from the cartel formation and graft of Petrobras contracts. This meant relocating the jurisdiction to the Curitiba court presided over by Sérgio Moro. Oliveira also pointed out several missing links in the accusation of the São Paulo prosecutors, and added that any request of preventive arrest to apprehend evidence was now rendered meaningless, since the prosecutor Conserino had already jumped the gun by conceding the interview to *Veja*.

On March 14, the case files were sent on to Curitiba – the same day that Lula's decision to accept nomination as minister in the Rousseff administration was made public. That day, before the leaked telephone recordings described in the previous chapter, Lula's nomination was interpreted in the national media as a way of ensuring that the Curitiba court would not authorize the preventive arrest of Lula. One example of this connection could be found in *Folha* on March 14:

> The ex-president was more willing to accept the nomination after the judge Maria Priscilla Veiga Oliveira, of the 4ª Vara Criminal da Capital, declined to authorize his imprisonment and decided to send the petition to be analyzed in Curitiba, where the PT leader is investigated in the Operation Lava-Jato.
>
> (Bergamo 2016, translation mine)

The following day, this interpretation became the dominant prism for understanding not just the nomination, but in particular the telephone recording between Rousseff and Lula that was leaked from the Curitiba court, described in Chapter 3.

The intervention of the STF judge Mendes ensured that the triplex case remained in the hands of both the Lava-Jato task force and Judge Moro in Curitiba. The prosecutors of the task force denounced Lula in September 2016, and the case went to trial a few days after the denunciation. The phase of testimonies lasted for six months, featuring ex-President Cardoso among others, concluding with a five-hour interrogation of Lula before Sérgio Moro. Lula continued to deny the allegations, claiming that he had never owned the beachside apartment and that the trial constituted a political persecution. Moro sentenced Lula to nine years and six months in prison on July 12, 2017, while the OAS president Pinheiro was sentenced to ten years and eight months for paying kickbacks to Lula in the form of the apartment, the interior design, and the extra elevator, amounting to

R$2.25 million. The kickbacks to Lula were allegedly drawn from a larger pool of R$16 million, originating in a Petrobras contract with OAS. Pinheiro's sentence in the triplex case was added to his previous sentences in the Lava-Jato case.

The Atibaia Ranch Case

Léo Pinheiro's close relationship to Lula during and after his presidential mandates was the target of another inquiry into kickbacks occulted in real estate. The *Veja* article of April 2015 detailed how a ranch in Santa Bárbara, Atibaia (in the interior region of greater São Paulo) was also under scrutiny as the ranch and the rapid renovation of the site possibly constituted kickbacks for Lula. A pool was enlarged, a porch added, and so on, allegedly at Lula's request, despite the fact the estate was not actually owned by Lula, but by friends of his. According to the investigation, the total value of the renovation amounted to around R$1 million.

On November 17, *Folha* revealed that the police were looking into the OAS accounts in order to determine what the company had been doing at the Atibaia ranch and exploring the possible relationship to the contracts between OAS and Petrobras (Ferreira and Rocha 2015). The case was largely forgotten in the final weeks of 2015, because Lula's acquaintance José Carlos Bumlai was arrested in the Lava-Jato probe, and Rousseff soon after faced impeachment proceedings. However, the Atibaia site became the focus of intense scrutiny in 2016, in parallel to the investigations into the triplex case. The two cases were often bundled together in media coverage, but actually had different trials in the Curitiba court (once the triplex case had returned from the digression of the process to São Paulo). According to the prosecutors, Odebrecht and OAS had split the construction costs for the ranch site and in return received political influence in government tenders via Lula. On August 1, 2017, a fortnight after being sentenced in the triplex case, Lula was charged in Curitiba in the case pertaining to the ranch in Atibaia.

The Palocci Case and the Instituto Lula

A third line of inquiry, also investigated and conducted in Curitiba, explored the evidence arising from the testimony of Marcelo Odebrecht. After leaving the presidency, Lula had given lectures and talks at various business events across South America. This activity had been the focus of interest in Brazilian news outlets, speculating that the payments were not merely the market price for the talks by an internationally renowned ex-president, but a way of making illicit transfers seem legitimate. Marcelo, the former president of Odebrecht, testified that his business empire had not only paid for some of Lula's talks in the period following his presidential mandate, but had also acquired a site in the Vila Clementina neighborhood of São Paulo for constructing a new building that would eventually have housed the Instituto Lula.

The institute, which was functionally a political communications office, was the base of Lula's post-presidential political oeuvre. To be more precise, the institute was the seat of Lula's political activities; at least until the police operations of March 2016 in the triplex case, when the offices were ransacked by police agents. After this, Lula increasingly took to traveling about the country, rallying political support. The institute, since it opened in 2011, had been located in the Ipiranga neighborhood of São Paulo, but according to the testimony and evidence presented by Marcelo Odebrecht, the company had purchased a new lot for the institute's offices. Hindered by red tape in the municipal authority, no building was ever constructed. As with the inquiry into the triplex, the case thus seemed rather hypothetical, since Lula could not really have enjoyed this bribe, and because the denunciation, like the earlier cases, was not linked to any specific political projects promoted by Lula while in office.

The originally fragile case was greatly helped by a plea bargain, however. By following the money, the PF succeeded in finding evidence that linked the site in São Paulo to Lula's former minister of Finances, Antônio Palocci. Palocci, also a founding member of PT, was arrested in September 2016 on these grounds and chose to plea bargain after six months of preventive arrest in Curitiba. In his plea bargain, he confirmed the story told by Marcelo Odebrecht, explaining how he had controlled a large fund of resources granted by the Odebrecht company in exchange for extended political goodwill. These funds, after Lula left office, had been earmarked in order to have Lula use his influence and act as a mouthpiece for the company's interest during the Rousseff administration. Rousseff, taking the mantle, was apparently not as aligned with the business elite. The Odebrecht family believed that Lula could sway her at the crucial moment if need be. Palocci admitted that he was the designated go-between for Lula and Marcelo Odebrecht, and furthermore, he claimed that he had accompanied Dilma Rousseff at a meeting where everyone present witnessed how well aware Luna was of the corruption in Petrobras.

The relationships between Lula in his post-presidential period, Odebrecht, and OAS, resulted in these three cases of alleged corruption in 2015, 2016, and 2017. Three more cases, not directly connected to Petrobras and the subcontractors, became trials in the courts of the Federal District of Brazil, as they investigated possible criminal acts committed by Lula while residing there as president.

Operation Zelotes and Tax Exemption by Provisional Decrees

In March 2015, a police operation investigating a systematic scheme of tax evasion was carried out. The operation, code-named Zelotes, had as its principal target CARF (*Conselho Administrativo de Recursos Fiscais*), a tax appeal agency under the Ministry of Finances. The initial estimates identified close to R$19 billion being withheld from the state during a period of five years, as the counselors of CARF had systematically favored a range of companies, including three major banks (Safra, Bradesco and Santander), the steel company Gerdau, and several construction companies. Furthermore, the inquiry targeted the

Globo-affiliated media company RBS. Perhaps due to the operation targeting the media conglomerate Globo, the Zelotes operation was mostly covered in the left-wing press: In April, the left-wing magazine *CartaCapital* pointed out that despite a month of coverage, other media, especially those from the Globo group, had been reluctant to report on the case. In contrast to the media-savvy style adopted by Curitiba's court, which readily published material from investigations, the Brasília-based court at which the probe was conducted did not disseminate material on the case. Like the Lava-Jato case, a task-force conducted the probe, under the auspices of federal judge Vallisney de Souza Oliveira and the federal prosecutor Frederico Paiva, but without the publicity and journalistic access.

As the next stages of the Zelotes investigation proceeded, evidence arose that linked some of the investigated companies to provisional decrees issued by the presidency (*medidas provisorias*). On October 1, 2015, the *Estado* front page featured the scoop that two law firms, SGR Consultoria Empresarial and Marcondes&Mautoni, had not only lobbied for lenient verdicts in the appeal council CARF, but also for specific tax exemptions for the automobile industry in Congress and with the executive branch. The exemption, according to *Estado*, was specified in the provisional decree MP 471, issued in 2009 by Lula, later ratified by Congress, with effects until 2015.[9]

Later in October 2015, the police investigations centered on one link in the supposed chain of bribes from the automobile sector: A paper trail that linked the law firm Marcondes&Mautoni, used by automobile manufacturers, to Luís Claudio da Silva, another of ex-President Lula's sons. Investigating this trail, the task-force obtained search warrants and examined the house and office of Luís Claudio da Silva. With this, the Zelotes case began to be covered by the mainstream press. While this paper trail was only one of the links between government and the automobile industry, a range of news items were produced on October 26 concerning the police action in his consulting service, as well as the law firm paying Luís Claudio da Silva for consultancy. The nature of da Silva's consulting services, the exact content of a report he delivered to the law firm, and possible plagiarism in the report was the object of the news. The frame, in other words, was the suspect nature of his consultancy, and that the report was only delivered to cover for the fact that the R$2.5 million paid for the service was, in fact, a (somewhat late) kickback for the provisional decree.

On these suspicions, the two lawyers behind Marcondes&Mautoni were arrested preventively, and ministers of the Lula and Rousseff administrations were subpoenaed. On January 6, 2016, Lula testified before the federal judge in Brasília. Both Lula and Rousseff were subpoenaed again in the case on January 21, as were many ex-ministers. Prominent testimonies followed, including the PT ex-ministers Gilberto Carvalho, Guido Mantega, and Miguel Jorge. Three months later, on April 30, 2016, the prosecutor of the case obtained the authorization of the court to open another line of inquiry, investigating senators Renan Calheiros, Romero Jucá, and Gim Argello (an ex-senator of the PTB party who had already arrested in the Lava-Jato case, 14 days before). Testimonies in the case had mentioned that some R$45 million had been offered to these senators to ensure that the *medida provisoria* was passed, favoring the car manufacturers. This probe was one of a dozen inquiries at that moment targeting President of the Senate Renan Calheiros.

The Zelotes investigations resulted in two trials against Lula, his son, the ex-minister Gilberto Carvalho, and a number of lobbyists and CARF councilors. In the first case, Lula was charged before the 10th court of the federal district for selling political influence to the Brazilian automobile industry and to the Swedish company SAAB (in order to secure the sale of 36 military aircraft), for money laundering and prolonging the MP 627 with criminal intent. In the second, Lula stood accused of corruption in the issuing of the tax exemption bill MP471.

Obstruction of Justice in the Cerveró Case

One of the former directors of Petrobras, Nestor Cerveró, was the object of intense interest in late 2015. While the director Paulo Roberto Costa had opted for a plea bargain back in 2014, Cerveró was only apprehended in January 2015, and did not admit to the charges while imprisoned in Curitiba. In Congressional hearings, the former director of Petrobras' International Division remained silent. As the months wore on, PT senator Delcídio do Amaral tried to find a way for Cerveró to flee the country – supposedly to avoid another incriminating plea bargain. Amaral, former Petrobras director during the Cardoso administration and former colleague of Cerveró, was secretly recorded on tape deliberating how to manage the escape. Cerveró's son Bernardo had participated in a meeting with Delcídio and decided to tape it. As he handed over the tape to the authorities, the extraordinary situation of apprehending a senator in public office became a reality. While this can only happen (as discussed in the Neves case) with the ratification of the Senate, few Senators had the nerve, under public scrutiny, and in the face of flagrant crimes, to deny the request for Amaral's immediate arrest.

The tape provided by Bernardo Cerveró was one of the conditions upon which the reduction of Nestor Cerveró's sentence rested. Cerveró also detailed how he had helped senators like Amaral and Renan Calheiros to channel money from Petrobras into their political campaigns, and claimed that the details of a remarkably bad Petrobras deal (the buy-out of the Pasadena refinery in Texas) was well-known to Dilma Rousseff, then director of the Administrative Board of Petrobras. Furthermore, he suspected that both Lula and Rousseff were well aware of the graft of the state oil company. Senator Amaral, in turn, claimed that his failed attempt at having Cerveró flee the country was actually a direct command from Lula. The PGR indicted Lula in May 2016, but the charges based on Amaral's testimony did not hold up to scrutiny: In September 2017, state prosecutor Ivan Claudio Marx requested that the inquiry be suspended and the 10th court of the Federal District discard the case.

Operation Janus

The operation named "Janus," on May 20, 2016, followed hot on the heels of the impeachment of Dilma Rousseff. The operation investigated one line of credit within the BNDES (the Brazilian state investment bank) extended to the construction company Odebrecht in a set of international sub-contracts in Africa, Cuba, and the Dominican Republic. On October 7, 2016, the prosecutors of the Federal District indicted Lula, Marcelo Odebrecht, and nine other men for fraud and corruption, securing credit lines in the BNDES, eventually leading to contracts between Odebrecht and the Angolan state. The alleged operator of the kickbacks, according to the denunciation, was a nephew of Lula's ex-wife, Taiguara Rodrigues, who channeled money through subcontracts between Odebrecht and his company Exergia Brasil. Some of these funds allegedly paid for monthly allowances to Lula's brother Frei Chico.

The court of the federal district was the scene of three more cases against Lula, of which one was rejected on the grounds of weak evidence and one was split into two formal denunciations. Furthermore, in the final days before the PGR Rodrigo Janot was substituted as head of the MPF by Raquel Dodge, Janot indicted Lula two more times, with one of these cases being redistributed to the federal district court. Janot's final indictments identified Lula as the criminal mastermind behind the Petrobras corruption.

The Criminal Mastermind behind the Graft in Petrobras

On September 5, 2017, Janot indicted Lula and the leaders of the PT for pursuing the grand scheme of corruption in Petrobras, resulting in kickbacks of R$1.5 billion in total. This case, by virtue of its objects and the history of inquiry, was sent straight to the STF. Together with three indictments targeting other political groups (the erstwhile coalition partner PP, as well as two separate indictments of the PMDB group in the Câmara and the PMDB senators), the indictment against Lula and PT detailed how the division of directories in the oil company was masterminded by Lula and the financial strategists of PT. The accusation also stated that Dilma Rousseff was conscious of the corruption and in cahoots with the PT Senator Gleisi Hoffmann, Hoffmann's husband Paulo Bernardo, and ex-Ministers of Finance Guido Mantega and Palocci.

Less than 24 hours after these indictments, the PGR filed another indictment, this time accusing Lula, Rousseff, and ex-Minister Aloízio Mercadante (a minister in both of their administrations), of once again obstructing justice in their attempt to prevent Delcídio do Amaral from negotiating a plea bargain. The indictment also denounced the criminal intent in nominating Lula for minister in the final days of the Rousseff administration. The PGR affirmed that the two indictments were interlinked but divided because the criminal organizations acting in the cases were distinct. Judge Fachin of the STF dispatched this second case to the court of the federal district three days later, since none of the targets enjoyed the *foro privilegiado* at this point, after the impeachment of Rousseff.

With one case discarded in the Federal district, Lula faced trials (or appeal processes) in eight cases total at the end of 2017. At the time of writing, they have had the following results so far:

1   (Curitiba) The ranch case: Lula was sentenced to 9.5 years of prison by Judge Sérgio Moro in July 2017, and the appeal court TRF-4 augmented the sentence to 12 years in January 2018.
2   (Curitiba) The beachside apartment case: Lula is charged.
3   (Curitiba) The Institute construction site case: Lula is charged.
4   (Federal district) The SAAB, automobile industry, and MP627 case: Lula is charged.
5   (Federal district) The provisional decree MP471: Lula is charged.
6   (Federal district) Influencing BNDES in Odebrecht's Angola operations: Lula is indicted.
7   (STF) The Petrobras graft mastermind: Lula is indicted.
8   (Federal district) The obstruction of justice through Mercadante: Lula is indicted.

The combined prison sentences of these trials may amount to more than 100 years in prison. Moreover, the Instituto Lula is under another investigation for money laundering, although the director of the Institute, Paulo Okamotto, has so far been acquitted in one of the cases involving Lula.

Outcomes of Judicial Actions in the Political Arena

In parallel with the Lava-Jato investigations, and frequently in consequence of events pertaining to that case, judicial actions have influenced and changed the political processes of Brazil. The outcomes of these judicial actions have not however been simply the punishment of political transgression in its various forms. Furthermore, the Lava-Jato case was not simply a case in which public office-holders lost their political capital. Rather, a myriad side-effects and macro-level changes are visible in the political arena as a result of the legal processes spawned during the Lava-Jato investigations. I will summarize these effects and categorize them as follows:

*   overturning elections;
*   rigging elections;
*   removing individuals from mandates of public office;
*   protecting individuals from actions against their mandates of public office;
*   extinguishing or severely damaging parties;
*   changing political capital and costs of forming coalitions.

Overturning Elections

Without a doubt, the legal actions leading to the impeachment of Dilma Rousseff and, subsequently, the acquittal of the campaign of Rousseff and the (then) vice-president, were the most the high-profiled judicial outcomes in the period 2014–2017.

Both the electoral court case and the impeachment processes against Rousseff and Temer could have overturned the result of the presidential election of 2014. This would constitute the ultimate judicial intervention in a democracy. None of these processes, however, actually convicted the election result of 2014 of corruption – despite the evidence produced and the political climate of crisis that characterized the period. As a result of the timing and the outcomes of the processes, Brazil lost a democratically elected president, and was left with an acquitted but still investigated president with record-low approval ratings. While the successful impeachment of Rousseff was executed on a quasi-legal basis (Wink 2017) grounded in fiscal delays, the electoral court case was dismissed on formal grounds pertaining to the scope of the original petition for cancelling the elections. Thus, both cases had to evade the specific revelations of the Lava-Jato case in order to create these particular political outcomes, despite the fact that neither process would have been initiated without the Lava-Jato probe.

Rigging Elections

Several of the Lava-Jato denunciations and trials are of critical import to the upcoming 2018 elections. Lula's sentence in the Triplex case, and the various delays in cases being judged before the STF will allow a number of investigated and denounced parliamentarians to run for office in 2018 (including the presidency), but keep the ex-president outside. Under normal circumstances, keeping a corrupt ex-president from running for the presidency should be beneficial to democracy. However, the denunciations against Lula after he left the presidency seem only tangential to the much larger problem of graft in state companies, in the sense that Lula was perhaps influential, if not exactly calling the shots. In economic terms, the real estate cases of Lula pale in comparison to parallel political corruption cases such as Cunha's and are dwarfed next to the tax evasion of some larger Brazilian companies.

Another situation triggered by the Lava-Jato case was a bill, proposed in parliament in 2017, that would change the method of allocating votes from proportional voting districts to a most-voted district system. Besides wasting many cast votes, such electoral reform would further help secure incumbent parliamentarians their seats thanks to greater access to funds (licit public funds as well as illicit ones), all the while remaining in office and maintaining their precious *foro privilegiado*. Thus, this legislation is just another means of rigging elections without losing the appearance of legitimacy, although the intention is anything but legitimate.

Removing Individuals from Mandates of Public Office

In this chapter, several specific cases have been highlighted, in which political actors have removed opponents from their mandates. In the cases of Dilma

Rousseff and Eduardo Cunha, such attempts were successful. There are three other individual cases which should be mentioned, however. The case of Renan Calheiros has already been described: Calheiros was removed as president of the Senate for a few days, through the monocratic intervention of STF Judge Marco Aurélio de Mello quickly overturned by the STF plenary. Senator Aécio Neves avoided a similar fate by one vote in the STF.

A more important case of this type of outcome pertains to President Michel Temer. Temer was not only denounced twice by the PGR, which, if the Congress had so chosen, would have removed him from office. Temer was also, even when still vice-president, the target of impeachment petitions. The first of these argued that what was true of the decrees issued by Dilma Rousseff which were interpreted as illicit loans outside of the Congressional license, also had to be true for identical decrees. Since Rousseff had been on several international journeys, Temer had in fact signed several of these decrees as acting president. This should have thus made him complicit in the same illegal act as Rousseff. Later impeachment petitions against Temer, once he assumed the mantle, based on obstruction of justice and breaches of decorum while in presidential office, revealed in the leak of the JBS owner Joesley Batista. These petitions were stalled indefinitely by the new president of the Câmara, Rodrigo Maia (of the party DEM) – and perhaps were perpetual political weapons held in reserve by Maia. This aspect of judicial or quasi-judicial action brings me to the next outcome, the protection from legal actions.

Protecting Individuals from Actions Against Their Mandates of Public Office

The president of the Câmara has proven to be of extraordinary importance in situations of political instability. This is due to prerogatives vested in the office. He or she is situated third in line for the presidency, while at the same time has the power to decide whether to pursue impeachment procedures. The scheduling of roll-call votes and sessions of the Câmara and the combined Houses must also pass through his or her office, potentially leading to significant delays in other proceedings such as disciplinary processes. Parliamentary votes may even be annulled on procedural grounds at the intervention of the president of the Câmara, who may decide to restart such a process. These are just some of the many instruments used (and abused) as protection or as a blackmailing device, as with the case of Eduardo Cunha.

What is perhaps even more extraordinary is the fact that aside from Eduardo Cunha, no internal cases for removal of mandate have occurred in three years in either house of Congress, despite – or perhaps rather because of – the mountain of evidence produced during the Lava-Jato investigations. An obvious explanation for this extended principle of silence would be the congressional fear of an all-in melee situation. Keeping up appearances in corruption scandals seems to be the easy way of tackling the negotiation problem that appears if central actors in Congress opt to threaten other actors' mandates. It is not just the president of the Câmara who holds protective powers; it is in effect all major parties that to some extent partake in the protection of mandates. This explains why, in the Lava-Jato case, we only see minor left-wing, non-establishment parties such as PSOL and Rede opting to denounce politicians in Congress. Aggression through Congress-internal disciplinary/judicial action, targeting political mandates, is normally shunned, especially so once the snowball of denunciations starts rolling. Such internal obstruction to action against mandates was also apparent in the case against Aécio Neves, where not only the STF declined to intervene, but the Senate plenary and the Senate disciplinary committee also protected his mandate.

Extinguishing or Severely Damaging Parties

Several legal steps have been taken to judicially or virtually extinguish the political parties PT and PP. PT is currently the target of a lawsuit in the TSE arguing that the party as a whole has been funded from sources abroad, which is prohibited, and that this should make the whole party ineligible. PSDB filed the action on January 20, 2016. STF and TSE judge Gilmar Mendes opened a similar case on August 5, 2017, prompted by the TSE action concerning illicit funding in Dilma Rousseff's presidential campaign. PP, meanwhile, is the object of a civil suit for administrative improbity to the amount of R$2.3 billion and the loss of mandates and rights to candidatures for most of the party leaders. The suit was filed by the PGR on March 30, 2017. Both of these legal actions – if successful – would have a huge impact in Brazilian politics, since PT and PP are the second and fourth-largest parties in Congress, respectively, commanding a full fifth of the seats in total. Neither of the cases have advanced, however. Furthermore, on October 6, 2017, the Congress passed a bill to protract the payment of such fines in civil suits. In effect, if found guilty, the fine of PP could be divided into 24,000 monthly fines, which would stretch the fine hypothetically across the next 2,000 years (Faria and Peron 2017).

Curiously, the parties are themselves perhaps the weakest link of all in the web of accountability institutions, and are not even considered as such in works on the subject (such as Power and Taylor 2011). Elsewhere, parties are producing accountability to signal distance, saving the image of the party, and minimize electoral consequences, often by expelling members accused or guilty of corruption. This has only occurred thrice in the Lava-Jato case, with the PT moving to expel members on each occasion. André Vargas was expelled early on (in 2014) for corruption denounced by Alberto Youssef, however since then only Antônio Palocci and Delcídio do Amaral have been expelled; in a strange twist to the case not due to confessions of corruption, but rather for lying and accusing the party leaders Lula and Rousseff of corruption.

The other twenty-odd PT politicians investigated or charged in the Lava-Jato case have not been targets of any party-internal accountability procedure, and neither has any politician in PSDB, PP, PMDB, PR, PSD, PTB, PTC, PCdoB, PDT, or DEM, to this date. This negligence can perhaps justify the move toward removing parties from the ballot, and it certainly shows that the parties do not consider it beneficial to strengthen their ethical position and public image by activating internal accountability procedures. Collective image, or the association between politician and party, may be very weak in Brazil, and the costs of potential infighting may anyway be too high for anybody to bother with this kind of initiative in a politico-legal environment already filled with legal actions.

Changing Political Capital and Costs of Forming Coalition

Ending, or attenuating, the rampant use of appointments to state companies and agencies in exchange for kickbacks, is perhaps the most positive effect of the Lava-Jato case. Even this effect has a problematic side-effect, strange as it may sound. As Brazilian executives lose this instrument of pork-style politics, the demand for other compensations from veto players in Congress (Tsebelis 2002) may rise, as may the political costs of forming coalitions. This could lead to increased use of (legal) pork-barrel policies and improved ideological cohesion of Brazilian governments. In theory, this should bode well for the moral condition of governing and forming coalitions. With the hindsight provided by the Lava-Jato investigations, it now seems probable that for decades, the use of illicit payments was an agglutinating factor in the coalition-building of Brazilian governments. It remains to be seen, when the dust has settled, if top positions in state company and clientelistic influence over tenders will once again be in demand as payment for votes in the fragmented Congress. The (hopefully) lower influx of illicit funding in the wake of the Lava-Jato case might obstruct the possibility of building and maintaining super-coalitions, thus bringing more deadlock situations to the Brazilian democracy (Avritzer 2016). The bargaining value of state company appointments may have been underestimated hitherto in the literature on Brazilian coalition formation (Pereira et al. 2016, Raile et al. 2011).

On top of these outcomes might be added two sub-goals of legal processes and interventions which help to reach outcomes such as the above. First, many legal actions, especially the range of appeals available in the Brazilian system, are used as a means of stalling for time – motivated by political intentions or for the sake of shifting the public agenda. This leads to the second instrumental use of legal processes, which is that of setting the media agenda, or at least filling that agenda. The latter use, agenda-setting, is considered in the following chapter, while the former sub-goal led to several of the outcomes discussed above: Michel Temer's court-packing of the TSE bench and the Senate's protracted and successful stone-walling of STF verdicts are but two of the outcomes of such delay tactics. In the final sections of this chapter, I will discuss the macro-level effects of these outcomes and the malleable character of justice and accountability in Brazil.

Lawfare in the Brazilian Debate and in International Research

What does the plethora of contested legal actions mean to Brazilian democracy and accountability? As we shall see in the following chapter, processual movements of legal actions are one of the main sources for political journalists in Brazil, generating much of the material in the newspapers sampled. In the above categorization, I have shown the functions of the judicial interventions in the wake of political scandal. However, this question must also be asked on a more abstract level.

I would avoid describing the contemporary context of Brazil, marked and marred as it is by corruption and the vested political interests and manipulations of justice, as "politicization of justice" or as "judicialization of politics," although superficially, both processes co-exist (Hirschl 2004, 2008, Tate and Vallinder 1995). That accountability mechanisms are activated by corruption scandals is, of course, to be expected. I will argue, however, that the term "politicization of justice" does not do the situation in Brazil justice, if the reader will excuse the pun. Rather, I prefer the term lawfare, because it opens the field of political science to legal-anthropological insights into the performative and contested aspects of law and the State – and possibly provides links to the context of contemporary media spheres and, especially, mediatized politics. This sensitizes research in a way better suited to capturing the events emerging from the Lava-Jato scandal, as opposed to research into changing discursive and organizational forms in Brazilian politics and laws. Simply put, lawfare brings emphasis to actors and actions, while the perspective of judicialization is more apt for theorizing societal change.

Cristian Zanin Martins, defense lawyer for ex-president Lula, raised the concept of lawfare in Brazilian media in October 2016. Zanin Martins used the concept as a response to an opinion piece in *Folha*, October 30, penned by two of the Lava-Jato prosecutors (Dallagnol and Martelo 2016). In the piece, Dallagnol and Martelo pointed out that the investigation was not politically motivated, since it targeted only the parties that had been in command of the graft in Petrobras. Contesting this claim, Zanin Martins repeatedly made use of the term "lawfare" during the following months, as in this critique of the Curitiba taskforce of Lava-Jato and the indictment of Lula for corruption in the triplex case:

After the hearings in Curitiba, it must be affirmed that this legal action of the triplex is another frivolous process, a part of the "lawfare" phenomenon that consists in utilizing judicial processes as a means to an end – an end which is political persecution.

(Zanin Martins 2016, translation mine)

Critique had emerged with the same tenor on the left wing of the Brazilian political arena since 2015. The main thrust of the critique was not just the obvious bias of the media attention and framings (described in the next chapter), but also the concerns about a bias of judicial and investigative attention. In particular, Lula's lawyers claimed that the corruption investigations against him were intentionally speeding up, in order to avoid Lula running for president in 2018, while other cases lingered in court dockets or stalled because of repeated reversals of rulings. Whether or not Lula was and is the victim of judicial-political persecution to a greater degree than Cunha, Neves, or other political opponents, the concept of lawfare is relevant to connect the judicial interventions to the role of the State.

In academic circles, the word "lawfare" was used once back in 1975 in the anthology *The Way Out – Radical Alternatives in Australia*, in an article concerning mediation in legal processes, and then forgotten. The authors, Carlson and Yeomans, wrote:

> Utilitarian law is the law of the State, of order, of business, of war, contract and crime – the law of ruthlessness, retribution and punishment. In the last 200 years, this law has uniquely dominated the Western world. It has swallowed the humane justice of humanitarian law, creating State monopolisation of law-making. Thus the inquisitorial or enquiry technique is gone, the adversary or accusatory procedure alone applies in our courts. The search for truth is replaced by the classification of issues and the refinement of combat. Lawfare replaces warfare and the duel is with words rather than swords.
>
> (Carlson and Yeomans 1975: n.p.)

The article departs from a Parsonian perspective and discusses various nations' use of mediation in legal disputes. Seemingly disconnected from the way Yeomans and Carlson used the term, it reappeared in legal scholarship dealing with warfare after the 9/11 attacks in the United States. Legal scholars, working on law, attribute the term to a U.S. Air Force lawyer, who asked, in November 2001, if law was "becoming more of the problem in modern war instead of part of the solution" (Dunlap 2001: 1). Here, the term takes on meanings parallel to judicialization, but limited to the context of international warfare: "Dunlap ... describes lawfare as attempts by opponents of the U.S. projection of power to use law to discipline and hamper that power" (Waters 2009: 891). Werner points out that the term is used as "a label to criticize those who use international law and legal proceedings to make claims against the state, especially in areas related to national security" (Werner 2010: 62). The restriction and encirclement of legislative branches by judicial branches, identified by Tate, Vallinder, Hirschl and other scholars discussing judicialization, is re-encountered in the restriction of warfare through international judicial processes and diplomacy.

In parallel, but unconnected to the above,[10] the term lawfare was included in the writings on the post-colonial condition by John and Jean Comaroff (Comaroff and Comaroff 2006). Here, the term almost has the inverse meaning, covering the abuse of socio-political state power dressed up as law in post-colonial contexts:

…what imperialism is being indicted for, above all, is its commission of lawfare: its use of its own rules – of its duly enacted penal codes, its administrative law, its states of emergency, its charters and mandates and warrants, its norms of engagement – to impose a sense of order upon its subordinates by means of violence rendered legible, legal, and legitimate by its own sovereign word. And also to commit its own ever-so-civilized, patronizing, high-minded forms of kleptocracy. Lawfare – the resort to legal instruments, to the violence inherent in the law, to commit acts of political coercion, even erasure … is equally marked in postcolonies, of course. As a species of political displacement, it becomes most readily visible when those who act in the name of the state conjure with legalities to act against some or all of its citizens.

(Ibid.: 30)

The Comaroffs also mentioned judicialization (here and elsewhere): "Not only is the non-postcolonial world more litigious than ever, but the judicialization of politics is proceeding apace everywhere" (Comaroff and Comaroff 2007: 148). "Lawfare" has since then been recycled by various anthropologists, while similar ideas have simultaneously emerged and created a burgeoning sub-field of anthropology, researching the juridico-political struggles at the margins of societies, legal systems, and states (e.g., Anders and Nuijten 2001, Das and Poole 2004, see also Gupta 1995). Here, the term merges with theoretical frameworks geared to the performative, transitive, and malleable aspects of "law" in everyday practices across the globe.

Lawfare, in the definition given by the Comaroffs, and the related anthropological interpretations of law as a range of instruments for coercion, seems both apt and somewhat imprecise to describe the situation of Lula and other politicians, however. First of all, in purely abstract terms, the anthropologists normally describe this coercion as subjugating national political subjects – in a word, citizens. Lawfare is not, in this literature, perceived as a homing missile targeted at individual, political actors (although in practice, all citizens coerced by the abuse of law would experience lawfare as such). The use of legal violence and state-legitimized oppression is frequently observed in marginalized groups, who are exploited or denied their right as citizens by political elites. In the abstract, to use the term lawfare to describe a tactic for overthrowing a singularly influential political leader, suspected of grand corruption, is a very uncommon use of that term.

Second of all, looking at Lula's concrete cases (to take the obvious example), we might doubt that the use of legal trials even constitutes coercion. Granted, Lula was forced to testify in March 2015, despite having testified voluntarily several times before and after. Similarly, he was denied the status of minister on grounds that were not applied to ministers of the Temer administration just months later (which I will detail below). However, the notions of violence, discipline, and bodily coercion are perhaps not as relevant in the case of Lula as with those cases normally explored by anthropologists. On the other hand, the symbolic violence to Lula's image is quite tangible and effective, most visibly seen in the street protests of 2015 and 2016 where inflatable dolls made to look like Lula in a prisoner's clothes were brandished by protesters. The imagery deployed here invokes the desire to see Lula behind bars, or in other words, to see him subjugated to the state's exceptional power.

This brings me to another theoretical question of the applicability of the term lawfare – namely, the role of the State. In the anthropological research, lawfare defined as intentional maladministration and abuse of legal power is the operational mode of kleptocracies and political elites with access to the ostensibly legitimate powers of states. In the Brazilian cases appearing in the Lava-Jato case, however, we need to reassess what we mean by the term "state." To begin with, we cannot fathom the MPF as "the state" in the same way as the legislative and executive branches of government are "the state." It seems, in the anthropological literature, that powerful elites in the post-colony cases are commanding the legal and coercive instruments of the state, but in the Lava-Jato case, sections of the political elite – the center-left parties along with the governing party PMDB – lost their grip on the investigative and judicial branches of government. Apart from Eduardo Cunha, two of Temer's former close associates and ex-ministers for PMDB are preventively arrested in the Lava-Jato case, while the current ministers Moreira Franco and Eliseu Padilha are under investigation in various cases, and also several aides have been arrested in 2017. Conversely, the continued survival of Michel Temer as president demonstrates that his presidency is legitimized by other actors, such as half the TSE bench, the STF judge Gilmar Mendes, and a majority in Congress.

In theoretical terms, the Brazilian case in general and Lula's case in particular are perhaps too complex to be subsumed under the concept of lawfare: When prosecutors and judges operate sometimes independently, and sometimes in tandem with the executive and legislative branches, terms from post-colonial studies are not adequate to describe the structures of political and intra-governmental struggle.

What is fruitful in the concept of lawfare, though, is the attention to the legitimizing effects of the instruments of law. I will quote here a recent study of contested jurisdictions that perfectly reflects one aspect of the partial and biased nature of the judicial decisions taken during the Lava-Jato case – a quote that, incidentally, also captures how legitimacy was bestowed selectively by the Supreme Court in Brazil. This study of law and the pragmatics of jurisdictions highlights how lawfare is present when discretion and legal power are distributed and spatially located within overlapping judicial systems:

These often hidden architectures (cf. Ford 1999), or cartographies, of discretion are both the condition of possibility for the distribution of official power and the targets of legal battles over where such power resides and how it can be expressed. Politicized legal warfare, or "lawfare" ... unfolds within the technically rendered routes, zones, and fractal hierarchies of jurisdictional space, relying on, contesting, and reinventing them in the process. By attending to the intricacies of these juridico-spatial formations and the poetic ... structures[,] they are expressed as performances both mundane and spectacular.

(Kahn 2017: 6)

This quote draws attention to the cases where Brazilian courts manipulate jurisdictions and the *foro privilegiado*, but superficially maintain the legitimacy: While Lula was barred from acting as minister in the last days of the Rousseff administration, Michel Temer successfully nominated Moreira Franco for minister in February 2017. The PMDB strategist Franco had been the government's executive secretary of the Program for Investment Partnerships since the first cabinet was put together by Temer, but as executive secretary he did not have the privilege of being judge before the STF. In February 2017, as the Odebrecht testimonies became authorized as evidence in the Lava-Jato case, Temer decreed (by way of a provisional decree) that the secretariat was now a ministry – changing nothing else in the cabinet composition, but endowing Franco with the *foro privilegiado*. This ensured that Franco would not be under the jurisdiction of the Lava-Jato task-force and Judge Sérgio Moro, who commonly authorizes preventive arrests.

As with the Lula case, various judges across the country intervened, but their verdicts were eventually overturned by the STF judge Celso de Mello. He ruled that the nomination could not constitute an obstruction of justice, since ministers are not made immune to investigation by the *foro* but must still respond to justice in the STF. The monocratic decision of Celso de Mello was thus exactly the opposite of the ruling by STF Judge Gilmar Mendes eight months earlier. Such conflicts of rulings in the STF can of course be questioned – but again, the timing of such appeals is determined by the judges, and the appeals can linger in the STF docket forever. The provisional decree making Franco's secretariat a ministry reached its deadline in September 2017, but was passed into law with a very tight margin of votes in the Congress.

Lawfare is also a performance of legitimizing interventions, not least through the creation or absence of scandalous coverage in the media. Thus, the tarnishing of Lula's image was not solely enacted through courts, but perhaps more so through the media coverage of the trials, as his project of performing as a credible virtual candidate was continuously undermined. The combination of investigations, legal actions, and the possibility of being barred by the Ficha Limpa law was repeatedly presented as his major political and legal problem (while the corruption charges were presented as the major image problem and moral problem for Lula and his party). Again, the timing of the legal actions is of interest: the possible PSDB candidates José Serra, Geraldo Alckmin, and Aécio Neves were all implicated in the Lava-Jato investigations, but since each of these politicians maintain the prerogative of being tried before the higher courts, neither of their cases had a celerity that could match the cases moving against Lula. This meant that either of the PSDB pre-candidates were in a much better judicial position than Lula – although they themselves were increasingly hampered in polls by allegations of corruption.

Even though the concept of lawfare, in its anthropological formulation, is perhaps more oriented toward the exclusion and coercion of social groups in post-colonial societies, it is also well suited as a sensitizing concept in the study of corruption scandals. As with the flows of information and leaks studied in the previous chapter, the selective application of accountability and legal measures in response to corruption denunciations is always of potential utility to some political actor. The cases of judicial intervention and non-intervention in the various case studies of this chapter demonstrate that law, even in a context with a seemingly abundant web of accountability institutions, is a malleable thing. Despite claiming to serve the universally legitimate combat against corruption, trials against corrupt politicians can have perverse effects – and may even be manipulated for political advantage.

Conclusion

The many dramatic judicial interventions into Brazilian politics and the equally spectacular lapses of justice have created a democratic, if not legal, impasse: When the law is executed only partially, and when this furthers political controversies while neglecting equality before the law, then that use of legal actions distorts the political field and undermines democracy.

During the Lava-Jato scandal, neither courts, congressional committees, nor judicial mechanisms could be relied upon to regularly produce accountability in an equilibrated manner, to resolve policy questions, or to promote a stable democratic State.

The existing literature on the flaws and merits of Brazilian accountability mechanisms has tended to assess such mechanisms, triggered by corruption scandals, based on whether justice was served or impunity prevailed. With the insights of this chapter, I draw attention to the systemic effects of accountability, sanctions, and interventions, because the mechanisms of checks and balances and accountability should not and cannot simply be measured by the results at the individual level.

The systemic ramifications of judicial interventions and legal struggles do not only influence jurisprudence and the day-to-day media agenda. As we have seen in the TSE case and Lula's cases, state-given laws, and the coercive power that resides as the ultimate boundary of such laws, can be deployed not only to coerce and suppress physically, but also to make or break political narratives. In this sense, "lawfare" is perhaps even more interesting as an analytical concept than the notions of judicialization of politics or politicization of the judiciary, because the concept of lawfare points to the discursive power and narrative capacity wielded by specific actors, through legal instruments and representations of trials and courts.

We might do well to keep in mind that the war, combat, or crusade against corruption are powerful metaphors, and the use of such metaphors legitimizes precisely the (symbolically or physically) coercive and violent manifestations of state power. In Brazil, parading politicians and businessmen in handcuffs from police transport vehicles into prison cells has enormous symbolic power, and the coverage of Lula being escorted from his home to testify in March 2016 was perhaps the moment most galvanizing to the impeachment of Dilma Rousseff. The incident clearly showed Lula as the passive object of law, rather than a politically vital subject. Since then, public opinion polls have been asking for the population's views on the imprisonment of Lula. Thus, the coercive threat of the State is discursively present and maintained on the media agenda – even if it never manifests into a concrete incarceration of the ex-president.

Notes

1 The vote in the Senate after the hearing of the nominated PGR is normally considered merely symbolic. Upon choosing Raquel Dodge, some discussion arose as to whether the president could disregard the order of the shortlist provided by the prosecutor's corporation. Dodge was only the second most-voted candidate on the list, behind the electoral prosecutor-general, Nicolao Dino. Nicolao Dino had, in the TSE trial a few months earlier, requested the cancellation of Temer's presidency and, moreover, is the brother of the communist governor of the state of Maranhão, Flávio Dino.

2 Supreme Justice Gilmar Mendes has repeatedly echoed the critique raised by Cunha and Temer, stating that prosecuting processes led by Janot lacked legitimacy, that Janot made a "complete mess" of the investigation, made a "sorry figure," and that the plea bargain negotiated in 2017 with the Batista brothers was the "greatest tragedy in the history of the PGR."

3 A number of crucial instances of judicial review may be mentioned here: Affirmative action in the public universities (the so-called racial Quota deemed constitutional in 2010), the 2011 affirmation of the constitutionality of gay marriage, and the ruling of 2016 where the STF acquitted doctors practicing illegal abortion, potentially paving the way for legalization of abortion in Brazil are three important examples. Stem cells, anti-Semitism, amnesty laws, and strike rights have also been the object of judicial review in the STF; see Koerner 2013: 699 for more examples.

4 In January 2018, only eight Congressmen were charged before STF: Gleisi Hoffmann and Vander Loubet of PT, Aníbal Gomes and Valdir Raupp of PMDB, Fernando Collor de Mello of PTC, and Nelson Meurer, Luiz Fernando Faria, and José Otávio Germano of PP.

5 The Supreme Tribunal of Justice (STJ) is the supreme appellate court dealing with non-constitutional issues. The court, composed of 33 judges, works to ensure homogeneous jurisprudence across the Brazilian courts, and the court also judges governors (in accordance with a special case of *foro privilegiado*).

6 The final step in the testimony phase saw both the imprisoned João Santana and his wife Monica Moura testifying to the TSE in April 2017. Nicolau Dino, the electoral prosecutor, concluded that the Rousseff-Temer ticket had used R$112 million illicitly, stemming from the corruption of state companies and channeled into the campaign via Odebrecht payments to João Santana (R$20 million), payments to three coalition partner parties (PROS, PCdoB, and PRB, R$21 million in total) and 4 million paid as compensation for the broadcasting slot of PDT during the race. Furthermore, R$17 million had been laundered by Odebrecht's subsidiary Petrópolis, and 50 million had been paid as delayed kickbacks for a tax exemption provisional decree (MP470 of 2009) which favored Odebrecht. The latter amount, according to Marcelo Odebrecht, had not been paid in full during the 2010 campaign, and had only been used in the 2014 campaign. With these testimonies and the final report of the prosecutor, the process of sentencing began in May 2016, but was interrupted as the court accepted the defendants' plea for more time and restarted on June 6, 2017. By then, Temer's

presidency had become embroiled in yet another mega-leak, threatening the stability of his government (see Chapter 3).

7 Zeze Perrella is notorious in Brazilian politics since the incident in which a helicopter owned by his company, packed with 455 kilograms of cocaine, was seized by the federal police. Perrella was not charged in the case.

8 The eight investigations targeting Neves in the STF can be reviewed at the Court's site, www.stf.jus.br, and found via search for the inquiries numbered INQ4246, INQ4244, INQ4444, INQ4414, INQ4423, INQ4436, INQ4392 and INQ4506.

9 MP 471 meant tax reduction incentives for car construction companies in the regions North, North-East and Center-West. Originally valid only in 2009, the decree was extended till 2015. The reduction was specifically to be determined from the expected value of the IPI (Imposto sobre Produtos Industrializados) and then return as reimbursement of two other product taxes, the PIS and the Cofins. In practice, the bill resulted in tax benefits for two car construction firms (MMC, linked to Mitsubishi, and CAOA, linked to Ford, Hyundai, and Subaru). Two more provisional bills, from Rousseff's government, also looked suspect to the investigation: The MP 512 (decree of 2010) was, like MP471, a tax reduction incentive, targeted at manufacturers of automobile motors, wheels, and other parts, again determined from the IPI and only for manufacturers in the regions North, North-East, and Center-West. The MP 627 (decree of 2013) annulled a temporary tax, the *Regime Tributário de Transição* (RTT), and changed the tax scheme for Brazilian multinational companies, as well as establishing an eight-year deadline for the Brazilian companies based outside of Brazil for paying two other taxes, the IRPJ and CSLL.

10 The Comaroffs were later made aware of the military-legal scholarship use (Comaroff and Comaroff 2007: 144) but had originally used the term to connote "the systematic effort to exert control over and/or to coerce political subjects by recourse to the violence inherent in legal instruments" (ibid.: 145).

References

Abramo, C.W. (2007) "Brazil: A Portrait of Disparities" *Brazilian Journalism Research*, vol. 3(1), 93–107.

Almeida, R. de (2016) *A Sombra do Poder. Os Bastidores da Crise Que Derrubou Dilma Rousseff.* Rio de Janeiro: Editora LeYa.

Anders, G. and Nuijten, M. (eds.) (2009) *Corruption and the Secret of Law: A Legal Anthropological Perspective.* Aldershot: Ashgate.

Arantes, R. (2002) *Ministério Público e Política no Brasil.* São Paulo: Sumaré/Fabesp.

Arantes, R. (2011) "The Federal Police and the Ministério Público." In T. Power and M. Taylor (eds.), *Corruption and Democracy in Brazil* (184–217). South Bend, IN: University of Notre Dame Press.

Araújo, C.M., Costa, S.F., and Fittipaldi, I. (2016) "Boa noite, e boa sorte: determinantes da demissão de ministros envolvidos em escândalos de corrupção no primeiro governo Dilma Rousseff" *Opinião Pública*, vol. 22(1), 93–117.

Avritzer, L. (2016) *Impasses da democracia no Brasil.* Rio de Janeiro: Civilização Brasileira.

Avritzer, L. and Marona, M.C. (2014) "Judicialização da política no Brasil: ver além do constitucionalismo liberal para ver melhor" *Revista Brasileira de Ciência Política*, n. 15, 69–94.

Barroso, R. (2017) *Questão de Ordem na Ação Penal 937.* Brasília: Supremo Tribunal Federal. Retrieved from www.stf.jus.br/arquivo/cms/noticiaNoticiaStf/anexo/AP937Q Orelator.pdf.

Benjamin, H. (2017) *Relatorio*. Brasília: Tribunal Superior Eleitoral. Retrieved from www.tse.jus.br/eleitor-e-eleicoes/eleicoes/eleicoes-anteriores/eleicoes-2014/prestacao-de-contas-eleicoes-2014/acao-de-investigacao-judicial-eleitoral-no-1943-58.

Bergamo, M. (2016) "Lula deve aceitar convite de Dilma para ser ministro" *Folha de S. Paulo*, p. A5, March 14. Retrieved from www1.folha.uol.com.br/colunas/monicabergamo/2016/03/1749879-lula-deve-aceitar-convite-de-dilma-para-ser-ministro.shtml.

Boydstun, A. (2013) *Making the News. Politics, the Media, and Agenda Setting*. Chicago, IL: University of Chicago Press.

Brooks, B. (2017) "Janot diz que Dodge e Segóvia estão desacelerando investigações de corrupção" *Reuters Brasil*, published on December 10. Retrieved from https://br.reuters.com/article/topNews/idBRKBN1DV52Q-OBRTP.

Bulla, B. and Moura, R.M. (2017) "Supremo indica maioria a favor de restrição do foro" *Estado de S. Paulo*, p. A4, November 21.

Campos, P.P. de (2017) "Juízes são mais duros que Moro ao revisarem penas em 2ª instância" *Veja*, edition #2538, published on July 12, 2017. Retrieved from http://veja.abril.com.br/politica/juizes-sao-mais-duros-que-moro-ao-revisarem-penas-em-2a-instancia/.

Cardoso, G. and Fatima, B. di (2013) "Movimento em rede e protestos no Brasil. Qual gigante acordou?" *Dossiê Mídia, Intelectuais e Política*, vol. 16(2), 143–176.

Carlson, J. and Yeomans, N. (1975) "Whither Goeth the Law." In M. Smith and D. Crossley (eds.), *The Way Out – Radical Alternatives in Australia*. Melbourne: Lansdowne Press.

Comaroff, J. and Comaroff, J. (eds.) (2006) *Law and Disorder in the Postcolony*. Chicago, IL: University of Chicago Press.

Comaroff, J. and Comaroff, J. (2007) "Law and Disorder in the Postcolony" (abridged version) *Social Anthropology* vol. 15(2), 133–152.

Cotta, L.C. (2008) *Adhemar de Barros (1901–1969): A origem do "rouba, mas faz."* Master's Thesis. São Paulo: Universidade de São Paulo.

Coura, K. and Marques, H. (2015) "Os favores da empreteira" *Veja*, edition #2423, April 29.

Couso, J., Huneeus, A., and Sieder, R. (eds.) (2010) *Cultures of Legality. Judicialization and Political Activism in Latin America*. Cambridge: Cambridge University Press.

Dallagnol, D. and Martelo, O. (2016) "Lava Jato, de onde veio e para onde vamos" *Folha de S. Paulo*, October 30. Retrieved from www1.folha.uol.com.br/opiniao/2016/10/1827555-lava-jato-de-onde-veio-e-para-onde-vamos.shtml.

Das, V. and Poole, D. (eds.) (2004) *Anthropology in the Margins of the State*. Santa Fe, NM: School of American Research Press.

Datafolha (2017) *Intenção de voto presidente – setembro de 2017, PO813939*. São Paulo: Datafolha.

Dunlap Jr., C.J. (2001) "Law and Military Interventions: Preserving Humanitarian Values in 21st Century Conflicts." Paper prepared for the Carr Centre for Human Rights Policy, November 29, 2001. Retrieved from http://people.duke.edu/~pfeaver/dunlap.pdf.

Edelman, L. (2016) *Working Law: Courts, Corporation, and Symbolic Civil Rights*. Chicago, IL: University of Chicago Press.

Falcão, J., Hartmann, I.A., and Chaves, V. (2014) *III Relatório Supremo em Números: o Supremo e o tempo*. Rio de Janeiro: Escola de Direito do Rio de Janeiro da Fundação Getulio Vargas.

Falcão, J., Arguelhes, D.W., and Recondo, F. (eds.) (2016) *O Supremo em 2015*. Rio de Janeiro: Escola de Direito do Rio de Janeiro da Fundação Getulio Vargas.

Faria, T. and Peron, I. (2017) "Reforma alivia dívidas dos partidos até com Lava Jato" *Estado de S. Paulo*, October 6, 2017. Retrieved from http://politica.estadao.com.br/noticias/geral,reforma-alivia-dividas-dos-partidos-ate-com-lava-jato,70002029781.

Ferraz, C. and Finan, F. (2008) "Exposing Corrupt Politicians: The Effects of Brazil's Publicly Released Audits on Electoral Outcomes: Evidence from Audit Reports" *Quarterly Journal of Economics*, vol. 132(2), 703–745.

Ferreira, F. and Rocha, G. (2015) "Polícia investiga sítio usado por Lula" *Folha de S. Paulo*, November 17, 2015, p. A4. Retrieved from www1.folha.uol.com.br/poder/2015/11/1707354-policia-investiga-sitio-usado-por-lula.shtml.

Greco, L. and Leite, A. (2014) "Die 'Rezeption' der Tat- und Organisationsherrschaft im brasilianischen Wirt-Schaftsstrafrecht" *Zeitschrift für Internationale Strafrechtsdogmatik*, vol. 6, 285–291.

Guimarães, J. (2016) "Midiatização Instrumental versus Publicidade Democrática na Operação Lava Jato." In J. Guimarães, M. Andrade Cattoni de Oliveira, M. Mont'Alverne Barreto Lima, and N. de Menezes Albuquerque (eds.), *Risco e Futuro da Democracia Brasileira: Direito e Política no Brasil Contemporâneo* (19–32). São Paulo: Fundação Perseu Abramo.

Gupta, A. (1995) "Blurred Boundaries: The Discourse of Corruption" *American Ethnologist*, vol. 22(2), 375–402.

Helmke, G. (2017) *Institutions on the Edge: The Origins and Consequences of Institutional Instability in Latin America*. Cambridge: Cambridge University Press.

Hirschl, R. (2004) *Towards Juristocracy: The Origins and Consequences of the New Constitutionalism*. Cambridge, MA: Harvard University Press.

Hirschl, R. (2008) "The Judicialization of Mega-Politics and the Rise of Political Courts" *Annual Review of Political Science*, vol. 11(1), 93–118.

Kahn, J. (2017) "Geographies of Discretion and the Jurisdictional Imagination" *Political and Legal Anthropology Review*, vol. 40(1), 5–27.

Koerner, A. (2013) "Judiciário e moralização da política: três reflexões sobre as tendências recentes no Brasil" *Pensar*, vol. 18(3), 681–711.

Lima, V.A. da (2004) "Sete teses sobre mídia e política no Brasil" *Revista USP*, São Paulo, no. 61, 48–57.

Lima, V.A. da (2009) "Revisitando as sete teses sobre mídia e política no Brasil" in *Comunicação & Sociedade*, vol. 30(51), 13–37.

Llanos, M. and Marsteintredet, L. (eds.) (2010) *Presidential Breakdowns in Latin America: Causes and Outcomes of Executive Instability in Developing Democracies*. London: Palgrave Macmillan.

McPherson, C.M. and Sauder, M. (2013) "Logics in Action: Managing Institutional Complexity in a Drug Court" *Administrative Science Quarterly*, vol. 58(29), 165–196.

Macaulay, F. (2011) "Federalism and State Criminal Justice Systems." In T. Power and M. Taylor (eds.), *Corruption and Democracy in Brazil. The Struggle for Accountability* (218–249). South Bend, IN: University of Notre Dame Press.

Macedo, I. (2017a) "Os senadores sob suspeita e o que eles dizem sobre as acusações em análise no STF" *Revista Congresso Em Foco*, vol. 26, July 18, 2017. Retrieved from http://congressoemfoco.uol.com.br/noticias/os-senadores-sob-suspeita-e-o-que-eles-dizem-sobre-as-acusacoes-em-analise-no-stf/.

Macedo, I. (2017b) "Quem são e o que dizem os 238 deputados e senadores investigados no STF" *Revista Congresso em Foco*, vol. 26, July 25. Retrieved from http://congressoemfoco.uol.com.br/noticias/quem-sao-e-o-que-dizem-os-238-deputados-e-senadores-investigados-no-stf/.

Marchetti, V. (2008) "Governança Eleitoral: O Modelo Brasileiro de Justiça Eleitoral" *Dados – Revista de Ciências Sociais*, vol. 51(4), 865–893.

Mariani, D., Lupion, B., and Almeida, R. (2017) "Qual é o grau de discordância e concordância entre os ministros do Supremo" *Nexo Jornal*, published on March 21, 2017. Retrieved from www.nexojornal.com.br/especial/2017/03/21/Como-os-ministros-do-Supremo-se-aproximam-ou-se-distanciam-entre-si-de-acordo-com-suas-decisões.

Mattoso, C., Casado, L., and Uribe, G. (2017) "Julgamento de Dilma-Temer no TSE já começa com disputa por um voto" *Folha de São Paulo*, March 29, 2017. Retrieved from www1.folha.uol.com.br/poder/2017/03/1870655-julgamento-de-dilma-temer-no-tse-ja-comeca-com-disputa-por-um-voto.shtml.

Mello, C. de (2016) *Voto*. Brasília: Supremo Tribunal Federal. Published on December 7, 2016. Retrieved from www.stf.jus.br/arquivo/cms/noticiaNoticiaStf/anexo/referendoADPF402CM.pdf.

Michener, G. and Pereira, C. (2016) "A Great Leap Forward for Democracy and the Rule of Law? Brazil's Mensalão Trial" *Journal of Latin American Studies*, vol. 48, 477–507.

Ministério de Planejamento, Orçamento e Gestão (2015) "Tabela 1 – poderes executivo, legislativo e judiciário." Retrieved from www.planejamento.gov.br/secretarias/upload/Arquivos/servidor/publicacoes/dados_ldo/anexo_i-tab1-quant_fisico_pessoal-pexec.pdf.

Moro, S. (2004) "Considerações sobre a Operação Mani Pulite" *Revista CEJ*, vol. 8(26), 56–62.

Netto, V. (2016) *Lava-Jato: O juiz Sergio Moro e os bastidores da operação que abalou o Brasil*. Rio de Janeiro: Editora Sextante.

Oliveira, G. (2014) "Cooperativa entrega triplex de Lula, mas três mil ainda esperam imóvel" *O Globo*, December 7, 2014. Retrieved from https://oglobo.globo.com/brasil/cooperativa-entrega-triplex-de-lula-mas-tres-mil-ainda-esperam-imovel-14761809.

Pereira, C., Melo, M.A., and Figueiredo, C. (2009) "The Corruption-Enhancing Role of Re-Election Incentives? Counterintuitive Evidence from Brazil's Audit Reports" *Political Research Quarterly*, vol. 62(4), 731–744.

Pereira, C., Rennó, L., and Samuels, D. (2011) "Corruption, Campaign Finance, and Reelection." In T. Power and M. Taylor (eds.), *Corruption and Democracy in Brazil* (80–102). South Bend, IN: University of Notre Dame Press.

Pereira, C. and Melo, M.A. (2015) "Reelecting Corrupt Incumbents in Exchange for Public Goods: Rouba mas faz in Brazil" *Latin American Research Review*, vol. 50(4), 88–115.

Pereira, C., Bertholini, F., and Raile, E. (2016) "All the President's Men and Women: Coalition Management Strategies and Governing Costs in a Multiparty Presidency" *Presidential Studies Quarterly*, vol. 46(3), 550–568.

Peruzzotti, E. (2006) "Media Scandals and Social Accountability. Assessing the Role of Scandals in Argentina." In E. Peruzzotti and C. Smulovitz (eds.), *Enforcing the Rule of Law. Social Accountability in the New Latin American Democracies* (249–271). Pittsburgh, PA: University of Pittsburgh Press.

Peruzzotti, E. and Smulovitz, C. (eds.) (2006) *Enforcing the Rule of Law. Social Accountability in the New Latin American Democracies*. Pittsburgh, PA: University of Pittsburgh Press.

Pontes, G. (2016) "Exclusivo: conheça os candidatos que caíram na Lei da Ficha Limpa" *Congresso em Foco*, September 30. Retrieved from http://congressoemfoco.uol.c.

Power, T. and Taylor, M. (eds.) (2011) *Corruption and Democracy in Brazil*. South Bend, IN: University of Notre Dame Press.

Polícia Federal (2017) *Estatística de Operações*. Retrieved from www.pf.gov.br/imprensa/estatistica/operacoes.

Presidência da República (2010) *Lei Complementar 135 De 4 De Junho De 2010*. Retrieved from www.planalto.gov.br/ccivil_03/Leis/LCP/Lcp135.htm.

Raile, E., Pereira, C., and Power, T. (2011) "The Executive Toolbox: Building Legislative Support in a Multiparty Presidential Regime" *Political Research Quarterly* vol. 64(2), 323–364.

Rennó, L. (2011) "Corruption and Voting." In T. Power and M. Taylor (eds.), *Corruption and Democracy in Brazil* (56–69). South Bend, IN: University of Notre Dame Press.

Speck, B. (2011) "Auditing Institutions." In T. Power and M. Taylor (eds.), *Corruption and Democracy in Brazil* (127–162). South Bend, IN: University of Notre Dame Press.

Supremo Tribunal Federal (2017) "Decisao de julgamento, ADI 5526." Retrieved from www.stf.jus.br/portal/processo/verProcessoAndamento.asp?numero=5526&classe=ADI&origem=AP&recurso=0&tipoJulgamento=M.

Tate, N. and Vallinder, T. (1995) *The Global Expansion of Judicial Power*. New York: New York University Press.

Taylor, M. (2011) "The Federal Judiciary and the Electoral Courts." In T. Power and M. Taylor (eds.), *Corruption and Democracy in Brazil* (162–183). South Bend, IN: University of Notre Dame Press.

Thornton, P. and Ocasio, W. (2008) "Institutional Logics." In R. Greenwood, C. Oliver, K. Sahlin, and R. Suddaby (eds.), *The SAGE Handbook of Organizational Institutionalism* (99–129). Los Angeles, CA: Sage.

Thornton, P., Ocasio, W., and Lounsbury, M. (2012) *The Institutional Logics Perspective. A New Approach to Culture, Structure and Process*. Oxford: Oxford University Press.

Tribunal Superior Eleitoral (2017) "Informações gerais sobre a Ação de Investigação Judicial Eleitoral nº 194358." Retrieved from www.tse.jus.br/imprensa/noticias-tse/2017/Marco/informacoes-gerais-sobre-a-acao-de-investigacao-judicial-eleitoral-no-1943-58.

Tsebelis, G. (2002) *Veto Players How Political Institutions Work*, Princeton, NJ: Princeton University Press.

Waters, C. (2009) "Beyond Lawfare: Juridical Oversight of Western Militaries" *Alberta Law Review*, vol. 46(4), 885–911.

Werneck Vianna, L., Carvalho, M.R., Palácios, M. de, and Burgos, M. (1999) *A judicialização da política e das relações sociais no Brasil*. Rio de Janeiro: Revan.

Werner, W. (2010) "The Curious Career of Lawfare" *43 Case Western Reserve Journal of International Law*, vol. 43, 61–72.

Wiarda, H.J. (ed.) (2004) *Authoritarianism and Corporatism in Latin America Revisited*. Gainesville: University of Florida Press.

Wink, G. (2017) "Judicialização da política ou politização da justiça? Uma Análise Crítica do Discurso do Libelo Acusatório contra a presidenta Dilma Rousseff no processo de impeachment" *Moara*, vol. 47, 152–177.

Winters, M. and Weitz-Shapiro, R. (2013) "Lacking Information or Condoning Corruption: When Do Voters Support Corrupt Politicians?" *Journal of Comparative Politics*, vol. 45(4), 418–436.

Zanin Martins, C., Zanin Martins, V.T., and Rafael, V. (eds.) (2017) *O caso Lula – a luta pela afirmação dos direitos fundamentais no Brasil* São Paulo: Contracorrente.

5 The Informational Cascades of Impeachment and the Lava-Jato Scandal

The previous chapters have demonstrated how disclosure of corruption emerges intermittently as leaks – when information is provided to journalists of the larger media outlets by the public prosecutors, by lawyers or even by the defendants – and how, subsequently, that disclosure is processed and instrumentalized throughout the judicial arenas of Brazil. Between the sudden leaks and the continuous grinding of the legal actions, the attention of the main Brazilian news outlets has been synced to the anti-corruption agenda, dancing to the tune of the leaky, legal processes. Even so, the various cases have not reached their end in an equal pace; many political actors under scrutiny have largely escaped accountability, and only a few cases have continuously been in the limelight. In this chapter, I will explore the distribution of information flows and attention. Whereas the previous chapters have given qualitative, historical and political explanations for the outcomes of the disclosure of corruption, both in the form of leaks and continuous coverage of legal action, this chapter works quantitatively, using the concept of cascades to understand the impact of disclosed information in the Lava-Jato scandal. The chapter contributes to the growing body of research on infostorms by developing an approach to tracing such information phenomena in the sphere of media.

Snowballing, avalanche-like informational media phenomena such as moral panics, media storms, and media hypes have been theorized before, but mostly as separate concepts within media studies (Thompson 2000, Tumber and Waisbord 2004, Welch et al. 2002, Wien and Elmelund-Præstekær 2009). In a certain sense, a mechanism similar to media hypes was also implied in more general media theories about agenda-setting. Agenda-setting theory predicts the relation between media coverage and the media audiences' perception of salience of issues (McCombs and Shaw 1972, McCombs 2005). Agenda-setting theory could be used to analyze the skew of salience transfer effects in the rapid surges of coverage that characterize scandals. This has rarely been explored (but see Boydstun 2013 and Walgrave et al. 2017), however, and such surges of media attention have only recently been linked to a general theory of information flows through the notion of informational cascades in social contexts (Hendricks and Hansen 2016).

Earlier concepts explaining the power of media scandals have sometimes been linked theoretically to various fields of sociology, but in distinct ways.

Where Thompson (2000) discussed the power of scandals in political fields using a Bourdieusian capital approach, the moral panics described by Welch and colleagues were conceived as a parallel to Durkheim's functional understanding of ritual, because surges of media panic acted to expel folk devils and confirm societal order (Welch et al. 2002). In a third strand of theory, the concept of media hype coined by Vasterman was connected loosely to framing theory. Several of these authors have pointed out that media-instilled panics and news waves entail social amplification of signals disproportionate to real frequency of the problem in question (e.g., Vasterman 2005: 516, Welch et al. 2002: 15). This conceptualization of news as signals in public spheres is a crucial component of the informational cascade framework as well.

In the following, I will explain the concept of informational cascades and operationalize this concept through a content analysis research design, drawing on agenda-setting theory. By using the concept of informational cascades, rather than ad-hoc theories defined by characteristics specific to certain media situations (such as hypes, panics, or storms), media theory may integrate these theories and link them to the general mechanisms of information flows and decision making. This integration requires an explication of the relationship between media systems and the collective processing of information in public spheres. Such an account may contribute to our understanding of chain reactions emerging between media, political actors, and public opinion; chain reactions that can be particularly nefarious in media environments rife with so-called "viral" news, "fake news," or "post-factual news." However, what is central here is neither "fake" news, although disinformation will be touched upon, nor the usual question of agenda-setting studies – for example, to ascertain how much of an impact media coverage had upon Brazilian audiences in the course of the Lava-Jato investigations. Such a study of the level of reception would require representative samples of both the population and the media coverage. Instead, this chapter will focus only on the information flows that emerged in the leading dailies during the Lava-Jato scandal and the build-up of salience in relation to particular political actors.

The analysis of this chapter helps explain the conundrum of the Lava-Jato scandal: How could the majority of the politicians implicated in the scandal escape social accountability and form a new government while embroiled in the very same corruption investigation that undermined the former government? Most theories of scandal affirm that the media holds great power during scandals, and the agenda-setting effects of media scrutiny are theoretically linked to this potential inherent in scandals: All else being equal, we would expect that more coverage of a political action (which is being characterized as transgressive and scandalous) would increase the likelihood of some kind of political response – resignations, public apologies, etc. While this expectation undoubtedly rings true in some political systems, it does not capture what happened in the Lava-Jato case. In fact, this corruption probe might, at a glance, seem paradoxically potent and impotent: The media reported ceaselessly on the case for three years, but while scores of businessmen were brought to trial and sentenced, with ample evidence of political corruption, very few politicians have been charged before the STF at the time of writing (although scores of congressmen are being investigated). Only two mandates have been annulled, and the political parties are completely unwilling to expel members who are denounced or sentenced for corruption. This flies in the face of the theoretical and common-sense expectations of political scandals, since the ongoing public shock of disclosed corruption has hardly affected the vast majority of the congressmen. The paradox of enormous media attention and limited accountability, I argue, can be explained partly as a problem of the informational cascade in the public spheres of Brazil.

In the following, I will consider theoretically how information about corruption can be shaped and passed on in cascades, expanding the theoretical apparatus presented in Chapter 1. Second, I operationalize the concept of cascades through a sampling strategy of print and web media, exploring the frequency, salience, and sequence of news on the various corruption cases and the impeachment proceedings. The data collected with this strategy provides a proxy for the general distribution of media attention in the public spheres of Brazil; and the distribution reflects editorial and journalistic selection processes, which are crucial in setting up an informational cascade in the media.

The findings of the content analysis demonstrate that the dominant news outlets' coverage of this wide-ranging scandal exhibited a centripetal pattern, leading to massive overexposure of three political actors, while information about other actors was marginalized and largely disregarded in the news. Two mechanisms of the media system were crucial: The overvaluation and the selective recycling of information about corruption. These mechanisms meant that news linking Lula to the Lava-Jato probe eclipsed news that dealt with other politicians' cases of corruption.

Delving into the processes where information was passed from political and judiciary elites, through mainstream media, and on to the stock markets of Brazil, I also find evidence that the informational cascade contributed to creating not just a moral crisis, but subsequently an economic and political crisis. The Lava-Jato scandal can be interpreted as an exemplar case, magnifying certain features such as skew and explosiveness inherent in media agenda processes (Boydstun 2013: 208). In the interplay of politics and media, these features yield information phenomena in the public spheres akin to financial bubbles (Hendricks and Hansen 2016).

The Concept of Informational Cascades

This chapter builds on the definition of informational cascade given in the first chapter. To unpack this definition further, I will expand three aspects of the theoretical framework before operationalizing the concept. First, I will briefly discuss the definition of information in the framework I am proposing, including the definitions of misinformation, disinformation, and information quality. Second, since this book works with media texts, it is necessary to link the abstract definitions of information to theories that deal with media objects; in particular, the theory of framing. Framing theory provides insights concerning the packaging of information in concrete media texts, which is an underdeveloped part of the informational cascade literature (but see Hendricks and Hansen 2016: 85ff.). Closing these preliminary remarks, I discuss how intertextuality is used in media texts on scandals to reproduce and extend certain journalistic frames. Intertextuality thus becomes a key aspect of journalistic narration in scandals, present in various clues (visual, textual, or metatextual, i.e., hyperlinks). Through such clues, audiences are invited to connect the dots between sequences of media texts, and cued intertextuality may thus be an important factor for the emergence of cascades and pluralistic ignorance in public spheres. The three theoretical considerations of corruption scandals and informational cascades, framing, and intertextuality provide the background for the sampling strategy and operationalization of the concept of informational cascade deployed.

As described in the first chapter, conceptually, informational cascades consist in rationally acting actors, who are sequentially passing along information through their public actions. The actors cannot derive private knowledge possessed by other actors, but nonetheless, all observing actors take the actions to be significant down the sequence stream. When making their respective choices, these actors might then base their actions on false assumptions about the private knowledge of others. A "cascade starts and new information stops accumulating" when the "preponderance of evidence supports one action" and actors repeatedly reproduce one public signal (Bikhchandani et al. 1998: 158).

Hendricks and Hansen warn that such sequences might bias the choices of an electorate or a group of decision-makers a great deal. They offer several illustrations of everyday situations where cascades harm our decision making. In one such illustration, they identify informational cascades in the environment of airports: Cascades occur when we are running frantically around an airport terminal, trying to find the right gate after only hearing half the announcement about a gate change. Observing other passengers with a calm, directed gait and tickets that are seemingly identical to ours, we decide to follow these apparently well-informed travelers. "They seem to know where to go, so I should follow them" goes the internal argument, which is potentially very wrong. This kind of thinking, they argue, occurs every so often in public spaces, or, indeed, in the formation of public opinion (Hendricks and Hansen 2016: 61, 245). Hendricks and Hansen point out how informational cascades might be harmful to democratic societies because cascades tempt citizens – voters as well as decision-makers – to make their choices based on the public informational sequence rather than the quality of the information.

Similar concerns were foundational for modern media studies. The simple model of media introducing ideas into the minds of the audience (like a highly effective hypodermic needle) was however debunked by Lazarsfeld and colleagues, who demonstrated more complex information flows: People adopt attitudes to political issues by first looking to local opinion leaders (which could be other people affiliated with a party, or simply people regarded as knowledgeable in political matters), rather than solely taking cues from media (Lazarsfeld et al. 1944). Individual actions, then, are based on the value invested in the signal sent by these opinion leaders, even though individuals will not know every aspect of the opinion leaders' internal deliberations and possible vested interests. In the limited-effects model proposed by Lazarsfeld and colleagues, the public signal of media (in campaign coverage) was attenuated or overridden by the signals of people's social environment. In both hypodermic-needle and limited-effect scenarios, however, individual decision-making was considered to be influenced by other social agents, sometimes in spite of private knowledge or convictions. Herein lie the roots of the problem of information, public knowledge, and signaling.

In Chapter 3, we saw how information is leaked or fed to journalists (usually those working for prestigious media outlets). These media outlets, in turn, disseminate the information, once journalists and editors have selected and packaged the information in specific framings (Entman 1993) and through specific formats and scripts (Altheide and Snow 1979: 10, van Dijk 1988: 34). The exact selection of information that will eventually reach audiences is limited by the gatekeepers of media and the sub-politics of the sources (Waisbord 2000: 93). Researchers should not naively assume that members of the audience cannot reinterpret the disseminated information in heterogeneous ways (Biroli and

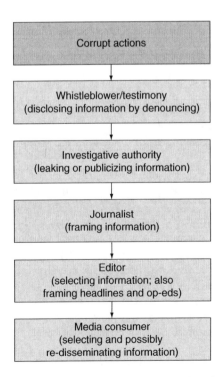

Figure 5.1 The chain of information in a denunciation of corruption.

Miguel 2013: 81), framing problems in other ways than the media framed them (see below): Signals of corruption could be disregarded or mistrusted by audience members, especially if one has private knowledge that contradicts the public signal of the media. However, in national corruption scandals, private knowledge about what goes on in the backstage of the political arena is naturally extremely rare. Even Brazilian congressmen, in fact, must sometimes rely on the rumors reported by the small news columns of *O Globo*, *Folha*, and *Estado*. Congressmen, unlike most of us, may however have a much better chance of understanding the implications of such rumors. Like ordinary citizens, even such insiders in political circles still stand at a fourth or fifth remove in the chain of information. Denunciations of corruption, for instance, conceptually look like this in a simple transmission model, ignoring the potential reinterpretations occurring downstream (see Figure 5.1 above).

The figure illustrates, in a simplified manner, how information is passed on to audiences via media actors. As described in Chapter 3, investigative authorities (MPF and PF) are not the only ones who can pass on information to journalists; defendants and their lawyers are just as capable of delivering information to journalists if they judge it to be beneficial to their case. Judicial actors in courts could also pass on information to journalists, but in the cases proliferating from the Lava-Jato investigations, information about probes normally comes to public attention months before the denunciations and documents are actually handed over to clerks of the courts. The notable exception to this part of the information flow is the judges. Judges with jurisdiction of a case, such as Sérgio Moro in the Lava-Jato case, see some elements of cases before they are investigated, because investigative measures such as arrests, telephone taps, or inquiries about telephone and bank registries need a judge's authorization, based on some manner of description of the circumstances of the case. Whistle-blowing can also happen outside of criminal investigations (which was the case in the Mensalão scandal, but rarely occurred in the course of the Lava-Jato case).

In any case, the information reaches the pages of political news, or the front pages, or even the daily news broadcasts. At this point, a bandwagon effect between media outlets might come into play, and when various media outlets repeat the same signal over and over again, an informational cascade might form. The bandwagon effect starts with the practical and epistemic job of the individual journalist, who, in order "to flesh out any one supposed fact … amasses a host of supposed facts that, when taken together, present themselves as both individually and collectively self-validating" (Tuchman 1978: 86). This means that many assumptions are continuously reproduced in news, and this recurrently validates the original assumption. The hegemonic interpretation of national politics, for example, could be reproduced over and over by journalists because this will present the shortest route to validating and interpreting new information culled from sources. The self-validation also occurs at the institutional level, where

[m]edia institutional actors rely extensively on each other not only as sources of reference but also as sources of institutionalized legitimacy, even

though they lack first-hand access to the event. This reflects the general tendency in contemporary journalism of including the perspectives of media institutions, commentators, correspondents and other media professionals in the news coverage as opposed to involving sources outside the media institutional realm.

(Kristensen and Mortensen 2015: 360)

Thus, when media outlets rely on other media outlets for information, and build on the same assumptions about issues, a feedback-loop emerges that reproduces the same signal many times over. This might then build up into a cascade, as visualized in Figure 5.2.

An informational cascade needs, as mentioned in the quote of Bikhchandani et al., enough weight to override the private knowledge and presuppositions. When people have little private knowledge, they confide in news texts (at least if the media outlet is perceived as trustworthy, which of course is not always the case). If all (trusted as well as distrusted) media outlets cover the same topic in the same way, private doubts might be dispelled. The cascade, or chain-effect, only triggers when there is "a preponderance of evidence [that] supports one action or the other by just enough to outweigh one individual's private signal" (Bikhchandani et al., *idem*). Once one actor decides to act upon that information, this constitutes another piece of evidence for others to see, because his or her action is also a signal. So, in a corruption scandal, when more and more people start to call for the resignation of a given politician, that call seems to be justified for yet more people, and joining the bandwagon, the call for action reinforces

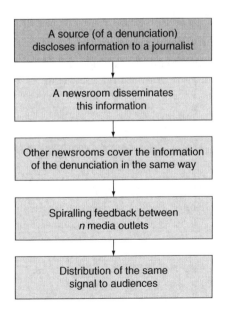

Figure 5.2 The informational cascade between media outlets.

itself until the proverbial mob with forks and torches materializes: The bandwagon effect results in a self-reinforcing feedback loop (Hendricks and Hansen 2016: 258).

In this chapter, I will attempt to trace exactly this dynamic in the media, working from a universe of 8,200 news texts on corruption from the two large media outlets *Folha* and *Estado*, as well as 1,335 headlines from the same outlets plus their competitor *O Globo*. With this dataset, I can track how some signals of corruption were repeated over and over in news texts, while others died out, and furthermore trace how the selected and disseminated information was carried into public spheres (through opinion polls and stock market data). Like the general model of a cascade, the particular informational cascade of the Lava-Jato scandal picked up steam gradually, until it reached a point where new information was promptly disregarded, no matter how relevant. Before describing the research design, the notions of information and information quality needs to be accounted for. Working from a definition of information, I will also prepare the ground for a discussion of how corruption is framed in news texts.

Information Definitions

An exceedingly broad range of information definitions has previously been proposed, deriving from such disparate disciplines as communication sciences, semantics, anthropology, cybernetics, and physics. In the following, however, only a few definitions will be discussed. This is done not just for brevity's sake, but also in order to grasp the kind of informational phenomenon most relevant to a contemporary media system.

Between the contributions of Floridi (2002, 2005, 2011) and Fallis (2009, 2011), the field of philosophy of information has inherited a central but debated distinction from thinkers such as Grice (1957) and Dretske (1981), concerning the element of veracity in information. For Floridi, information can only be defined as "well-formed, meaningful and truthful data" (Floridi 2011: 80), while Fallis tries to take contextual factors such as imparting processes, intentionality and semantic layers into account. Fallis (2011) objects to this, claiming that untrue information might still convey meaning that can be verified. Fallis tries to sort different kinds of lies into the categories of misinformation, disinformation, and information, depending on the intention behind defective semantic content. Obelitz Søe (2014, 2016) has usefully clarified the conceptual intersection of different kinds of information discussed by Floridi and Fallis, proposing a framework of four categories: information (which is verifiably true), disinformation (which is intentionally false), misinformation (unintentionally false), and information-as-natural-meaning (in the sense of Grice 1957, in which natural meaning refers to states of reality that are true independent of any observations and discursive statements). So, while this latter category cannot include meaning determined by social conventions, the former three frequently do include information determined according to social norms, practices, and linguistic usage.[1]

Actual political and social agents may very well choose to deteriorate information quality for specific communicative purposes and political goals, and so for pragmatic purposes, more than conceptual precision, defective, derived, and even alethically distorted information is still regarded as information here. This thrusts the concept of information toward the notion of framing found in media studies (Entman 1993, Sniderman and Theriault 2004). I return to this move shortly.

A media text (including material broadcast through radio, internet, or television) can be understood as a signal containing many bits of information. For example, the introductory sentence or paragraph called a "lead," as defined by most journalists, normally establish the who, the what, the when, the where, and the why of a news item (Carey 1986: 148, Tuchman 1978: 100). Leads establish several facts, purported to be true. A report on a statement by a politician, for instance, is a speech act from which various bits of information are extracted by the reporter. The speech act itself and the extracted information can be interpreted as one or more discrete signals, e.g., as evidence, as a denial, or as parts of a testimony. While all of the informational content of the speech may be intentionally false (which means it is disinformation, strictly speaking), the fact that the politician spoke is still verifiable. News in scandals can include disclosed information of the Gricean, natural-meaning variety (a person caught on tape, for instance, leaving a physical mark, or an audio-visual mark, or a signature). More commonly, information about corruption in news texts is of the convention kind (e.g., allegations about a transgressive and prohibited action, performed by a public agent or agents, which could not have been performed unknowingly nor innocuously by that agent). In either case, the information is framed as corruption intentionally by the journalist through textual or visual markers. That is, both information of the conventions kind and information-as-natural-meaning need to be packaged along with other bits of information to make the transgressive nature of a political action clear.

Framing of Information in Corruption Scandals

Related to the question of information quality, the concept of framing covers the way in which information can be formed and then imparted exactly and truthfully, but partially, in a way to create states of potential misinformation with the audiences. Partial transmission of information is possible in larger packages of information, such as the bundling of information we find in news. Deliberate deterioration of information in order to create misinformation – what is commonly called spin – is an element of specific political and journalistic practices of shaping information textually. Although framing has already been mentioned in the second chapter, I will briefly revisit the concept of framing and argue why, ultimately, a study of the various framings of corruption is not a fruitful research design, although theoretically linked to the topic of information flows.

The academic perspectives on framing range from cognitive to constructivist approaches across discursive and symbolic environments. In one formulation, framing involves selecting a few aspects of a perceived reality and connecting them together in a narrative that promotes a particular interpretation. Frames can perform up to four functions: define problems, specify causes, convey moral assessments, and endorse remedies ... Framing works to shape and alter audience members' interpretations and preferences.

(Entman 2010: 391)

Logically, framing also entails de-selecting some information, for example leaving out other potential causes or remedies; the aspect of de-selection is also relevant to the aggregate level of news framing, to which I return below. Some scholars have broadened Entman's definition, viewing "frames as structures that draw boundaries, set up categories, define some ideas as out and others in, and generally operate to snag related ideas in their net in an active process" (Reese 2007: 150). This means that some media researchers tend to view frames as discursive formations, while other researchers (e.g., in the field of journalism studies) would name the journalistic and editorial activity of selecting and packaging information "framing." In this more limited sense, framing is a professional practice linking events to a repertoire of storyable forms – reporting, say, on politics as a horse-race or a conflict – using specific metaphors and locating actors textually within certain scripts (van Dijk 1988).

As argued in the second chapter, the frames utilized by Brazilian journalists to cover political corruption are highly predictable: Suspicion is cast upon a political actor or a political action, and the suspicion is the object of conflict, being contested or affirmed to varying degrees by the involved actors (such as whistle-blowers, prosecutors, police agents, political supporters or opponents, and of course the denounced actors themselves). In the media texts reporting on the Lava-Jato investigations, various reasons for condemning corruption are brought up: Respect for the Constitution, in the name of democracy, or the electorate, to save the Petrobras company, or with reference to morality, economy, or national industrial development. But no matter who is voicing such concerns in the news texts, and regardless of the explicit presence of any condemnation of corrupt acts, the frames of the texts imply political transgression from some perspective (Damgaard 2015). Whether or not responsibility is clearly attributed to an identifiable political actor (Iyengar 1990), the transgression lies at the heart of the frame, as the device that defines the problem, moves the plot, and makes the news item newsworthy.

Alternative frames may spin off from the simplistic denouncement narrative as the story develops, but in terms of public signals of corruption and information quality, the framing of spin-off news hardly matters. At the intertextual level, spin-off news items still refer to the original narrative of transgression and denunciation. For this reason, framing is not useful in this study: When news mentions a corruption case, it can be understood as a public signal that the accused politician is corrupt, even when competing frames (Sniderman and Theriault 2004) are present in the same text. This argument brings me to a final consideration, regarding the ways that the Lava-Jato scandal grew into a vast discursive behemoth, looming over both the impeachment proceedings and the various strategies of lawfare discussed in the previous chapter: The mere reference to the Lava-Jato probe linked a multitude of disparate texts together intertextually.

Intertextuality

Earlier research has discussed the role of intertextuality in scandals, which may shed light on the narrative linkages in the coverage of the Lava-Jato scandal. Elizabeth Bird notes that new information in corruption scandals connects to earlier disclosure intertextually, like strings on a bead, which gives an episodic quality to scandals. Scandals take on forms dissimilar to "the terse, inverted-pyramid, 'news' style" and develop through follow-up stories (Bird 1997: 101). A particular news item in the coverage of a scandal can be considered as "one element in a mesh of stories," emerging from a broader repertoire of cultural narratives, stereotypes, and scripts (ibid.: 104). That is, the news items are discursively linked. Wortham and Rhodes (2012) argue that in general, discourse connects across speech events, and linked speech events are essential to social life. Because of this structuring, events can be recognized as such, belonging to a set or being distinct from the background noise of history. The events connected thus constitute narratives, which "are joined together in chains or trajectories, through discursive processes that link speech events to each other, such that signs and individuals move along chains of narrating events that occur in different spatio-temporal locations" (ibid.: 161).

Brazilian news texts commonly represent the Lava-Jato corruption case as an ever-expanding episodic narrative – almost like a feuilleton or the Brazilian soap opera genre *telenovela* – that engulfs many actors in the political spectrum. Usually, this was marked by the simple inclusion of a reference to the Lava-Jato case itself. By referencing the Lava-Jato case, or one of the parallel investigations of grand political corruption, neither headlines nor leads of news texts or broadcast news need to include words like "bribe" or "corruption." The intertextually established newsworthiness of the Lava-Jato investigations and high-profiled politicians is what signals corruption. Even media outlets which are normally highly trusted by Brazilians to produce quality coverage can utilize certain strategies to imply corruption without explicitly labelling an action "corrupt." It is enough that some bit of information can signify a transgression from some societal perspective (Damgaard 2015).

Intertextual implicature is a framing strategy that can help journalists evade libel lawsuits and enhance the news value in certain news items. For example, information about the rebuilding of the Presidential Palace's swimming pool was included as news by *Folha* in November 2016, because no contract was encountered, while at that moment, the construction company Odebrecht was under much scrutiny, as was the ex-president Lula. The renovation of a public building – indeed, buildings which are part of the national heritage of Brasília – could thus be cast as possibly corrupt, although the renovation in all probability will never become the centerpiece of a trial. However, the signal was one in a range of signals apparently testifying to the corrupt relationship between the ex-president and the private company.

In this vein, associating an agent's action, indicated by disclosed information, with transgression, is a politically potent signal, even in cases where the action does not qualify as a legal transgression. The information about the swimming pool was not misinformation, because it was not incorrect; rather, we may say that the publicizing of this information is characteristic of disinformation because it is not newsworthy unless it testifies to corruption. In other words, the inclusion as a news item in itself signals that something fishy was going on – otherwise, one could not make sense of the information as "news." Perfectly ordinary actions may thus be bundled in the media along with other information and come to be associated with transgression or even substituting for evidence of transgression. If perceived "correctly" (that is, from the view of the manipulative imparter), members of audiences might then hold false beliefs about the information – believing some politician to be corrupt – although no disinformation nor misinformation was disseminated, only circumstantial information that implied corrupt dealings.

Intertextual implicature, furthermore, has ramifications for the sampling strategy, because the construction of a corpus of news texts about corruption need to go beyond criteria of simple key words. It is also necessary to include texts that report on the companies, businessmen or political actors involved, where the spin-off relation to a case of political transgression is merely a relation of allusion or implication. I will turn to this and related questions of sampling in the following.

Operationalization and Sampling Strategy

In the following, I will discuss a methodology for exploring an informational cascade in the news. While Hendricks and Hansen (2016) analyzed the decision-making problems arising from cascades, the problem of this book is rather the emergence of a cascade and the institutional configurations leading to such a phenomenon. Other researchers have addressed similar phenomena recently, and their methods could be adapted for this purpose: Amber Boydstun, although constructing a study around the term "media storm" and patterns of media attention, sampled news items of front pages and coded the news items for issues (Boydstun 2013: 11, 82). Russell and Waisbord, analyzing so-called "news flashpoints," or bursts of coverage, also analyzed frequencies of news items (but only items related to the Snowden leaks). Both examples dealt with the *New York Times*, and both worked with a content analysis methodology (Russell and Waisbord 2017: 860).

By opting, like these two studies, for a research design based on content analysis, the present study could connect to agenda-setting theory, which in its original formulation explored the relation of media content and voter perceptions of societal problems (McCombs and Shaw 1972). McCombs and Shaw utilized a macro-level content analysis method, coding the overall thematic content of various news items. Later, agenda-setting scholars tried to integrate framing as a second level of agenda setting in order to get to a more detailed and context-sensitive level of analysis (Ghanem 1997, McCombs 2005). Researchers of information phenomena in public spheres view agenda setting as "a concept which may be studied using tools from formal epistemology and network theory to evaluate the differences between the mobilization of both robust knowledge and ignorant belief configurations in networks" (Wiewiura and Hendricks 2017: 2). With the studies by Boydstun, Russell, and Waisbord in mind, I will argue that the inverse should be equally feasible: Detecting cascade-like informational phenomena through content analysis and understanding cascades through agenda-setting theory.

In the following, I therefore undertake a content analysis of the news items that deal with corruption. The content analysis does not compare the amount of news on corruption to news dealing with other issues but aims at the distribution of news items devoted to the plethora of corruption cases in the political system of Brazil. Comparing the Lava-Jato scandal and impeachment to other issues in Brazilian public spheres would simply underscore something obvious, namely that the political situation was the object of intense media attention.

The goal here is also not to find agenda-setting effects of the media coverage at the level of reception, as looking for agenda-setting effects of the several years of intense media coverage of corruption would not go far enough: There is ample evidence in various surveys that can be correlated to the reception of the corruption scandals and the impeachment: During the sample period, the topic of corruption, for the first time, overtook unemployment, security, and health as the problem considered most important for society (Datafolha 2015: 3) – despite being the South American country with the lowest bribery rates (Pring 2017: 31). Both the Rousseff and the Temer administrations experienced record-low approval ratings (Datafolha 2017), and trust in political institutions and parties was the lowest on the continent (Latinobarómetro 2017: 25–27). None of this, of course, can be tracked to specific news items or events, since the barrage of information on corruption dominated the political news throughout 2015 and 2016.

Rather, the first goal here is to map out the evolution of media attention (operationalized as news items) to the various national corruption cases (defined below). Second, this content analysis might detect feedback patterns in the coverage of particular cases, where coverage heaps up, drawing away resources and attention to other cases. To construct the content analysis, I will first define a corpus of texts, and argue for the validity and utility of this particular sampling of the Brazilian media system.

Sampled Media Outlets

Corruption is a topic being dealt with across a totality of interlocking media discourses, which are fluid and engage in never-ending intertextual dialogue, and so the analysis of the national media agenda is in principle an almost infinite endeavor. However, given the extant knowledge of information distribution and vertical integration in Brazil, summarized in the second chapter, we know that the media system is quite concentrated (Cabral 2017, Lima 2004, Matos 2008), and that a few newsrooms drive the media agenda. In the above-mentioned content analysis research designs, the authors similarly constructed representative samples of the national media agenda (e.g., Boydstun 2013: 82). In Boydstun's study, the outlet sampled was picked out to be exemplary, representative, and a driver of the national media agenda. Along the same lines, I will argue that it is methodologically sound to narrow the research object by sampling from only three media outlets.

First off, due to the vertical integration of media outlets, there are only a few newspaper and broadcasting network newsrooms covering the national political scene. These newsrooms distribute information through their associated networks of news agencies and regional subsidiaries in radio, television, and print. Abramo showed that in the mid-2000s, 90 percent of agency-credited news originated with *Estado* and *Folha* (Abramo 2007: 99). Furthermore, as demonstrated in Chapter 3, the leaks of the Lava-Jato case largely appear in these two media outlets and in *Globo*, *Veja*, and *IstoÉ*. In other words, to detect a cascade of information about political corruption, we must begin with these news outlets.

The prestigious daily papers, in contrast to broadcast news and weekly magazines, are particular useful news platforms on which to gauge regular information distribution, because daily newspapers have dedicated (and, usually, fixed) space and resources to devote to political coverage. The newspapers report on politics every day, which might not be the case for, say, the evening news. Daily coverage of political issues gives a sense of the waxing and waning attention of the media. In this sense, broadcast news journals and weekly magazines are less reliable, because their selection criteria for inclusion are constrained in different ways than web and print media of the prestigious newspapers. TV news are limited to specific time slots, and will balance political news with other topics, thus giving incomplete pictures of politics on days where other issues crowd on the national agenda – sports, international terrorism, natural disasters, etc. Weekly magazines of Brazil are similarly constrained to a format in which a certain amount of items deal with political scandals. Across the duration of a week, daily newspapers may report on a variety of cases, whereas the political reporting (or scandal coverage, as it were) of the Brazilian weeklies are normally feature articles of some length with a single topic, often expanding the front page's framing of the most notable (or most scandalous) news item of that week.

In other words, for this part of the study, I leave out broadcast and weeklies, not because they do not matter, but because their particular formats filter the coverage of political matters much more tightly than do the newspaper format. Whereas the agenda of weeklies and televised news, on any given day, is negotiated between politics and other topics, this is not the case in the print and web news of the quality newspapers. In aggregating the landscape of news in the daily papers, we get a better sense of the relative weight of different corruption cases, including smaller cases that may eventually grow in importance, and avoid the methodological complication of media formats with stronger selection pressures, where political news competes with international news, sports, and other topical features.

Briefly stated, as a representative sample of the various news media of Brazil, I have picked out a few central media outlets and organizations (those that get the scoops and distribute news along their vertical networks of agencies and subsidiaries). Two sets of sampled data were collected: A sampling of front pages and a sampling of articles. The daily journals selected for front page sampling were *O Globo*, *Folha*, and *Estado de S. Paulo* – the three largest and most prestigious papers of Brazil. The headline samples provide an index of the salience of each corruption case on the national media agenda on a daily basis. If a corruption case is mentioned on one or more front page, there is a chance that it may also reach the news broadcasts. The article sampling, meanwhile, took both printed and web-publicized news items and opinion pieces from *Estado* and *Folha*, leaving out *O Globo* in order to avoid excess data redundancy.

This second sample provides an index of how attention to all cases of corruption was distributed by including the cases that did not make it to the front pages. The front-page count is inherently weighted, since only so many headlines can fit in a front page, while a sampling of all published articles of print and web face fewer restrictions. The print versions of quality newspapers, as pointed out above, normally have many pages dedicated to the coverage of politics, while their online versions face no restrictions inherent in the format. Thus, these kinds of media give a measure of the resources and attention given to scandals and investigations independent of other news of national or international importance.

The sample of articles includes articles published on the newspapers' online editions. With the increasing internet access rates across Brazil, and the increasing reliance of web media as sources for news, it would be unwise not to take online news outlets into account. The print news media and the regularly scheduled newscasts are no longer the first to arrive at the scene and report breaking news. Often, newsrooms will present a scoop or a breaking story online immediately, gradually building up some commentary and perspective and printing some of it on the following day, along with a report of the event. When examining disclosure of corruption, it is not infrequently the online news outlets that come into focus. Beyond that, it might also be relevant to consider how online news are mediated doubly – not only as a particular media format in itself, but also as content that may be more or less shareable on social media. For these reasons, I have also stored the available social media statistics published on the media outlets content pages, although such statistics comes with their own methodological problems.

Let me briefly summarize this section: In addition to the front pages of the three national newspapers, I opted to collect both web and print versions of news items on corruption from *Estado* and *Folha* in a single SQL database structure with various metadata and a coding of the issues being reported. The database is one of two results of an archiving strategy, with the other result being a full-text collection of the article content. As the web constantly changes, it was necessary to fixate the texts of the corpus. Therefore, on a daily basis, I collected all textual material pertaining to Brazilian corruption cases publicized in the two media outlets. I did so by checking each of the index sites listing the whole range of political news items, and cross-checked with the print versions of the same outlets. From these lists of publicized online material, I selected each and every one relating to political corruption and downloaded the whole text while also noting down a range of metadata. In a few instances, the news item had a steadily developing form (such as live updated material from votes in Congress or STF), and in those cases, I copied the material after the final update, usually between 3 and 24 hours after the last update.

Sampled News Items

The problems of defining corruption conclusively have consequences for the ways in which one can operationalize "information about corruption" in a research design dealing with media texts. Understanding corruption as a framed and constructed object, it becomes problematic to use legal definitions as the yard-stick for determining what is and what is not corruption. Linguistic criteria could then be imagined; i.e., including all news items that contain synonyms for corruption, fraud, etc. Both of these criteria fall short, however, because news items are not necessarily dealing with corruption explicitly (as in the swimming pool example above) but may merely imply this assessment of political actions by connotation or association through framings that emerge intertextually.

Therefore, I opted to study the research object "media texts with information about corruption" from a minimalist and heuristic definition: Information about corruption can be found in political news items that have, as primary cause of their newsworthiness, a possible political transgression. It is, admittedly, almost tautological to define corruption news as news items treating corruption as the newsworthy object. However, this definition eliminates news items about other issues that merely mention corruption in passing. Meanwhile, the "aboutness" criterion is not a tautology, but a pragmatic identifier, and this criterion is implied in the definition when pointing to the cause of newsworthiness. This is the crucial part: If a news item is newsworthy because the events described are said to be caused by (or intertextually linked to) a political transgression (alleged or actual), then it should be included in the sample. In other words, the inclusion criterion requires that the primary issue of the news item is "corruption."

It is certainly not a perfect definition, because some kinds of news items can slip through the cracks. When, say, Congressional debates are paralyzed because of corruption allegations, a news item reporting on this fact would count as a news item about corruption, while coverage of Congress debates merely mentioning corruption allegations would not be included – although both could be construed by audiences as containing signals about corruption.

In a few cases, news items have been left out which could arguably have been included. In general, I included all articles covering political corruption or corruption in state companies (since these have politically appointed executive officers), as well as all articles treating or discussing alleged improper economic or political conduct of the President, ex-presidents, ministers or ex-ministers, since these articles are partly overlapping thematically (see the discussion regarding the problem of fluid corruption definitions above). This means that the articles concerning impeachment petitions were included, though they in many cases do not deal with corruption per se, but certainly deal with perceived illicit political actions. This inclusion was fortunate, because it allows for comparisons between the most visible political topics of the sampled period – impeachment and the Lava-Jato case.

However, I excluded articles about corruption in national and international football associations, as well as articles about the train cartel of São Paulo, as that case was running out of steam and went on to disappear totally from the media agenda. Articles about ex-president Fernando Henrique Cardoso's mistress were also excluded, as the framing in most of these articles (whatever the population in general may think) did not cast the Cardoso case as corruption, but as extra-marital activity, making it scandalous for sexual-moral reasons rather than for public-office moral reasons.

Leaving aside those caveats, I have deployed the definition given and kept track of the various corruption cases and their spin-off probes, identifying news items related to these cases and the politicians under scrutiny. Many of the cases have already been described in the previous chapters, while this chapter provides insights into the general distribution of media attention, albeit only with an approximation of the aggregate universe of media discourse.

Sampling Period

In the front-page sample, the headlines of the three daily papers were collected for six months leading up to the vote of the Câmara, on April 17, 2016, approving the removal of Dilma Rousseff as president. The database of all news items on Brazilian political corruption in *Estado* and *Folha* encompasses a slightly longer period, until May 12, 2016, the date when the Senate approved the removal and Michel Temer assumed the presidency. In both samples, the sampling period starts in October 2015. The events of the sampled period were crucial in setting up the political outcome of the impeachment process, as momentum gathered in favor of ousting the president. Specifically, this was the period in which the impeachment petition that eventually was the cornerstone of the impeachment proceedings was handed in, but also the moment where the Lava-Jato investigations reached the critical phases of denouncing top politicians, including Lula and Cunha. The period is therefore interesting because it is the period of converging scandals – the stories of political corruption and potential removal of the head of state intertwine in this period throughout the media sphere. The theme of impeachment first appeared as a serious possibility in the selected media outlets during this period, and the political consequences of the Lava-Jato investigations are only manifested from this period onward, with the initiation of the disciplinary process against Eduardo Cunha. Impeachment had been mentioned at distinct moments before this period – most notably immediately after the elections and in February and March 2015 – but the onset of this topic as a common front-page topic can be dated to October 2015.

The total sample amounts to 1,335 headlines concerning corruption cases and 8,200 news items in the database of articles. The database and the tally of headlines and topics are available online, at the time of writing, at the University of Copenhagen's Centre for Latin American Studies site (www.clas.hum.ku.dk/research).

Cascading Corruption News: A Content Analysis

In this section, I will present the findings of the content analysis of sampled articles and front-page headlines dealing with corruption. This is done first diachronically, to illustrate how news media built up the informational cascade, and then synchronically, showing how the total coverage appeared across the sample period. By aggregating the frequency of news items, I can demonstrate how news on certain cases was largely disregarded in the total coverage of political corruption. The coding of issues in the content analysis, as discussed above, is based upon the attribution of responsibility, or, if no transgressive actor appears, the investigation. Because all different cases and the denounced actors were coded in this sample, it allows for relatively fine-grained analysis of media attention.

The sample period had a few lulls, with days with only one or two headlines dealing with political corruption, but during most of the sampled weeks, the national newspapers ran two or three front-page headlines daily and many articles about the Lava-Jato investigations, impeachment proceedings, or other cases of political corruption. During the period, corruption or other forms of political transgression were attributed to dozens of political actors in the 188 distinct cases identified. At the beginning of the sample period, in October 2015, the headlines and articles treated a diverse range of corruption subjects: Lula, Cunha, the CPI of Petrobras, as well as the case of the *pedaladas* and the TCU decision to reject the accounts of the state (see next chapter). However, the diversity was gradually reduced, as only a few cases, which have been described in the previous chapters, attracted sustained attention in the sampled outlets.

The news items and front-page headlines presented in Figure 5.3 deal with Eduardo Cunha, then president of the Câmara, the various inquiries of the Lava-Jato investigations targeting him, as well as his maneuvers in the Conselho da Ética to avoid being removed from office. Though Cunha's house and offices were searched by police agents in mid-December, and the PGR requested his removal the following day, the headlines of the week before Christmas mostly focused on the debate of the STF regarding the regulations for conducting an eventual impeachment. The holidays and January 2016 had declining attention to all corruption news, including the impeachment and Cunha's cases. A few

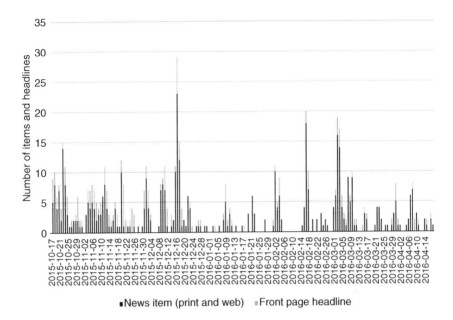

News item (print and web) ■ Front page headline

Figure 5.3 Number of headlines and news items on Eduardo Cunha's corruption cases.

peaks of attention to Cunha's cases are present from January until he conducted the impeachment vote of the Câmara in March. These peaks appear on the dates where his (first) trial was on the STF agenda (February 16 and March 3). News dealing with Cunha's corruption cases had been increasingly infrequent since the PGR requested his removal on December 16, 2015. After the impeachment vote, Cunha was temporarily removed from the position of president of the Câmara in consequence of his ongoing corruption trial, and this generated 76 articles (mostly web-based) the following day in *Folha* and *Estado*.

While news attention to Eduardo Cunha remained mostly steady during the period, news on Lula's corruption cases eventually eclipsed news concerning Cunha, starting at the turn of the year. Events related to Lula commanded the attention of the media at several moments (see the previous chapter for details). Figure 5.4 demonstrates the frequency of news items, broken down into six of these cases, as well as the frequency of headlines. In October 2015, the part of the Zelotes investigation related to Lula was made public. In November, the arrest of his acquaintance, the cattle king José Carlos Bumlai, drew headlines. In the last week of January and all of February, attention increased steadily to the two real estate cases (the ranch in Atibaia and the beachside triplex in Guarujá). In early March, the media focus on these cases dovetailed with the breaking news of Lula's testimony in the Lava-Jato case, Lula's indictment by the São Paulo state prosecutors, and, after two months of scandal coverage, his ultimately unsuccessful nomination for minister. The increasing media attention to

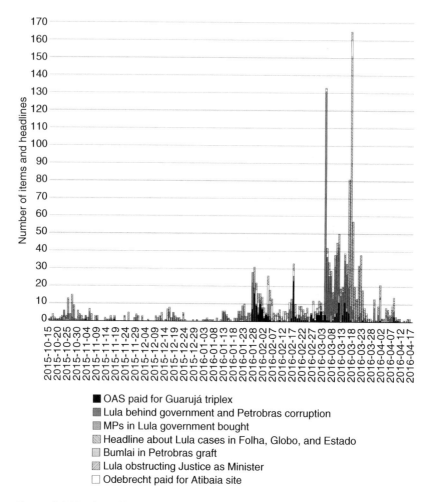

Figure 5.4 Number of headlines and news items on Lula's corruption cases.

Lula's cases (and activity in the investigations) also coincided with the great street protests of 2016, which I return to below.

Figure 5.5 shows the 1,176 headlines concerning the main actors of Brazilian politics that were sampled in the six-month period from October 2015 to April 2016. In the same period, 150 other headlines dealt with corruption allegations or probes against other actors (governors, the vice-president, senators, and mayors foremost among these). The company most frequently denounced for corruption in the headlines is Odebrecht, but this is not anywhere as frequent as news items on the corruption of politicians.

As discussed in the methodological sections of this chapter, the information flows leading to cascades must be understood as dynamic phenomena. This

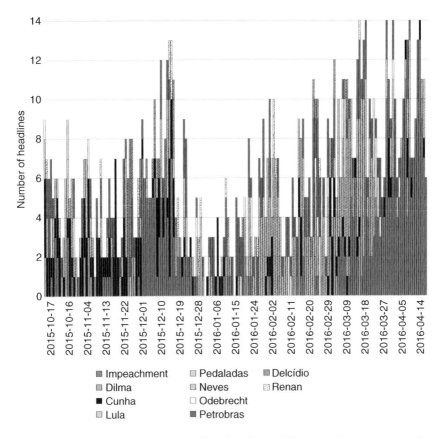

Figure 5.5 Number of front-page headlines in *Globo*, *Folha*, and *Estado* on corruption cases.

means that when signals are amplified, other signals may be attenuated and eventually lost in the din, as this graph of the most covered corruption cases demonstrates The attention to Lula and Cunha continued into November, with a spike of attention as the PT senator Delcídio de Amaral was also arrested in the Lava-Jato probe, followed by peaks of media interest in the first half of December, when Cunha signaled the start of the impeachment process. October and November's variety of signals about corruption was drowned out in early 2016 as the newspapers dedicated their attention to cases of Lula. The Carnival and the zika virus attracted attention in February, which meant that the front pages had a brief lull in attention to corruption. On March 4, 2016, the graph demonstrates that as Lula was taken to testify in São Paulo airport and the marketing expert of Rousseff was arrested, the intensity of media attention to corruption increased and, shortly thereafter, decisively shifted the focus toward the question of impeachment.

The pivotal point of Figure 5.5 is the days following the leak of recorded conversations with Lula, on March 16, where Lula's cases began to be overtaken by headlines dealing with the impeachment. From that point on, impeachment news gathered speed and grew tremendously, dwarfing and eventually (in May) completely suppressing other news about politics and corruption.

Frequency of Corruption News Items across the Sample

Looking at the total sample of news items from the printed and online versions of *Folha* and *Estado*, it is apparent how the impeachment process and the corruption cases of Cunha and Lula were massively exposed. In comparison, news

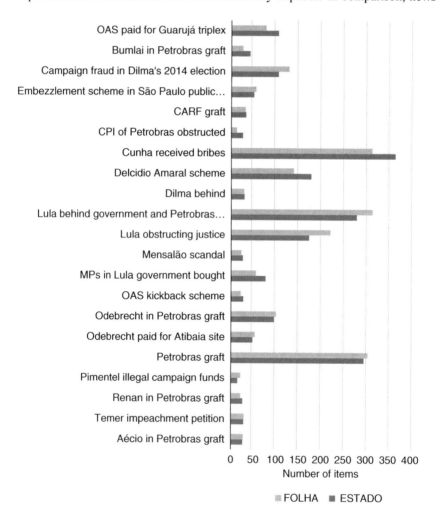

Figure 5.6 Comparison of number of news items on corruption cases between *Folha* and *Estado*.

items on other investigated politicians (both opposition and the erstwhile-government partner PMDB that jumped ship) were few and far between. The following graph shows the frequency of the most reported topics (with more than 30 news items in total) besides news on the impeachment. The impeachment was covered in 1,651 news items in *Estado*, while *Folha* publicized 1,727 news items in the sample period from October 15, 2015, until the ousting of Rousseff on May 12, 2016. Between *Folha* and *Estado*, there is very little variation in the relative distribution of attention to the range of corruption cases:

Apart from the 3,378 news items concerning impeachment proceedings (left out in the graph), the most covered cases were the various investigations of Lula (with a total of 261 front-page headlines and 1,507 news items across six cases) and the PT senator Delcídio do Amaral (320 news items in total). The only story that rivaled those about the PT was the complex story of Eduardo Cunha's disciplinary process and various corruption investigations (675 news items and 160 front-page headlines). News about corruption in Petrobras in general, most frequently mentioning PT and/or PMDB with no specific politicians associated, reached 600 in the sample period. Items concerning Dilma Rousseff's involvement in the Petrobras graft and laundered money from the Petrobras scheme feeding her 2014 campaign reached more than 290 items in total, while impeachment news items numbered more than ten times that figure (3,378) in the two news outlets.

This intense focus on these four persons (Rousseff, Lula, Cunha, and Delcídio) outshone by a considerable margin the attention to the rest of the investigated politicians. At the top of the second tier, the president of the Senate, Renan Calheiros, was the focus of 60-some news items (summing news items on several cases), just ahead of Aécio Neves. While Neves was only subjected to formal investigations later in the Lava-Jato probe (outside of the sample period), Calheiros accumulated investigations in 12 different instances in the period. The alleged corruption of other central politicians (such as the senators Romero Jucá of PMDB and Antônio Anastasia of PSDB) was not even half as frequent a topic as news on Calheiros and Neves. Like the once-impeached president, now senator, Fernando Collor de Mello, these third-tier politicians were the objects of fewer than 25 news items each in total across the two news outlets. Meanwhile, the sons of ex-president Lula (Luís Claudio and Fabio Luís) were mentioned in more than 50 news items about political corruption, in spite of the fact that neither of them ever ran for public office.

In relative terms, the attention to the impeachment of Dilma Rousseff and her possible relation to the Petrobras graft outsized all news topics concerning corruption. For instance, the ousting of the president was covered five times as often as the investigation of the president of the Câmara, and impeachment was covered 11 times as often as the case of the senator Delcídio do Amaral. The relative weight of corruption news between news on Rousseff and Neves can be expressed in the ratio 73:1, while the ratio between news on Lula and Neves was 32:1, and Cunha relative to Neves 15:1. News on corruption probes into PMDB senators like Romero Jucá (later to take office as Minister of Planning and

Budgets) and Valdir Raupp were almost lost, about 500:1 in relation to impeachment news, and about 250:1 relative to news on Lula's corruption cases.

The former PT minister José Dirceu and the former PT treasurer João Vaccari Neto were both on trial in the sample period. Both were objects of several headlines, and their trials were the topic of 70 and 32 articles, respectively, reporting on several cases.[2] This added to the general directionality of the cascade: That PT was behind the corruption in the oil company.

Frequency of Corruption News Headlines in the Sampled Front Pages

On the front pages in the sample period, a similar pattern was evident. The table below presents the frequencies of the most frequent cases in the headlines, including headlines and front-page items which cover corruption in Petrobras in general without responsibility attributed to specific political actors. The issues of impeachment and fiscal delays (*pedaladas*, described in the next chapter) are separated from other headlines that cover Dilma Rousseff's alleged corruption.

Like in the sample universe of articles in print and web media, the headlines demonstrate a PT-centric focus of the front-page space of *Estado*, *Folha*, and *O Globo*. As was the case in the article sample, only Cunha had a visibility close to Rousseff and Lula, though, as the impeachment proceeded, not nearly rivaling it. Apart from the above-mentioned actors, the most-mentioned corruption cases of the headlines included an embezzlement scheme in São Paulo public schools apparently run out of the state assembly (12 headlines), the trial of José Dirceu (19 headlines), the improbable but still newsworthy potential probes into the ex-president Fernando Henrique Cardoso (5 headlines), as well as several of Lula's ex-ministers.

Michel Temer, before taking over the presidency, was mentioned in five headlines in relation to corruption cases in the sample period. Temer, furthermore, was mentioned twice in headlines concerning the electoral court process determining the validity of the 2014 campaign, and twice in relation to the stalled processes of impeachment petitions requesting his removal from office. Despite many testimonies mentioning Temer and PMDB leaders, media attention only shifted toward them as the party grabbed influential cabinet positions following Temer's ascendancy. That attention had effects, however: Within 34 days of Temer seizing power, three ministers had stepped down (see Chapter 3).

In the chronological analysis, it is clear that the prestigious Brazilian media outlets, across the board of the political beat and on various platforms, developed

Table 5.1 Number of front-page headlines in *Globo*, *Folha*, and *Estado* on corruption cases

327	61	33	261	206	160	48	43	22	15
Impeachment	Dilma	Pedaladas	Lula	Petrobras	Cunha	Odebrecht	Delcídio	Calheiros	Neves

an increasingly narrow focus in the sample period. Even after the PGR requested the STF to have Cunha removed, the news media tended to devote less and less attention to the president of the Câmara while he orchestrated the process of impeachment, eventually commanding the session of the vote. Other political actors denounced for corruption were intermittently present on the agenda, but never for long. The only political actor that received sustained attention until right before the impeachment of Rousseff was Lula. While the leak of Lula's conversation and the coverage of his testimony presented Lula as the key political actor under fire, the coalition parties of the government signaled that they would jump ship, like Cunha and PMDB, and vote for the impeachment. This would allow Temer to form a new cabinet with the center-right parties. The diachronic analysis, meanwhile, shows that the corruption cases involving exactly these actors had only been covered fleetingly by the sampled media outlets.

These findings prompt the following question: Why did the newsrooms of the large media organizations prioritize the news items as they did, placing the spotlight on the impeachment process and denying agenda space to reporting on corruption with the political parties coming into power? The findings of the content analysis above, naturally, cannot explain the editorial selection processes nor the information gathering or leaking that preceded editorial choices. To understand organizational conditions that determine informational cascades of scandals such as the Lava-Jato and the impeachment of Dilma Rousseff, I will discuss two information phenomena found in the media: the selective recycling of information and overvaluation of information about corruption. Both are information selection pressures that became crucial for ousting Rousseff, as well as legitimizing her impeachment. Before doing so, I will consider the organizational environment of media scandals and market pressures that may have contributed to the emergence of these information phenomena.

The Attention Economy and Investment of Media Actors

The environment of "big media" – such as the prestigious Brazilian newspapers and the top broadcasting networks – is an economy of attention, and a highly important measure of the success of each media outlet is audience outreach. Maximization of the audience by way of attracting attention is the central logic or imperative of such media (Landerer 2013). Once information from corruption investigations has been disclosed to journalists, the leak enters into a special economy of attention inside the newsrooms: A scandal, to editors, represent an attention-grabbing pool of different stories that can be mined continuously with a certain amount of recycled information. Therefore, dedicating manpower to a scandal is a relatively cheap investment compared to the number of stories it can yield (Beale 2006: 401). That editors work with this continuous mining of corruption cases for information and new spin-off news is clearly visible in the graphs presented above.

Furthermore, as scandals usually beg the question, "did somebody else know this?" it is easy to escalate the scandal to other governmental actors or to a national level, if locally contained. Such an escalation holds the promise of a greater potential audience. Thus, scandals tend to inflate enormously in terms of space and attention, but in some cases only ephemerally – what Vasterman has termed *hype cycles* (Vasterman 2005, Wien and Elmelund-Præstekær 2009).

Corruption scandals involving national politics are prime news material that checks all news value boxes, meaning a potentially nation-wide audience. So, in terms of audience, the newspaper with a scandalous headline is assumed to sell more, meaning more advertising revenue. It is therefore of utmost interest to competing media organizations to break such news before competitors, as this will give the organization with the scoop the upper hand in relation to sales, clicks, and views. In a situation of stagnant or dropping audiences, if advertising is central to the business case of the newspaper or network, then scandals will especially be in demand. Dropping audiences, common to the majority of print media systems today, also threatens media industry of Brazil. Like the editors, media owners and shareholders thus have a weighty incentive to invest in scandals, although in their cases it is actual financial investments that are at stake in this economy of attention.

To editors as well as owners, the question of sources, credibility, and individual professional careers is usually of less concern than it is to the journalists. Journalists, on the other hand, invest time, reputation and goodwill from their sources in bringing new aspects of the scandal to the table. What they potentially gain from this is of course professional status, and the perks that come with it. What they might lose, in the case of false allegations, is the trust of their sources, access to corridor talk and a dent in their professional image. Various techniques are used to write up news items deriving from information in corruption cases so as to protect journalists from status loss.

Principally, the risk-free asset of the scandal is the well-researched and objective news item. Unfortunately for normative theories of the public sphere, there is a number of ways in which the journalist might jump the gun, overstate the case, trust an untrustworthy source, or frame the issue beyond fairness. This constitutes a risky investment of credibility in such a less-than-optimal news construction (Liebes and Blum-Kalka 2004: 1154ff.). In some media systems, of course, the repercussions may be minor, either to the media outlet that can wash the hands by firing the reporter and hiring another journalist, or to the reporter him- or herself who might weather a few months of bad standing with the powerful, as long as the position, payroll, and byline is still secure. Sources that blow the whistle have even more to lose, no matter if their story catches on or not.

The short-term investment of covering scandals holds a potentially very large promise of returns for the journalist. Since the Watergate case, the idea of the investigative journalist that brings about the downfall of a president has hovered as the fixed star of the journalistic profession (Schudson 2004: 1234). The ideal incorporates within it the notions of the media as the fourth estate, media as the watchdog of society, and the guardian of public truth. Scandals, when they have political repercussions, confirm this idealized role of the journalist. The ideal of unmasking power also leads to many frenzy-like situations, barrage-questioning politicians and corporate bosses in full run, in the hope that the stellar exposés written by one heroic journalistic protagonist may secure democracy, along with Pulitzer prizes.

In most media systems, legal frameworks exist to govern and guard against slander, unfounded allegations and fanciful denunciations. However, the worth of a scandal, in terms of sold copies and air-time, may very well surpass the cost of a lawsuit to the newspaper or broadcasting network. Especially in cases where evidence is sparse, but likely to trigger formal investigations, the investment in the scandal promises great returns. Thus, editors with economic incentives and journalists with ideological and prestige-oriented incentives constitute the two intertwined sets of actors in a media system that combine to produce the bandwagon behavior: Cascades of news items that take their cue from one another lead to a circular orientation to the original allegation of the scandal (which may or may not be true). The cascade may in turn feed into the decisions of other actors (say, in the political system), and eventually media bandwagon effects may emerge across an entire media system: Everybody wants a piece of the action and therefore needs to join the fray, truth be damned, if nothing else then just to cover the resonance of the media hype. The bandwagon effect generated by media covering media, results in a feedback loop and more amplification, magnification, and stimulation of coverage (Vasterman 2005: 511).

The Centripetal Recycling of News

At the systemic or organizational level, the vertical ties between Brazilian media outlets are likely to amplify a cascade, which results in the reproduction of certain information and the tendency to ignore other events. As mentioned before, Brazilian news media are organized in a few powerful conglomerates, with much vertical as well as horizontal integration between different regional outlets and different media types. A few newsrooms control the gates of the political system, and the information admitted through these gates propagates through networks of news agencies and inter-media shoveling (Paterson and Domingo 2008).

The incipient research field of gatekeeping in digital media spheres furthermore suggests that when news dissemination moves online, fewer news gatekeepers become more influential than before (Bro and Wallberg 2015, Welbers et al. 2018). In a vertically integrated media system like Brazil, where only a few news agencies distribute most of the news (Aguiar 2014: 55), the fragmentation and multiplication of online news sources has its counterweight in this inwards spiral of attention of news media. Fewer issues, touching only selected societal bases, stay on the agenda of mainstream media for longer periods and are replicated by online news media, whether associated or independent. The centripetal pattern of shutting out minor news issues and focusing intensely on nation-shaking crisis news was evident in the Lava-Jato case online as well as offline.

The selective recycling of only a handful of corruption cases – in a scandal that seems to have capillaries reaching almost every corner of Congress and most state governor seats – is a democratic problem. The mainstream media, *Folha*, *Estado*, and Grupo Globo and their affiliated media groups downstream, in particular, have been accused of an ideological slant. The charges of anti-PT bias might be true in some individual instances, most evidently in the weekly magazines, but the problem of recycling information about a not-representative portion of the corruption cases might also be a systemic problem:

> the mostly noble intentions of journalists can result in a media agenda that is far from most normative ideals. These noble intentions get filtered through a complicated system of organizational and marketplace incentives and disproportionate information processing. As a result, such intentions are not always reflected in the news and its patterns.
>
> (Boydstun 2013: 209)

A major marketplace incentive is the audience profiling of newspapers and the resurgence of the party press strategy mentioned in the second chapter (Lattman-Weltman and Chagas 2016). The disproportionality introduced by the media system integration and the newsrooms responding and to scoops of other newsrooms by recycling the scoops and then covering the same item from other angles is another filtering effect behind the recycling.

Finally, the group-think mentality of editors in scandals may be caused by the fact that the news values of a scandal story are usually given an equal assessment by editors, leading them to locate the stories at the same level of importance in newspapers or in newscasts. This is a pattern generally found (Shoemaker and Vos 2009: 52) – the most prominent news items are reported in essentially the same way – and it is especially true for Brazilian mainstream media reporting on scandal cases. The observation that certain events, dealing with political corruption at the national level, are unanimously considered "good news," leads me to the problem of overvaluation: When the assessment of news values is distorted by bandwagon effects among editors and cascade effects between media outlets, democracy cannot rely on media as producer of accountability. In the following section, I will explore the notion of value of information in news media.

Value of Information and Overvaluation

The information flow of a scandal involves not just disclosure of information, but also the anticipation of value, and the a priori realization of this value. This flow is shared between media and the political system, broadly speaking. By value, I designate the possible usage of some information in accountability processes, such as the various judicial actions mentioned in the previous chapter. This usage is obviously political in nature, but is reflected and shaped by the media.

What I term value here goes beyond the usual sense of "news values" in the literature (a classic term, see Galtung and Ruge 1965). News values "reflect ideologies and priorities held in society" (Bell 1991: 156), and are thus not neutral constructs outside of the particular journalists and editors who decide to include or exclude information. Rather, the attribution of value varies contextually. In corruption news, the factors for determining value include the relevance of disclosed information to institutional processes or accountability processes (what can be included, what will count as evidence, etc.), and the eventual trajectory of the processes triggered by disclosure (what is the ultimate outcome, e.g., how much damage can disclosed information inflict on the careers of the denounced?). This is linked to the ideal of watchdog journalism discussed in the sections above. The potential repercussions of a scandal are also determining factors in the editorial processes and the redissemination after publication; editors need to prioritize what disclosed information merits a follow-up story, and consider what will likely be retweeted, liked, and shared, etc. All of these questions are strongly oriented to the future horizon of political and public action. In other words: An information, as element in the scandal, is only as interesting as its potential political value. This value derives from its disruptive potential, but more importantly, the value is relative to the perceived center of political agency.

The proximity to perceived centers of power is an important factor in determining what information will be transmitted in mainstream media's information flow. It is common to the news criteria of most national media systems to value coverage of power-holders, although certain positions of power might be excluded from scrutiny (Thompson 2005: 43). News production in national politics is strongly centralized, and this is mirrored in the allocation of journalistic attention: "in a presidential system[,] media tend to reinforce the emphasis on the administrative aspects of government, rather than on party politics" (Albuquerque 2012: 91). With unclear party lines, indistinguishable ideological stances between parties, and heterogeneous government coalitions, political agency is often made a matter of persons rather than parties – and the person of the president is viewed as the central political force, dwarfing party leaders and governors. Thus, the presidential political system also influences the relative value of news items concerning political actors.

Media attention to information is thus modulated by the perceived potential value of that information, just like in markets of other assets. Unlike most tradeable assets, however, information does not lose value by being copied. On the contrary, in scandals, given greater attention, the dissemination of the original scandal will instead create increased demand for new information on the topic. This feedback structure of information demand in scandals is essential to creating the conditions for a bubble-like situation, where certain information is valued greatly and other information that would normally be of public interest, is systematically undervalued.

Following the impeachment and successive indictments of the PMDB politicians and Michel Temer, it is obvious that the usage value of information is neither necessarily nor sufficiently determined by its belonging to categories of misinformation or disinformation. Disinformation and misinformation, even when understood to be such, might still have scathing potential. Therefore, in scandals, verifiably true information is not guaranteed to be as interesting and therefore demanded as disinformation or misinformation. Rather, assumptions of value are based on the potential impact of the news, and this impact is partly determined by the position of the denounced actor. These assumptions play out somewhat like speculation on a stock market, where actors move resources in expectation of future returns. In the same way, the anticipation of the value of information is part and parcel of how media operates in scandals.

Interpreting the editorial selection processes of Brazil in these terms, we may imagine that journalistic production dealing with the impeachment of Dilma Rousseff was in high demand by editors because this process was perceived to actually produce consequences and likely to change the political landscape. Meanwhile, the processes which stalled (e.g., legal actions against PMDB leaders and the ex-president Collor) were less in demand, as they were either perceived or actively framed to be dead-end stories, with no likely consequences and little relation to the center of power.

The same reasoning could be used to explain the apparent contradictory over-valuation of news items on Lula's corruption cases: Although Lula was not in public office, the fact that he was considered a likely presidential candidate in 2018 made his trials much more interesting than any other part of the Lava-Jato investigations. The disruptive potential, as described in the previous chapter, of denying Lula the possibility of running for president, would have considerable consequences for all parts of the political spectrum. Although other ex-presidents – Collor, Cardoso, and Sarney – were also implicated by testimonies, denying Lula's political agency in 2018 would have much more impact. Thus, despite allegations against Cardoso, the PGR requesting Sarney's arrest and indicting Collor, it was Lula's sentence in 2017 that came to be framed as "historical."

Further Stages of the Informational Cascade

Having discussed the intra-media stages of the information flows in the Lava-Jato and impeachment scandals, I now turn to a number of societal spheres where disclosed information trickled down and influenced collective behavior and decision-making processes. The particular cases analyzed in the previous chapter demonstrated that news on corruption in the media may activate various accountability mechanisms, but the activation of institutionalized accountability processes usually requires sustained media scrutiny, and various political influences may obstruct accountability processes. The cascade of information documented in this chapter, meanwhile, may trickle down in other contexts and dimensions of the public sphere than accountability processes. The dimension of electoral accountability cannot be directly connected to the scandals of 2015–2017, due to the electoral cycle of Brazil (and the fact that Brazil is anyway a country with limited electoral accountability; see the previous chapter). However, I have picked out several examples that may illustrate the ramifications of the media's informational cascade in other contexts.

The assumption of this section is that media attention is correlated (and maybe causally related) to other spheres where information is valued, and that the media agenda may drive the processes of information flows there. I will briefly review four such spheres, using four secondary sources of data, to establish how and to which extent the information emerging in the Lava-Jato scandal reached Brazilian publics. In each of these spheres, information pathologies may arise.

First, while collecting metadata of the sampled news items, the social media statistics of each web-published article were also harvested (where available). Such data gives a glimpse into the afterlife of online news items; usually ephemeral, but in some cases brightly flaring. While the most scathing leaks and allegations obviously get attention by social media users, that attention is not consistently reflected in editorial decisions of follow-up stories. The inconsistency of editorial selection and audience sharing of news speaks volumes concerning the uptake and viral potential of news items on specific political actors. Second, as several public opinion institutes regularly conduct surveys in Brazil, the impact of corruption news upon approval ratings, audience perceptions of societal problems, and the political agenda can be explored. Third, the fluctuations of the stock markets of Brazil provide yet another set of interesting data. The concept of information flows seems particularly apt when noticing how smoothly and rapidly information disclosed and leaked to the media was fed into the financial and monetary flows of the Brazilian and international finance market. Events on the political scene deemed important in the media triggered immediate reactions from actors on the financial markets, and those steps of the cascade sequence were visible in aggregated financial indicators, such as stock markets and exchange rates. Finally, since social mobilization and political participation is linked to the (social) media agenda (Boulianne 2015), it is reasonable to compare the sampled coverage of corruption to the street protests occurring in the sample period.

Social Media

While collecting metadata of news items, I also collected the social media statistics of each article provided by embedded widgets on the news site (where available). This is a data source that needs to be treated with reservations in order to generalize, because the online audience of each of the prestigious newspapers sampled is not at all representative of Brazil in general. But the distribution of likes and shares certainly does provide some hints as to which corruption cases attracted the most (or the least) amount of attention on a short-term basis. Because the data provided by the media platforms regarding social media distribution continuously varies for each article, the data is rather unreliable: Likes are retracted, profiles are deleted, and the scripts of the embedded widgets on the news sites are developed and changed without any transparency to the researcher. Furthermore, script errors and deliberate manipulation of bots can introduce false data or manipulate the counters.

The most shared news item in the sample period on *Folha*'s website, from October 25, 2015, revealed that Lula's son was being investigated in the Zelotes investigation. This item was shared 293,000 times, according to the embedded counting script. That this item should be top-ranked seems plausible, since this was the first news item in *Folha* directly associating Lula's family to corruption – albeit not the last. The most shared news item in the sample period on *Estado*'s site *Estadão* was an item published on November 11, 2015, reporting on ex-STF judge Joaquim Barbosa (the judge rapporteur of the Mensalão case). In the article, Barbosa commented on the situation of Petrobras, foreseeing Brazil's "humiliation" in the legal processes running in the legal system of the US. This item was shared 132,300 times according to the counter.

Among the top-ten shared news items of both outlets, there is surprising diversity: One denunciation of Aécio Neves' corruption reached 42,100 shares on *Estadão*, while *Folha* had two reports, dealing with two other denunciations implicating Neves, that reached 110,000 and 87,000 shares. *Estadão*'s other most-shared items dealt with Cunha's cases (two items reaching around 40,000 shares) and Lula (55,000 shares of another article in the Zelotes case). An *Estadão* item about the hostile reactions to Neves and São Paulo governor Geraldo Alckmin during street protests in March reached almost 59,000 shares. Apart from Neves' and Lula's cases, the most shared items of *Folha*'s site in the sample period detailed two other inquiries targeting PSDB (Alckmin and the late national president of the party, Sérgio Guerra), both items reaching 93,000 shares. Outside of the sampling period, other breaking news on *Folha*'s site dealing with arrests (of PT leaders such as Dirceu and Vaccari Neto) reached around 60,000 shares. Many other politically intense moments in the sample period were described in series of articles, which would likely divide the frequency of shares among several news items, meaning that these moments are not visible as outliers in the dataset on the parameter of social media shares.

Despite the attention of social media users, the three cases relating to Neves and the two other cases linking PSDB to political corruption did not become objects of more front-page news and little investigative journalism afterwards. These stories are one-shot items on the graphs presented in the previous sections, in contrast to the sustained media attention to Lula. Somehow, the social media interest did not translate into editorial prioritization of these sub-scandals emerging from the Lava-Jato investigations. The data cannot reveal whether this is due to political bias in newsrooms, or the sub-politics of information flows and source relations in the accountability institutions, but it is nonetheless significant that some storylines which gained much traction online were promptly disregarded in the media.

Public Opinion Polls

Opinion and agenda polls registered a doubling of the amount of respondents that noticed and remembered negative news concerning the Brazilian government more than doubled in the six months following the 2014 elections. The survey respondents registering negative news about the Rousseff government reached 72 percent in March 2015, and that amount was steady in the following surveys (Indicadores CNI 2015a, 2015b). During the same period, President Dilma Rousseff's approval ratings in polls fell from around 50 percent during the 2014 elections, 40 percent around Christmas 2014, to 12–13 percent (Indicadores CNI 2016, Datafolha 2016b) in March 2015, to 8–10 percent in July–August 2015 (Datafolha showing the lower figure, surveyed in early August 2015; ibid., 14).

Government approval ratings for the months corresponding to the media sample presented here is very similar to the fluctuations of corruption news:

Baptista (2017) has demonstrated that the government approval ratings and surveys of trust in the Rousseff administration, in the various polls conducted during 2015 and 2016, correlated significantly with the negative coverage of corruption on the front pages of the weekly magazines – more negative news covariates with lower trust in government and lower approval ratings. The only moment where this was not true was immediately after the 2014 elections, when both approval ratings and negative coverage grew.

Reactions on the Stock Market

The stock market fluctuations to the political events in the sample period provide a third source of data, which could be interpreted as stages of an informational cascade. Specifically, the initiation of each step in the impeachment process

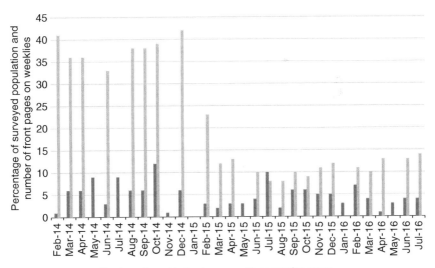

Figure 5.7 Approval ratings of government and coverage of scandals, 2014–2016.

Source: Baptista 2017.

triggered immediate reactions from actors on the financial markets, visible in aggregated financial indicators such as stock markets and exchange rates. Just like other actors observing the signals of the political events, traders and shareholders reacted to the publicly available signals: When news indicated impeachment of Rousseff as likely, Brazilian stocks increased in value, and inversely decreased in periods without news on the impeachment, because the Rousseff administration was depicted as unable to implement economic reforms. Although theoretically, the sudden concerted moves of shareholders scattered across the world could be mere correlation, I will argue that the events that gradually brought about the ousting of Dilma Rousseff, because they were internationally visible and of obvious consequence to the economic policies of Brazil, were in fact causing these fluctuations.

As an example, a spike in Brazilian stock value is visible on the day when the impeachment petition was accepted (December 3, 2015). The São Paulo stock market Bovespa rapidly reacted, breaking a steady decline, rising 3.29 percent on average within the day, with Petrobras preferred stock rising 6.12 percent and the Banco de Brazil leading with an 8.4 percent rise.

As the Supreme Court intervened in the impeachment process shortly thereafter, and it became clear that the initiation of proceedings would only take place after the Carnival, the Bovespa index fell into decline again (while the dollar-real exchange rate climbed). However, coinciding with news that heralded the impeachment of Rousseff (e.g., the imprisonment of Rousseff's marketing strategist João Santana on February 23, and new plea bargains alleging corruption in Rousseff's campaign on March 4), that trend was broken again.

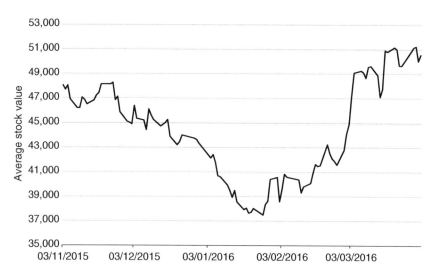

Figure 5.8 Bovespa index, November 2015–March 2016.

Source: BM&F-Bovespa 2018.

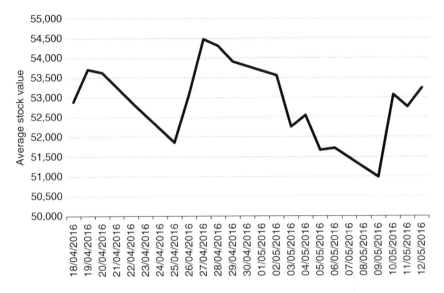

Figure 5.9 Bovespa index, April 18–May 12.
Source: BM&F-Bovespa 2018.

Zooming in on the last days of Dilma Rousseff's presidency, Figure 5.9 shows the Bovespa index from the day of the vote in the Câmara to the day of the vote in the Senate.

In response to the Câmara ratification, the Bovespa index rose with a brief interruption until April 27, continuing the trend of March and April. On the 28th, the Central Bank chose to maintain the interest rate at 14.25 percent and the market cooled off for a fortnight, only to rise again with the two-day debate in the Senate heralding the removal of Rousseff on May 12. The collective of actors known as "the stock market," in the aggregate, viewed the impeachment optimistically and responded positively to each step of the impeachment process.

The exchange rate between the Brazilian real and the US dollar also reflected the market activity and the possibility of impeachment. In Figure 5.9 the tendency is therefore the same (although graphically inverted): The real steadily lost value vis-à-vis the dollar throughout the second half of 2015, and only recuperated with the string of negative news for Rousseff that started in February and became plainly visible from March onward.

Not surprisingly, the actors of the stock market react on possibilities – in this case, on the possibility of impeachment, trying to buy stocks cheap before other actors realize that their value may increase after the impeachment. This explains the rapid spikes, rather than prolonged value increases, of the market: Short bursts of speculative activity and no real changes in the economic realities of Brazil, because the Congress stalled economic reform during the whole period while waiting for the impeachment.

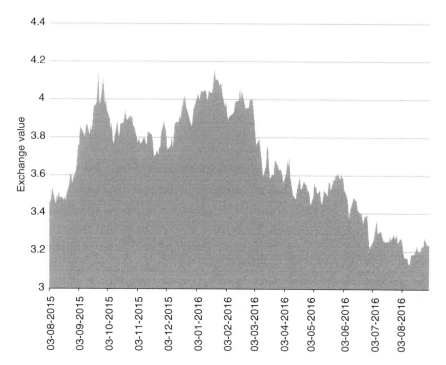

Figure 5.10 Exchange rates BR$–US$, August 2015–August 2016
Source: Banco Central do Brasil 2018.

The media system and the financial markets are linked empirically, but the underlying phenomenon of information value also links them theoretically: The value of (scandal) information on the media market, just like on the stock market, is anticipated (that is, potential) value.

Street Protests

Although the sample period of the media data presented here comprises seven months of coverage, it is worthwhile to consider both the street protests of the sample period and the period preceding it. Immediately after the presidential elections of 2014, right-wing groups voiced concern with the election result, and the leading opposition party PSDB filed several actions in the electoral court, as described in the preceding chapter. The same political spectrum, galvanized around three online movements, mobilized crowds for street protests during 2015 and until the vote of impeachment in the Câmara on April 17, 2016. While the mobilization of these protests and the size of the crowds are obviously not only related to the news on corruption, but determined by many factors, it is fair to assume that the degree of success in mobilizing large groups against political corruption would be influenced by news on exactly that topic. Therefore, I will venture a few observations concerning the relation between news on political corruption and the street-level support of the various protests in Brazil in 2015–2016. The majority of these were cast as anti-governmental, while a number of street rallies supported Dilma Rousseff and PT, denouncing the impeachment process as a coup d'état. The anti-government street protests were planned some time ahead, mostly by the same three groups Movimento Brasil Livre, VemPraRua and Revoltados Online (as well as minor participation by SOS Forças Armadas and the right-wing party Solidariedade) (Chaia et al. 2017: 9). Because of the identical organizational setup combined with the varying information flows of media, we can think of the news as the independent variable that, to some unverifiable extent, has influenced the dependent variable of street rally turnout.

In 2015, the largest protests took place on March 15 in a range of south-eastern Brazilian state capitals and larger cities. The figures reported for the number of participants varied wildly: While the organizing groups claimed that millions protested in total, and the police of São Paulo claimed that 1 million had participated in the protest in downtown São Paulo, the survey institute Data-folha more modestly counted 210,000 participants at the peak that day (Data-folha 2015a). In Rio de Janeiro, the police gave an initial estimate of 15,000, while the organizers claimed 50,000 participants were present. In Brasília, the police estimated 40,000 protesters, and in Belo Horizonte, 24,000. The most covered events of the news that immediately preceded these protests against government corruption were the imprisonment of the PT treasurer and the inquiries being opened into 47 high-level politicians from the government coalition. Furthermore, the week before these protests, several affluent neighborhoods of Rio and São Paulo had "panelaços": People slamming pots and pans together from their windows in protest – a protest targeting the televized speech of Dilma Rousseff commemorating the International Women's Day.

Later anti-government protest of 2015 did not reach the same levels of mobilization. Although, again, estimates disagreed, they were all lower relative to the estimates of the March protests – in São Paulo on April 12, Datafolha counted 100,000, and in August, 135,000. Police reported 25,000 in Brasília on August 16, while their colleagues in Rio refrained from reporting numbers on the same day. On December 13, the lowest turnout of the anti-government protests was registered: Estimates clocked in at 30–40,000 protesters in São Paulo and some thousands in Brasília, Belo Horizonte, and Rio. The low turnout could be correlated with a string of bad news for the main forces moving the impeachment along: The disciplinary process against Eduardo Cunha was underway, Michel Temer was being ridiculed for a leaked letter to the president complaining about his lack of duties as vice-president, and the STF had overturned the procedure of impeachment initiated by Cunha. The counter-protests on December 15 had more success, gathering 55,000 in São Paulo, according to Datafolha, and 100,000 according to the organizers (which here consisted of trade and student unions as well as left-wing movements). Earlier pro-government rallies had gathered on April 7 and August 20 with less support, but with the narrative of a looming coup d'état firmly grounded in the coverage of the pending impeachment proceedings, the left-aligned movements and unions had more success on the streets in December.

The groups Movimento Brasil Livre and VemPraRua once again called for street protests in March 2016, and these turned out to muster massive support. This time around, the call for impeachment overshadowed the anti-corruption agenda and the support for the Lava-Jato investigations; or perhaps more precisely, these topics were mixed together now. Both *Folha* and *Estado* dedicated their front pages to illustrating the crowds massing in São Paulo, reporting that the protests were the largest seen in Brazilian history, with estimates of the police reaching 1.4 million and the Datafolha counting 500,000 protesters downtown (Datafolha 2016a). The Rio police force again did not give an estimate, while the organizers claimed one million protesters marched in the protests. More than 200 other cities had registered protests. Preceding this successful mobilization was three weeks of the largest build-up of negative news for Rousseff and Lula especially. As seen in Figure 5.2, the attention to the Lula cases exploded with his testimony in early March, more Petrobras revelations, and the arrest of the PT marketing strategist João Santana in February. News on impeachment also climbed in this period, with PMDB leaving the governing coalition wholesale and paving the way for a supermajority against Rousseff in the Câmara. However, as mentioned above, the mood of the great street protests in São Paulo was hostile to the political establishment in general, and the PSDB leaders Neves and Alckmin had to retreat from the public protest.

The circulation of corruption news can be interpreted as one stage of an informational cascade that feeds into the mobilization of street protests. I would argue that the mobilization of protests is possibly correlated with (but not solely determined by) the media agenda, and I can demonstrate empirically that the coverage of the protests amplified the informational cascade, as the sampled media outlets produced massive amounts of coverage of the largest anti-government protests. The coverage of the protests, of course, also tied in to the coverage of corruption and the impeachment. On the other hand, the anti-impeachment protests of the following week, which still got mentioned on the front pages of *Folha* and *Estado*, saw much less article coverage, and the layout and photo editors of both newspapers chose to run much smaller images of the anti-impeachment protests. In size, frequency, and staying power, the anti-impeachment was a lesser item on the media agenda.

Conclusion

I will summarize the argument of this chapter by highlighting an effect of the media coverage that is distinct from the agenda setting or salience transfer effects discussed in classic media studies.

In the attention economy of modern media organizations, agenda space is a limited resource, as is the resource of journalists in newsrooms. The Brazilian media had an exceedingly diverse menu of corruption cases to look into, and, as demonstrated in Chapter 3, many agents were interested in pushing information pertaining to particular cases. Such conditions result in heterogeneous pressures for selection of information. In addition to this, the same media organizations are pressed to maximize their audience by providing information relevant to a national public, rather than a local one. The outlets, furthermore, have strategic goals of keeping certain kinds of news consumers as paying clients. While the input side of the information flows was perhaps diverse in 2015, the journalistic and editorial product of *Folha*, *Estado*, and *O Globo* increasingly came to focus on scandals implicating Lula in early 2016. As demonstrated above, the virtual audiences were apparently attentive to many other cases in addition to Lula's, and the large street protests of March 2016 called for large-scale political reno-vation as well as impeachment of Rousseff. The combination of large-scale street protests and intense media coverage of Rousseff's increasing isolation, Lula's failed nomination, and the imprisonment of PT's marketing expert, however led the government coalition partners to jump ship. Sensing that impeachment was a real possibility, the media coverage intensified while the markets reacted positively.

Since the very start of the Lava-Jato investigations, key non-PT politicians had been the objects of sporadic media exposés: Vice-President Michel Temer, Senate President Renan Calheiros, and a number of other senators and congress-men, all from PMDB. The name of the 2014 presidential runner-up Aécio Neves, likewise, had cropped up in the denunciations from time to time, with short-lived media attention. These politicians became the key actors in the formation of a new government. With the leaks of conversations between Lula and Rousseff, government coalition parties found a convenient excuse to jump ship, and news on impeachment immediately flooded the landscape of media. In the two months from the great street protests in March to the preliminary removal of Rousseff on May 12, the media outlets were engrossed in the proceedings and the spectacle of the impeachment. Ignoring the investigations implicating the parties coming into power, the intense media focus paved the way for the ousting of Rousseff, and legitimized her impeachment.

The informational cascade in the media had not just agenda-setting effects, but more insidiously, the informational cascade had the unfortunate effect of eclipsing accountability mechanisms and confusing the political scenario of impeachment with corruption investigations. Rather than concerning themselves with the increasingly real possibility of corrupt politicians taking power in order to save their own hides, the collapse-of-government frame dominated the polit-ical news with increasing salience. Failing to hold the future government accountable, the informational cascade of the media reproduced the same signal and, on top of that, created a media event around the ousting of Rousseff. In the following chapter, I will review the ways that the media event of the impeach-ment came to be intertwined with the Lava-Jato investigations and the discourse of corruption, despite the fact that the effective legal ground of the impeachment was neither corruption nor related to Petrobras.

Notes

1 Floridi argues (2011: 104) that derived information is really meta-information, and that a definition of semantic information, strictly speaking, cannot include indirectly emerging data, but must inherently be truthful. Floridi would therefore reject this categorical scheme used here on ontological grounds. For the purposes of this chapter it is necessary to encompass the (derived or direct) variants of information that are not truthful, although this, to Floridi, would merely be communication which does not entail truth value (ibid.: 96).
2 Due to the diverse codings of the cases involving Vaccari and Dirceu, neither politician appears in the graph of the most-reported topics.

References

Abramo, C.W. (2007) "Brazil: A Portrait of Disparities" *Brazilian Journalism Research*, vol. 3(1), 93–107.

Aguiar, P. (2014) "Marx explica a Reuters: economia política das agências de notícias." In J.A. Silva Jr., M.C. Esperidião, and P. Aguiar (eds.), *Agências de Notícias: perspectivas contemporâneas* (38–78). Recife: EdUFPE.

Albuquerque, A. de (2012) "On Models and Margins." In D. Hallin and P. Mancini (eds.), *Comparing Media Systems beyond the Western World* (72–95). Cambridge: Cambridge University Press.

Altheide, D. and Snow, R. (1979) *Media Logic*. Los Angeles, CA: Sage.

Banco Central do Brasil (2016) *Cotações de fechamento de Dólar dos Estados Unidos*. Retrieved from www4.bcb.gov.br/pec/taxas/port/ptaxnpesq.asp?id=txcotacao.

Baptista, E. (2017) "Corrupção e opinião pública: o escândalo da Lava Jato no governo Dilma Rousseff." PhD Dissertation. Belo Horizonte: UFMG.

Beale, S. (2006) "The News Media's Influence on Criminal Justice Policy: How Market-Driven News Promotes Punitiveness" *William and Mary Law Review*, vol. 48(2), 397–481.

Bell, A. (1991) *The Language of News Media*. Oxford: Blackwell.

Bikhchandani, S., Hirshleifer, D., and Welch, I. (1998) "Learning from the Behavior of Others: Conformity, Fads, and Informational Cascades" *Journal of Economic Perspectives*, vol. 12(3), 151–170.

Bird, E. (1997) "What a Story! Understanding the Audience for Scandal." In J. Lull and S. Hinerman (eds.), *Media Scandals: Morality and Desire in the Popular Culture Marketplace* (99–121). New York: Columbia University Press.

Biroli, F. and Miguel, L.F. (2013) "Meios de comunicação, voto e conflito político no Brasil" *Revista Brasileira das Ciências Sociais*, vol. 28(81), 77–95.

BM&F-Bovespa (2018) *Cotações*. Retrieved from www.bmfbovespa.com.br/pt_br/servicos/market-data/cotacoes/.

Boulianne, S. (2015) "Social Media Use and Participation: A Meta-Analysis of Current Research" *Information, Communication and Society*, vol. 18(5), 524–538.

Boydstun, A. (2013) *Making the News. Politics, the Media, and Agenda Setting*. Chicago, IL: University of Chicago Press.

Bro, P. and Wallberg, F. (2015) "Gatekeeping in a Digital Era" *Journalism Practice*, vol. 9(1), 92–105.

Cabral, E.D.T. (2017) "Mídia Concentrada no Brasil: Até Quando?" *Revista Latino-Americana de Ciencias de la Comunicación*, vol. 13(24), 49–59.

Carey, J. (1986) "The Dark Continent of American Journalism." In R. Manoff and M. Schudson (eds.), *Reading the News* (146–196). New York: Pantheon.

Chaia, V., Maranhão, C., and Martinho, S. (2017) "O Brasil da telenovela e do jogo político: um estudo de caso do impeachment de Dilma Rousseff e a estética das telenovelas brasileiras no ano de 2016." Paper presented at ANPOCS 41st conference at Caxambu, Minas Gerais, October 24, 2017.

Damgaard, M. (2015) "Multiple Margins and Mediatized Transgression" *Ephemera –Theory and Politics in Organization*, vol. 15(2), 411–434.

Datafolha (2015a) *Manifestação na avenida Paulista. 15/03/2015*. São Paulo: Datafolha.

Datafolha (2015b) *Avaliação da presidente Dilma Rousseff – novembro de 2015, PO813824*. São Paulo: Datafolha.

Datafolha (2016a) *Manifestação Avenida Paulista. 13/03/2016*. São Paulo: Datafolha.

Datafolha (2016b) *Avaliação da presidente Dilma Rousseff – abril de 2016, PO813859*. São Paulo: Datafolha.

Datafolha (2017) *Avaliação do presidente Michel Temer – novembro de 2017, PO 813942*. São Paulo: Datafolha.

Dretske, F. (1981) *Knowledge and the Flow of Information*. Cambridge, MA: MIT Press.

Entman, R. (1993) "Framing: Toward Clarification of a Fractured Paradigm" *Journal of Communication*, vol. 43, 51–58.

Entman, R. (2010) "Media Framing Biases and Political Power: Explaining Slant in News of Campaign 2008" *Journalism*, vol. 11(4), 389–408.

Fallis, D. (2009) "A Conceptual Analysis of Disinformation." Preprint of *iConference* 2009. Retrieved from www.ideals.illinois.edu/bitstream/handle/2142/15205/fallis_disinfo1.pdf?sequence=2.

Fallis, D. (2011) "Floridi on Disinformation" *Etica & Politica/ Ethics & Politics*, vol. 13(2), 201–214.

Floridi, L. (2002) "On Defining Library and Information Science as Applied Philosophy of Information" *Social Epistemology: A Journal of Knowledge, Culture and Policy*, 16(1), 37–49.

Floridi, L. (2005) "Semantic Conceptions of Information." In *Stanford Encyclopedia of Philosophy*. Retrieved from https://plato.stanford.edu/entries/information-semantic/.

Floridi, L. (2011) *The Philosophy of Information*. Oxford: Oxford University Press.

Galtung, J. and Ruge, M. (1965) "The Structure of Foreign News" *Journal of Peace Research*, vol. 2(1), 64–91.

Ghanem, S. (1997) "Filling in the Tapestry. The Second Level of Agenda Setting." In M. McCombs, D. Shaw, and D. Weaver (eds.), *Communication and Democracy: Exploring the Intellectual Frontiers in Agenda Setting* (3–14). Mahwah, NJ: Lawrence Erlbaum Associates.

Grice, H.P. (1957) *Studies in the Way of Words*. Cambridge, MA: Harvard University Press.

Hendricks, V. and Hansen, P.G. (2016) *Infostorms. Why Do We "Like"? Explaining Individual Behavior on the Social Net*. 2nd edition. London: Springer.

Indicadores CNI (2015a) *CNI/Ibope Avaliação do governo, septembro 2015*. São Paulo: Confederação Nacional da Indústria.

Indicadores CNI (2015b) *CNI/Ibope Avaliação do governo, dezembro 2015*. São Paulo: Confederação Nacional da Indústria.

Indicadores CNI (2016) *CNI/Ibope Avaliação do governo, março 2016*. São Paulo: Confederação Nacional da Indústria.

Iyengar, S. (1990) "Framing Responsibility for Political Issues: The Case of Poverty" *Political Behavior*, vol. 12(1), 19–40.

Kristensen, N.N. and Mortensen, M. (2015) "Amateur Sources Breaking the News, Meta-sources Authorizing the News of Gaddafi's Death: New Patterns of Journalistic

Information Gathering and Dissemination in the Digital Age" *Digital Journalism*, vol. 1(3), 352–367.

Landerer, N. (2013) "Rethinking the Logics: A Conceptual Framework for the Mediatization of Politics" *Communication Theory*, vol. 23, 239–258.

Latinobarómetro (2017) *Informe Latinobarómetro 2017*. Santiago de Chile: Corporación Latinobarómetro.

Lattman-Weltman, F. and Chagas, V. (2016) "Mercado Futuro: A Economia Política da (Re)Partidarização da Imprensa no Brasil" *Dados*, Revista de Ciências Sociais, vol. 59(2), 323–356.

Lazarsfeld, P., Berelson, B., and Gaudet, H. (1944). *The People's Choice: How the Voter Makes Up His Mind in a Presidential Campaign*. New York: Columbia University Press.

Liebes, T. and Blum-Kalka, S. (2004) "It Takes Two to Blow the Whistle: Do Journalists Control the Outbreak of Scandal?" *American Behavioral Scientist*, vol. 47(9), 1153–1170.

Lima, V.A. da (2004) "Sete teses sobre mídia e política no Brasil" *Revista USP*, São Paulo, no. 61, 48–57.

McCombs, M. and Shaw, D. (1972) "The Agenda-Setting Function of Mass Media" *Public Opinion Quarterly*, vol. 36, 176–187.

McCombs, M. (2005) "A Look at Agenda-Setting: Past, Present and Future" *Journalism Studies*, vol. 6(4), 543–557.

Matos, C. (2008) *Journalism and Political Democracy in Brazil*. Lanham, MD: Lexington Books.

Obelitz Søe, S. (2014) "Information, misinformation og disinformation. En sprogfilosofisk analyse" *Nordisk Tidsskrift for Informationsvidenskab og Kulturformidling*, 3(1).

Obelitz Søe, S. (2016) *The Urge to Detect, the Need to Clarify. Gricean Perspectives on Information, Misinformation and Disinformation*. PhD Thesis. Copenhagen: University of Copenhagen.

Paterson, C. and Domingo, D. (eds.) (2008) *Making Online News: The Ethnography of New Media Production*. New York: Peter Lang.

Pring, C. (2017) *People and Corruption: Latin America and the Caribbean*. Berlin: Transparency International.

Reese, S. (2007) "The Framing Project: A Bridging Model for Media Research Revisited" *Journal of Communication*, vol. 57, 148–157.

Russell, A. and Waisbord, S. (2017) "The Snowden Revelations and the Networked Fourth Estate" *International Journal of Communication*, vol. 11, 858–878.

Schudson, M. (2004) "Notes on Scandal and the Watergate Legacy" *American Behavioral Scientist*, vol. 47, 1231–1238.

Sniderman, P. and Theriault, S. (2004) "The Structure of Political Argument and the Logic of Issue Framing." In W. Saris and P. Sniderman (eds.), *Studies in Public Opinion: Attitudes, Nonattitudes, Measurement Error, and Change* (133–165). Princeton, NJ: Princeton University Press.

Thompson, J.P. (2000) *Political Scandal: Power and Visibility in the Media Age*. Cambridge: Polity Press.

Thompson, J.P. (2005) "The New Visibility" *Theory, Culture & Society*, vol. 22(6), 31–51.

Tuchman, G. (1978) *Making News. A Study in the Construction of Reality*. New York: The Free Press.

Tumber, H. and Waisbord, S. (2004) "Introduction" *American Behavioral Scientist*, vol. 47, 1143–1152.

Van Dijk, T. (1988) *News as Discourse*. Mahwah, NJ: Lawrence Erlbaum.

Vasterman, P. (2005) "Media-Hype. Self-Reinforcing News Waves, Journalistic Standards and the Construction of Social Problems" *European Journal of Communication*, vol. 20(4), 508–530.

Waisbord, S. (2000) *Watchdog Journalism in South America. News, Accountability, and Democracy*. New York: Columbia University Press.

Walgrave, S., Boydstun, A., Vliegenthart, R., and Hardy, A. (2017) "The Nonlinear Effect of Information on Political Attention: Media Storms and U.S. Congressional Hearings" *Political Communication*, vol. 34(4), 548–570.

Welch, M., Prica, E., and Yankey, N. (2002) "Moral Panic over Youth Violence: Wilding and the Manufacture of Menace in the Media" *Youth and Society*, vol. 34(1), 3–30.

Wien, C. and Elmelund-Præstekær, C. (2009) "An Anatomy of Media Hypes: Developing a Model for the Dynamics and Structure of Intense Media Coverage of Single Issues" *European Journal of Communications*, vol. 24(2), 183–201.

Wiewiura, J. and Hendricks, V. (2017) "Informational Pathologies and Interest Bubbles: Exploring the Structural Mobilization of Knowledge, Ignorance, and Slack" *New Media and Society*, Article first published online: January 10, 2017 – https://doi.org/10.1177/1461444816686095.

Wortham, S. and Rhodes, C.R. (2012) "Narratives across Speech Events." In A. De Fina and A. Georgakopoulou (eds.), *The Handbook of Narrative Analysis* (160–177). Malden, MA: Wiley-Blackwell.

6 Coup d'état or Constitutional Act?

At the outset of this book, I asked how the failures of accountability processes in Brazil could happen in plain sight of the population and the media, and how the checks and balances of the Brazilian democracy, that supposedly had become more and more consolidated, so quickly could give way. How could the initial success of the Lava-Jato investigations, apparently ending the rule of impunity for the business elite and the politicians benefitting from corruption and cartelization, turn into a media crusade against corruption that undermined the rule of law?

I will retrace the steps of this book in order to answer that question. By doing so, this chapter can also shed light on the question frequently raised in debates during and after the impeachment: Was the impeachment of Dilma Rousseff really a *golpe*, or coup d'état, or was it a congressional act within the limits of the Constitution – an exit to the deadlock of Brazil's faltering coalitional presidentialism under Rousseff?

First, I will revisit the theoretical line of this book. In scandals, media matters in several ways: because media attention signals importance to society and sets the agenda, and because this agenda-setting effect may trigger accountability processes (Peruzzotti 2006: 255, Smulovitz and Peruzzotti 2000: 152, Waisbord 2000: 230ff.) and call decision-makers to action (Walgrave et al. 2017). While media agenda setting in scandals can have electoral consequences and also lead to the mobilization of street protests, it is the ability to set the stage for horizontal accountability that is most interesting here, because exposés in agenda-setting media may partly determine who is to be held accountable (Porto 2011: 122).

There are many factors that determine what gets covered by media and what does not. Media agendas are usually characterized by skew (Boydstun 2013), generated by the incentives and restraints of media institutions. Media agenda congestion, policy-maker attention and the institutional set-up of news media covering political life combine into two feedback mechanisms – internally in particular media organizations, and between media actors. Such feedback is especially likely in a vertically integrated and concentrated media system such as Brazil's (Cabral 2017), because the same news items propagate down a chain of media outlets within the same conglomerate. Though scandals are likely to also be characterized by explosiveness, sudden spikes of attention may still turn into a sustained media storm (Walgrave et al. 2017). This happens when an informational cascade (Hendricks and Hansen 2016) emerges between various actors (such as media outlets, political parties, and financial actors), repeating and recycling the same signal many times over. All of this will exacerbate the bias (Feres Júnior and Sassara 2016) of an already skewed media agenda.

While the scrutiny of political corruption and improbity in media exposés normally triggers accountability processes (Porto 2011), a radically skewed media agenda may counteract accountability, by exposing only a select few of many different corruption cases. Some cases then linger in court dockets and on police desktops, while others are hastened through without due consideration. In a judicial system where corruption trials may drag out for a decade or more (Taylor 2011: 172, Falcão et al. 2014), rapidly executed processes are perceived as exceptional, obtain more coverage in the short run, and stand out on the media agenda. Insiders of investigations and trials may leak or push information to media outlets to exacerbate this pattern. Leaks that can scandalize members of the political elite are more likely to make it past the gates of a media system for three reasons; because this kind of news deals with actors in the eye of the public, because it ticks all the boxes of news values (Galtung and Ruge 1965), and because media outlets (even without access to the leaked information itself) cover the repercussions as well as the original coverage; "in this way, the coverage becomes in part coverage of the coverage" (Kristensen and Mortensen 2013: 361).

In sum, by continuously leaking information of corruption investigations on a large scale, these actors may drive the media agenda, which in turn triggers accountability processes and supports mobilization of discontent. Even when journalists create or yield space to competing frames, the leaky sources hold power to initiate cascades between media actors, if these choose to recycle the leaked information, and thereby to create the momentum for accountability processes. This book has aimed at exposing and discussing this systematic link between leaks from concealed sources, the web of accountability institutions, and the Brazilian media system.

The link between leaked disclosure of corruption, media, and accountability processes, influences politics in three ways. Reforms and bills are proposed to remedy the democratic deficits, but this might merely be a strategy of signaling and maintaining legitimacy (Seligson 2002). Political actors can also utilize information from leaks and media exposés to initiate further legal actions. If they are able to influence courts' decisions and jurisdictions, they have the option of not only waging lawfare (Comaroff and Comaroff 2006), but also reinforcing the media attention to those cases from which the legal actions derived. In addition to this, political actors may capitalize on the momentum of informational cascades, skewed media agendas, and accountability processes, by strategically jumping ship (Balán 2011). The use of denunciations of corruption as an intra-government instrument to claim more power may thus look like a genuinely ethical act on the surface, but in reality cover an intra-elite power struggle where political dominance is sought through non-democratic means (Waisbord 2000). If media actors fail to acknowledge this and act upon it, they are contributing to the construction of manipulative publicity in the public sphere (Habermas 1989 [1962]: 178), to the detriment of true accountability.

In Chapter 4, I described the failure of the Brazilian horizontal accountability processes since 2015 to produce equal and timely interventions into politics, although the Lava-Jato probe was frequently represented as exceptionally effective. Nonetheless, the successes of the Lava-Jato eclipsed several prominent failures of accountability institutions, and the horizontal accountability failures were thereby compounded by the media-borne vertical accountability deficits in equilibrating the overall attention to the actors coming into power, as analyzed in Chapter 5. Chapter 3, meanwhile, described the moments where various political and judicial processes were kick-started by leaks in the media, most notably the gradual disintegration of the governing coalition in 2015 and early 2016. The net result of these stacked failures, leaks, and scandals was the impeachment of Dilma Rousseff and the quickening of court trials involving Lula (relative to the delays of legal processes involving non-PT politicians).

To demonstrate that this cascade of leaked information and political responses actually contributed to the ousting of Rousseff and the inauguration of Michel Temer, I will now outline the process leading to the impeachment. I can then conclude the book by considering how the impeachment and the array of other consequences produced by leaks and lawfare affected the general condition of the Brazilian democracy. Finally, I will consider the lessons of Lava-Jato and the impeachment in theoretical and practical terms.

Fiscal Delays and the Impeachment of Dilma Rousseff

The impeachment petition, submitted in October 2015, that eventually led to the ousting of President Rousseff in August 2016, was based on several charges, many of them related to the corruption of Petrobras. However, according to the law defining impeachment proceedings (law 1079 of 1950), acts anterior to the mandate of the incumbent cannot legally ground an impeachment process. That clause meant that even if conclusive evidence of Rousseff's active or passive acceptance of corruption in Petrobras before 2015 had surfaced, she would have been shielded from such charges (although the allegations or evidence could still be used in TSE trial). Despite this restriction of the impeachment law's scope, the arguments concerning Rousseff's role in the graft of Petrobras contracts were still present in most of the stages of the process: In the initial petition, in the public debates and the votes of the Câmara and Senate, as well as in the final accusation, the *libelo acusatório* (Wink 2017). So, in order to provide a firmer ground for initiating the process of impeachment, the opposition had to frame the impeachment petition around Rousseff's personal responsibility for certain fiscal delays. These were dubbed *pedaladas fiscais*, and a description of the impeachment demands a brief exposition of the history of those delays. The following section cannot do the complexity of the constitutional and fiscal intricacies justice, but may give the reader some sense of what the delays came to signify in public discourse.

During 2014, the Finance Ministry had expanded an existing and common practice of delaying transfers of funds between the State Treasury and public banks. Three public financial institutions (the Caixa Federal, the Banco do Brasil, and the FGTS) transferred money to citizens in several conditional cash transfer programs, as well as to companies through several lines of credit for industrial companies and agribusinesses, but the State Treasury would then "pedal" for a while, only dispensing funds some days later. Shifting temporarily the financial burden of the programs onto other public institutions, the delays somewhat masked the fact that the state accounts were in bad shape after years of plummeting oil prices and the great slow-down of the Chinese economy, the most important export market of Brazil. The expansion of this practice, reaching at one point R$3.5 billion in delayed funds from day to day, was revealed by journalists from the financial beat of *Estado* in April 2014. While the secretary-general of the State Treasury, Arno Augustin, denied that this constituted an illegal budget maneuver, the government still stopped that practice in 2014. The Lava-Jato scandals and the elections pushed the case of the *pedaladas* from the headlines. Therefore, the topic lay dormant since August 2014, save for one front-page headline on January 11, 2015, in *Estado*, but it had been on the agenda of an audit inquiry internally in the TCU, the Tribunal of Union Accounts. On April 17, *Estado* and *Globo* highlighted the leaked report of Julio Marcelo de Oliveira, Prosecutor of TCU. Oliveira then presented the tribunal with an audit report that pointed out that *pedaladas* infringed the Law of Fiscal Responsibility (Villaverde 2016: 177ff.). Meanwhile, impeachment re-emerged in the media in February, March, and April 2015 (e.g., Zalis 2015), and opposition parties gladly commented on the issue.

José Mucio, one of nine TCU judges, was assigned to the case. He agreed with the auditor and recommended that the court plenary decide on the culpability of all involved in the fiscal maneuvers of 2014. Despite strong protests from the government, headed by the Attorney-General, protests from a number of ministers from the 2014 government and presidents of public banks testifying in the court, the other TCU judges concurred. The maneuvers and the defenses of government occupied journalists covering the financial beat in the daily newspapers in June, July, and August 2015 (Villaverde 2016: 181ff.). However, in 2015, the practice of *pedaladas* had already been stopped. The only delayed payments between the State Treasury and the banks were transfers to back up an agribusiness line of credit promoted by the government called the Plano Safra. This credit line, totaling R$5.6 billion, had nominal payments in January and June 2015 that were only eventually paid in December 2015.

While the case was under scrutiny in the press and in the TCU, on July 17, the first crack in the government coalition appeared when Eduardo Cunha stated that he considered himself in opposition to PT, and that he wanted all of PMDB to leave the government with him. Cunha had suffered two days of journalistic barrage because a leaked testimony in the Lava-Jato case implicated him. Cunha criticized the PGR, and claimed the government was covertly attacking him through the corruption investigations. Cunha also began to undermine the stability of Rousseff's position by signaling the viability of the impeachment petitions he had received as president of Câmara. Through his position, he was vested with the power to deny or proceed with the impeachment process. Removing Rousseff would bring Vice-President Temer, also national president of PMDB, to the presidency, and in the event of the vice-president's removal as a result of the ongoing TSE trial, Cunha would be the next in line to claim the presidency (see Chapters 3 and 4 concerning Cunha's corruption cases).

Despite Cunha urging his party to jump ship, PMDB remained in the coalition and even gained more posts: In the cabinet reshuffle on October 2, the party gained one additional minister position for a new total of seven (Almeida 2016: 89), but almost half of the party's members in the Câmara began to stray from the government line in votes. Soon after Cunha broke ranks, Michel Temer declared at a press conference that "someone" would now have to ensure political unity to govern the country. The vice-president implied that the president could not be entrusted with this responsibility, underscoring the growing tension between PMDB and PT (ibid.: 58). Nonetheless, PT could not govern without PMDB, but many PMDB Congressmen were voting for conservative bills, spearheaded by Eduardo Cunha. In late July, Cunha also added two new elements to his pressure. First, a range of expensive bills (called the *pautas-bomba*) that would force the government into a budget deficit; and second, Cunha stated that he was now analyzing one particular petition filed by Hélio Bicudo, former PT member and founder, and Miguel Reale Junior, former PSDB Minister of Justice in the last year of Cardoso's government. The two senior lawyer-politicians (aided, from August onwards, by the younger professor of law Janaína Paschoal) marshalled three overall arguments in three different versions of their impeachment petition:

- The corruption in Petrobras (linked to the Mensalão case).
- The *pedaladas* (eventually interpreted to be legally identical to the delayed payment for the Safra credit line in 2015).
- The state budget of 2015, then moving toward a deficit.

The final argument was included when the lawyers realized that expenditure totaling R$2.5 billion in presidential decrees had been announced by the government in July and August 2015. However, at the moment of issuing the decrees, the Congress had not ratified a state budget deficit, and spending in excess of the state budget could therefore be considered an unauthorized loan and a breach of the Law of Financial Responsibility, article 36, just like the *pedaladas*. A revised petition penned by the trio of lawyers was handed in to Cunha on September 17, and resubmitted in October 15, in a final revision. Both submissions became media events through the coverage of the large print and broadcast media. In the final petition, the president was deemed responsible for the delays, which according to the petition were crimes against the state. Both pieces of information were contested: The practice of delaying payments is wide-spread at both federal and state level in Brazil, and Rousseff's hand in cooking up quite specific fiscal transactions was debatable (but see Villaverde 2016).

Meanwhile, TCU had scheduled the verdict of the 2014 state accounts for October 7. The report of Oliveira, the TCU auditor, concerning the *pedaladas*, became the grounds for rejecting the accounts, and with this sentence, TCU reinforced Reale's, Paschoal's and Bicudo's interpretation of delays, ruling *pedaladas* to be in violation of the Law of Fiscal Responsibility. Only once before, in a crisis of the Vargas government in 1937, had the tribunal rejected the state accounts. To deny that line of argument in an eventual impeachment process, the government also tried to remedy the situation of delays in 2015, including the paying back of interest to the public banks, adding R$55.8 billion to the deficit.

With the rejection of the 2014 state accounts in the TCU, the outlooks for the accounts of the state in 2015 turned even bleaker, and Minister of Finances Joaquim Levy was struggling to find a way of ensuring that the state budgets of 2015 would not end up with a deficit, in spite of declining tax income. The noticeable problems for the government of ensuring a budget surplus conspired to make Standard & Poor's lower the investment grade of Brazil (Almeida 2016: 69ff.). This was seen as a blow to Levy. The economic goal of the state, the *meta fiscal*, was revised several times, for an extraordinary deficit at the end of 2015. The revisions also contributed to the lowering of the country's international investment grade with the other major international grading agencies.

The approval of the state budget only passed the floor of the Congress very late in the year. With the hope of pushing the Rousseff administration into another breach of the Law of Fiscal Responsibility, the vote for approving the budget was postponed several times in November 2015 by the opposition and Cunha at the helm of Congress. With the unexpected arrest of the senator Delcídio do Amaral, the budget wound up on the agenda in the last week of the parliament working year. The Congress ended up ratifying a total state budget deficit of R$119.9 billion, and Levy left office shortly. The media represented his resignation as a response to the congressional deadlock.

A Skein of Scandal and Legitimacy

As described in Chapter 4, in November, Cunha repeatedly stated that the petition for impeaching Rousseff was almost cleared for take-off in Congress. This was interpreted by journalists and pundits as a bargaining chip in his own struggle to avoid a disciplinary process in the Conselho da Ética. The PT representatives in the Conselho voted for opening a process against Cunha, on December 2, and the same afternoon, Cunha declared that he would accept the petition filed by Bicudo, Reale, and Paschoal. In the absence (at that time) of any investigations targeting Rousseff specifically in the ongoing corruption probe, the negative evaluation of her administration's fiscal policies and management of state accounts became the kernel of the impeachment process.

A number of maneuvers masterminded by Cunha dominated the agenda of Congress in the week that followed. Cunha established a set of rules that allowed dissenters of government coalition parties to be elected for the special

Congressional commission that would be installed to analyze the impeachment petition. Through secret vote-casting for the candidates for this commission, the Congressmen could ignore party discipline (and the normal rules of Congressional commissions), by voting for lists consisting of dissenters. Protesting against this, several ballot boxes were smashed in the Congress by Rousseff allies during the tumultuous vote. Aiming to stop the chaos of the Câmara, the STF judge Barroso preliminarily revoked Cunha's rules and urgently put the question of due process in the impeachment on the agenda of the STF for the following week. This helped Rousseff to a certain degree, as the intervention of STF on December 16 and 17 annulled the special commission installed by Cunha and made the coming stages of the impeachment process less volatile and subject to his artifices. However, even with a fixed set of rules defined by STF, the government was still facing the fact of the crumbling coalition.

What was less visible at the time of the intervention was the STF's stake in securing the constitutionality of the impeachment process. Fully aware that with an indicted politician running the process, the impeachment looked less than legitimate, STF's president (at the time, Ricardo Lewandowski) agreed to hear Cunha's complaints the day before Christmas. The meeting between the president of the Câmara and the president of the STF was made open to journalists, however, and Lewandowski denied every issue taken up by Cunha. This had the double effect of showing that the STF was both committed to securing the constitutionality of the process and that the Court did not confide in Cunha, who left the audience chamber of the Court embarrassed. Crucially, the STF had also unanimously denied the government's request for stopping the entire process due to Cunha's indictment. The initiation of the impeachment might be a part of Cunha's grab for power and hope of immunity against prosecution, but the STF maintained the position that it was entirely legitimate.

Following leaks of conversations between Lula and Rousseff (see Chapter 3), and the arrest of their marketing strategist João Santana, dissent grew in most parties of the government coalition. The special commission that was eventually installed in March 2016 contained a majority of Congressmen in favor of impeachment. The dissent was probably also motivated by *Realpolitik*: At this moment, the federal government was unable to guarantee much influence to their allies, and with another state budget deficit looming, the gains from pork-barrel politics were expected to be minimal. Furthermore, the possible removal of Rousseff would result in a new cabinet, meaning entirely new horizons of influence. An eventual new governing coalition could pick out new persons for the many positions of confidence in state companies, agencies, and entities, and continue to meddle in public tenders.

No matter the motivation, the special commission approved a report in favor of impeaching Rousseff on April 11, with the votes 38 for and 27 against. The registration for the final meeting of the commission even saw physical infights between substitutes of absent commission members. The commission's concluding report (Arantes 2016) repeated that government credit lines without backing to the banks doling out the money were effectively unauthorized loans, like the *pedaladas*, and the report affirmed that Rousseff was ultimately responsible for this practice. An addendum to the impeachment law 1079/50 links this law to the Law of Fiscal Responsibility, so that budgetary movements not ratified in the annual Budget Law are defined as crimes of the Executive, and this meant that Rousseff transgressed both laws. The major scandals of the PT government (now defined as crimes of administrative improbity) were again mentioned in the special commission's report, despite the delimitation of the temporal scope in the impeachment law. Thus, the Lava-Jato investigations, the Zelotes case, and PT's and Rousseff's involvement in the corruption of Petrobras anyway snuck into the process (ibid.: 10ff.).

Cunha then scheduled the vote of the Câmara plenary for the following Sunday, April 17, and 73 percent of the Chamber of Federal Representatives voted in favor of the petition for impeaching Dilma Rousseff. Of the 511 representatives voting, virtually none cited the explicit justification of the petition – the delays of transfers from the Treasury to the public banks. However, scores of representatives stated that by voting for impeachment, they voted against corruption, frequently reproducing the exact narrative about Rousseff that first emerged in 2014 with the initial disclosure of corruption in Petrobras.

Cunha was removed as president of the Câmara shortly thereafter (as described in Chapter 4), and his substitute, Waldir Maranhão (of the PP), revoked the vote of April 17, but then retracted that revocation within 24 hours. The Senate ratified the Câmara's vote on May 12, removing Rousseff for a maximum of 180 days. Between the vote in the Senate that temporarily removed Rousseff and the final vote in August, a technical report made by Senate clerks demonstrated that no internal document corroborated the theory of Rousseff's personal involvement in masking budget deficits through the fiscal delays (Pederiva et al. 2016: 212ff.), but that the decrees for extra expenditure in July and August 2015 should have been previously ratified in Congress. The technical report pointed out that in the process of executing the decrees, no decision-makers in government were made aware that delays of payment for these decrees would impact upon the budget goal.

Nonetheless, the special commission of the Senate produced a report in favor of ousting Rousseff permanently during June and July, again bringing in arguments about Rousseff's role in the graft of Petrobras, and the commission ratified the report with the votes 14 to 5 on August 4. Ricardo Lewandowski, finishing his period as president of the STF with this process, could then conduct the final stage of the impeachment process in the Senate in the end of August, sitting beside Senate President Renan Calheiros of the PMDB, also investigated by the Lava-Jato task-force. The Senate voted on August 31, after two days of political-juridical proceedings, with 61 senators in favor and 20 against impeaching Rousseff.

In spite of the fact that the two issues were legally separate, the Lava-Jato scandal fed into the impeachment process in no small way, tangling together questions of political responsibility, hidden motives, and corruption. Despite these extra-processual intrusions along the way, from Cunha's maneuvers to the final charge, the STF maintained a shroud of legitimacy under the auspice of then-President Lewandowski. Although no other executive or governor in Brazil has been removed for fiscal delays, despite doubts about Rousseff's personal responsibility in the transfer of funds between state entities, and despite the fact that Rousseff was never charged in a civil or criminal suit for administrative improbity, STF secured the execution of impeachment according to the letter of the constitution.

Perhaps because the judges viewed this as a viable exit from the political deadlock of the Congress, or maybe because they believed in the accusations floating concerning Rousseff's role in the graft of Petrobras, the STF became a stunted instance of checks and balances: By merely allowing the Legislative to demand accountability of the Executive, without bothering to hold accountable the Congressmen playing the jurors of the impeachment, the STF deliberately unbalanced the equilibrium in the Brazilian separation of powers. This was obvious in the way that the impeachment was conducted as a solely political trial, without the ambition of upholding the rule of law beyond the letter, and it became even more obvious in situations involving STF and TSE Judge Gilmar Mendes the following year. Here, impunity for Temer (in the TSE trial), his cabinet (e.g., Moreira Franco or Romero Jucá), and supporters (such as Aécio Neves) was prevalent, while Lula, Rousseff, and their ministers enjoyed no protection through similar interventions.

The vertical dimension of accountability mattered little in relation to the shroud of legitimacy bestowed by the STF, as the scholars of law and the bar association paid more attention to the impeachment itself than to the role of STF in securing the process. Furthermore, media attention worked to the detriment of the vertical dimension of accountability, as clarified in the previous chapter: The agenda-setting outlets systematically over-exposed the impeachment process and reduced attention to the cases involving every PMDB leader but Cunha, paving the way for replacing Rousseff with her vice president, Michel Temer. At that point, Temer himself had been implicated by five different individuals in testimonies of the Lava-Jato probe, and, like Rousseff, he was indicted by the PGR in September 2017 for his role in the corruption of Petrobras.

Although Rousseff may someday be found guilty in the Petrobras case, for passively or actively maintaining the model of political control over directorates (and tacitly or expressly accepting the derived kickback payments to PT and the coalition partners), the impeachment process rested on other legal grounds. These grounds were fragile, but the STF judges upheld a façade of legitimacy, and they went out of their way to secure the execution of the impeachment, while never stopping to question whether the culpability for personally attributed crimes, defined by the impeachment law as *crimes de responsibilidade*, actually extends to acts committed down the chain of command. Was Rousseff really personally ordering the delays and the specific technical realization of credit lines of the Plano Safra? If there were protests against the delays in the State Treasury, had she herself demanded the silencing of these protests from her subordinates? And if these quasi-*pedaladas* of 2015 were deliberately executed to cook the books of the state budget and uphold the country's investment grade, should it be considered a crime against the state, or a defense of the nation's financial assets? And if Rousseff actually did all of this maliciously, did the penalty of losing the presidency equal the gravity of the crime?

Given these deficiencies, the impeachment was arguably a coup, in the sense of an illegitimate take-over of government with no consulting of the electorate, although the process was effectively dressed up as a constitutionally legitimate act. While the legality of the proceedings was observed, I will argue that the legitimacy of the impeachment was thoroughly impaired as Temer and his party were participants in the graft of the state companies and benefitted from the corruption. To add insult to democratic injury, grabbing the reins of the presidency also provided Temer with the instruments for stopping the TSE trial and curtailing other corruption probes. In a way, the greater scandal was really the skein of legitimacy and scandal, which permitted the maintenance of the façade. In this entanglement of media coverage of impeachment, lawfare, contradictory judicial rulings, faltering checks and balances, and openly failing accountability mechanisms, it was never consistently questioned whether prosecutors and judges, while dredging information up, speeding up or dragging out cases, were also dragging the Brazilian democracy onto thin ice. With Temer's narrow escape from the TSE trial and two indictments in 2017, impunity was restored, leaving the ice to thaw and closing around the hole left by the sinking legacy of PT's ex-presidents.

Crusade Against Corruption in a Crumbling Democracy

The two preceding sections have given a partial answer to the question posed in the introduction, concerning the power relations between the Brazilian Executive and Legislative branches. A decade ago, Brazilian democracy seemed well-consolidated, competitive, and increasingly accountable (Avritzer 2016: 27, Power and Taylor 2011: 266), orbiting around the office of the president. The strength of the presidency made scholars of Brazilian politics (e.g., Amorim Neto 2007, Pereira and Mueller 2000) argue that the Executive branch of the Brazilian government in fact held too much power relative to the other branches. After the impeachment of Rousseff and the two obstructed indictments of Temer, this perception needs to be reformulated. Now, what matters is really the power of veto-players in the Congress to form alternative majorities. In other words, the lesson of the Lava-Jato case and the impeachment to political science was that a Brazilian president is dependent on Congress, and not the other way around.

The president, moreover, is only to a limited extent able to influence judicial affairs. In the analyses presented here, we see that the STF acts incongruently but independently of the executive branch (even when a majority of the bench is appointed by the prevailing party's presidents), while the TSE remains heavily influenced by the president. The Ministério Público and the PF act independently, albeit with a possibly vested political agenda, but a Congress (super-)majority can shield presidents from investigations – and this is a central bargaining chip in the power game determining Executive prerogatives. The checks and balances of Brazilian politics is a complex game, and the Congress – not the president – is situated centrally to fix the weights of the balances, as the arbiter of impeachments, deadlocks, and veto powers against accountability mechanisms initiated by the MPF.

The considerations of checks and balances above leads me to the fourth and final question posed initially. Could it be that independence of the judiciary is not beneficial to democracy? In the introduction to this book, I remarked that we generally perceive the independence and impartiality of the judiciary as a bedrock of the rule of law. The independence of the Brazilian public prosecutors and the courts has grown tremendously since the 1990s, so much that the debate has now seen a sea change: Could independent courts and prosecutors turn out to be a problem for democracy? This is a complex debate best left for another full-length study, but certain elements of this answer have cropped up in the course of this book.

First, when key actors of Congress and the Executive work toward ending the combat against corruption, independence of the judiciary is obviously of utmost import. No more than two weeks after the impeachment, it became clear that substituting Temer for Rousseff would not bode well for the Lava-Jato investigations. Leaked recordings published by *Folha* in May 2016, produced before the impeachment became a reality, featured a key witness in the Petrobras case discussing the removal of Rousseff with major political actors of PMDB. In the conversations, the politicians (Renan Calheiros and ex-President Sarney, for instance) agree with their interlocutor that it is necessary to end the corruption probes into the political establishment, which threatened to "put an end to the political class." Another key actor, PMDB Senator (and later Minister) Romero Jucá, affirmed on the tapes that it was necessary to "stop the bleeding" of the political class by changing government and ending the PGR's and the Lava-Jato task force's project of cleaning Brazilian politics:

> We have to stop this shit … We have to overthrow the government in order to stop the bleeding. To stop [the project seeking to] finish off the political elite, and construct a new caste of politicians, pure, that aren't corrupt … they would fall. All off them. Aloysio, Serra, Aécio.
> (Cited in Valente 2016, translation mine)

The growing suspicion that a group within the political elite of Brazil was interested in removing the President Dilma Rousseff with the intention of saving their own hides was thus confirmed. With this leak and others to follow, the exertion of sustaining the façade of legitimacy was negated by events taking place between May 2016 and 2017. In consequence of the above-mentioned leak, Jucá and two other ministers of the Temer cabinet were forced to resign. The testimonies of Odebrecht leaders that gradually leaked in November and December 2016 made it clear that many decision-makers in Congress and in governor's offices would also be interested in "stopping the bleeding." In May

2017 the Temer administration and the key supporting senator Aécio Neves became embroiled in scandal again, through yet another leak of the Lava-Jato investigations. Temer was discussing hush money to stop Eduardo Cunha from negotiating a plea bargain in his prison cell, while Neves had requested bribes for paying his lawyer's bills in the Lava-Jato case. This time, with the dissemination of recorded conversations and the tracking of carry-on bags of cash delivered to Temer and Neves' aides, there was no denying that kickbacks and bribes continued to play a role in the backstage politics at the highest level, and that political actors were more than willing to obstruct justice.

However, the flip-side of independent prosecutors and judges is the willingness to leak and prosecute politics in ways that actively disrupt democracy and deliberately distort the distribution of media attention. Holding politicians accountable is a good thing, but when the information game of lawfare and media hunt becomes more viable than court trials, the electorate is not served, and neither is the sense of justice.

Despite a strong professional identity, the prosecutors aligned at different moments with various political forces, undermining first Lula, then Rousseff, and later Temer, by leaking information at critical junctures. So, with the strategic option of leaks available, judicial actors can bypass the institutionally designed spaces for resolving or mediating conflicts, relying on media hype to create the necessary legitimacy for the very procedure of bypassing. But where medical bypass surgery necessitates delicacy, the effects of this targeted transparency is rarely surgical in its incisions into institutional settings. Ignoring due process and individual rights to privacy for extended periods can result in dysfunctional institutional relations and constitutional crisis, as seen at various moments.

The fact that the STF, TSE, and MPF in conjunction have been calling the shots during the unfolding scandals meant that general elections of 2018 were determined by judiciary actors at the outset. The outcome of the 2018 elections – unknown at the time of writing this book – will also be shaped by the climate of the Lava-Jato investigations and impeachment, in addition to the campaign donation reform of 2015 plus the historically abnormal situation of presidential candidates from both PT and PSDB being discredited in the media. At a more tangible level, however, judiciary interventions and the timing of legal processes may keep some corrupt politicians in the running for presidency and Congress while stopping others due to the tardiness of legal processes and the Ficha Limpa law. Presidential candidates and the scores of investigated federal representatives and senators alike maintained or lost their eligibility at the mercy of the timing of the accountability institutions, while a polarized and volatile political context resulted in many voters looking to outsider candidates perceived to be "clean."

Another problematic consequence of judiciary independence is the speculation flowing from leaks. Setting the stage for conspiratorial media interpretations, leaky accountability serves political interests by tarnishing images and disregarding due process; this was the case of Judge Sérgio Moro's online publishing of phone conversations that documented the anxiety of Rousseff and Lula in relation to Lula's appointment as minister, but hardly showed criminal master-minds at work. The publication of the Rousseff-Lula dialogue was however swiftly picked up by the mainstream media to reinforce the narrative of a political crisis.

The combat of corruption became a crusade with vested party interests, always unknowable to the electorate despite the apparent increased transparency of legal processes. This great innovation of the Lava-Jato case – the unceasing publication and pushing of information – has certainly shown its political worth. While still largely ineffective at the individual level of Congress, the Lava-Jato scandal created the conditions for the impeachment of a president, and with it, a regime change – not just a change of governments, but, as a corollary of that change, a regime change in crucial policy aspects. These policy changes have included a redrawing of the role and the size of the state, education, reforms of social security and pensions, and a wave of privatizations, to name a few. Thus, the power of publicity does not necessarily reside at the individual level, where a scandal might mean the end of a particular political career. At the institutional level, the scandals have changed the framework of the intersection of public information flows in media systems and political systems, and this has repercussions, as described in the previous chapter, for public opinion, stock markets, and the mobilization of political resistance. In the wake of the Lava-Jato scandals, impeachment, and leaks, a tale often told about Brazil persists: 97 percent of the population thinks the government governs for personal gains and only 13 percent of citizens are satisfied with democracy (Latinobarómetro 2017: 9–10), political corruption is perceived to be rampant and increasing (Pring 2017), and the disapproval of Congress is the highest since the return to democracy (Datafolha 2017). Trust in government and political institutions is very low, and the percentage of voters declaring their intention to vote blank in the 2018 general elections was record-high less than a year before the elections.

Post-Politics in the Light of Leaks and Scandals

The profound effects on Brazilian democracy of the Lava-Jato probe may generate insights into the effect of political scandals and leaks beyond the Brazilian border. First, based on the case studies of this book, I suggest that leaks should be considered a part of a broader post-political climate. I would argue that post-politics comprise not just the projection of alternative facts or the viral spread of damaging (fake or real) news, but also the use of bulk information to produce institutional rupture. Like the leak of US Democratic National Committee emails prior to presidential nominating convention in 2016, or the devastating allegations made against François Fillon in the French presidential elections in 2017, the Brazilian case shows how political or institutional actors become pitted in antagonistic relations through leaks – and for sure, neither the Lava-Jato leaks nor the Fillon allegations cropped up randomly. Both are intentional, designed to wreak a certain amount of havoc in a political arena. This havoc, however, rapidly undermines the stability of the political institutions and settings in which they work. Since the leaks of Lava-Jato have made every politician a possible target, each politician is prepared to transgress the normal rules of democratic conduct if need be. These transgressions have become weapons, pure and simple, in an ongoing institutional conflict, and we may expect more conflicts of the sort in the future.

The second consequence of leaks in post-political environments is the ever-increasing suspicion cast upon political actors. In cases such as Brazil, that suspicion arises for very good reasons, to be sure. But leaks, through the technological and organizational setup of whistleblowers, data journalism, servers, etc., simultaneously configure disclosure and secrecy in order to protect the sources. The leaking is naturalized as the morally correct thing to do, maintained and protected as a private, heroic act, and rarely questioned in its political intent. The new mediated visibility (Thompson 2005) of political actors does not extend to the individuals or collectives who work through leaks, and the transparency demanded of politicians is not reflected in the accountability of leaky organizations (Wahl-Jørgensen 2014). But public information is not necessarily transparent or innocent, and media professionals partaking in the leaks-and-journalism assemblage should be wary of mindlessly recycling leaked information. In this theater of shadows, the power of leaks not only consists in the bypassing of normal media gatekeepers and fact-checking, but also provides a slippery entry point for the post-politics of allegations, denunciations, and leaks thereby to underpin and strengthen certain kinds of defamatory speech about politicians easily detectable in social media.

Finally, while leaks do not necessarily contribute to the post-truth problematic of contemporary democracy, they do in fact play into the distinction of knowledge types by projecting the leaked information as "a superior mode of knowledge, a cultural signifier of unmediated objective information" (Hansen and Flyverbom 2014: 2). Leaks, in the public sphere of media disseminating these leaks, occupy a privileged space relative to the claims made by political actors, who are rendered suspect a priori by virtue of their presence in the leaked information. The apparently "hard" facts found in leaked files command the top position of the hierarchy of public knowledge, and leaks thereby create the conditions of qualifying, disqualifying, and delegitimizing information.

Theoretical Implications and Remaining Questions

The post-political climate of leaks eclipses ideology, but also challenges key theoretical terms. Where earlier literature saw the positive contributions of leaks to public accountability, especially in global context of fiscal havens and international networks of corrupt and secretive offshore shell companies, I would like to draw attention to the dynamic of leaks in terms of information flows. Leaks may shake a web of accountability institutions, but the media limelight can be attractive not just to kick-start investigation but also for political instrumental reasons. This means that the accountability theory model (Mainwaring and Welna 2003, Porto 2011) needs to be reinterpreted as inserted into *Realpolitik* and struggles for symbolic capital (Thompson 2000). The vertical and horizontal dimensions are intersected by vectors of political force that bend and stretch the web of accountability. An investigation or a trial, with solid evidence or without substance, can be of utmost value – not for democracy nor for accountability, but to eclipse other cases or as a stepping stone for launching political candidatures. Information flowing from such legal actions can drive the media agenda and contribute to the formation of informational cascades between the agenda-setting media outlets. Watchdog media becomes a hollow term, then, not because of political or ideological bias, nor because of singular instances of recycled fake news, but because the emphasis of the infostorm redirects attention and precipitates pluralistic ignorance in public spheres (Wiewiura and Hendricks 2017).

With the emergence of such infostorms, the actual content of news items may be subsumed in the avalanche of signals. For theoretical and methodological purposes, this means a reorientation of research from media texts to media spheres, from news frames to agendas, or from micro to macro. While particular texts – such as initial disclosures or leaks – may have much agenda-setting influence, derived social proof only becomes manifest when the same signal is retransmitted, disseminated, and recycled again and again. A political crisis may lurk on the horizon, only to flare up when herds of political actors conjure the crisis into being, and the self-fulfilling prophecy of crisis becomes reality. This was the case in Brazil, when declining economic indicators such as export revenue and tax revenue became exacerbated by the cascades of news on political turmoil and the derived effects on investors, stock markets, and exchange rates. A political crisis, in this sense, could be conceptualized as a bubble: a rapidly growing, bootstrapping informational phenomenon.

Scandals and leaks about corruption are effective catalysts for the phenomena discussed here; infostorms, cascades, and bubbles can be set in motion by when media actors flock around a case of political transgression and act in a herd-like manner (Hendricks and Hansen 2016). Departing from this observation, the case studies of this book may generate an important question for media system theory: What does the uniformity (or pack-mindedness) of a country's media agenda mean to political issues, and does media research have adequate conceptual tools to establish the degree of group-think in media systems? These questions cut across newsroom ethnography, journalism, and agenda-setting studies, and could in time open up new avenues of research on agenda fragmentation, pluralization, or polarization of public spheres, and democratic participation in a wider sense. If democracies are founded upon the premise of access to transparent and dependable information on affairs of state, then it is vital to establish how media institutions funnel and filter information, and to what extent such filtered information trickles down into the blogosphere, social media, and ultimately civic society.

Perhaps media institutions should not be conceptualized (as accountability theory commonly does) as one institution among others in the web of accountability? When the attention and visibility staged in the media generate distorted policy-maker agendas, driven by backstage interests, I fear that media act rather as political stakeholders. The same doubts could be raised for the new variety of indignant online movements that capitalize on the information flows about political transgression to produce hateful speech toward entire segments of populations and ideologies associated with these segments.

Aside from theoretical implications for accountability and scandal theory, media system research, and agenda-setting studies, several practical implications of the Brazilian case are left at the end of this book. First, it is important to find models that can ensure and qualify the separate independence of society's watchdogs – understood here to be not only media but also courts and prosecutors – since the combination of lawfare and scandal creates a toxic and opaque political atmosphere. How to avoid that the barking of one watchdog instills a frenzy in the rest of the pack, without restricting freedom of speech and Constitutional procedures? In less poetic terms, the question remains as to whether and how the feedback mechanisms of Brazil's accountability and media institutions could be dismantled and reassembled into something more democratic, equilibrated, and informative. Second, the imbalance of the Brazilian system's checks and balances is on display in the cases presented here, but a viable way to improve the checks and balances seems a long way off as long as the Congress is situated comfortably in a dead zone of accountability; largely untouched by the corruption investigations and largely unwilling to let go of elite privileges and the possibility of obstructing interventions from the judiciary branch.

Finally, the data presented in this book can be mined and interpreted in many more ways, and I welcome suggestions and attempts to do so. As most parts of the previous chapter's dataset on media coverage and leaks are published in the public domain, scholars from diverse fields can perhaps think of novel ways of reassembling the complex and remarkably skewed interplay of information flows, media dissemination, and corruption allegations in Brazil. To be sure, the possibilities of detecting patterns and gaining insights are not limited to the brief content analyses provided in the previous chapter, and so I invite scholars to interrogate and expand the data, as well as to introduce new questions and approaches that can expand the scope of the present inquiry.

References

Almeida, R. de (2016) *A Sombra do Poder. Os Bastidores da Crise Que Derrubou Dilma Rousseff.* Rio de Janeiro: Editora LeYa.

Amorim Neto, O. (2007) "O poder executivo, centro de gravidade do sistema político brasileiro." In L. Avelar and A.O. Cintra (eds.), *Sistema político brasileiro: uma introdução* (123–133). São Paolo: UNESP Press.

Arantes, J. (2016) *Relatório.* Brasília: Câmara dos Deputados. Retrieved from www2.camara.leg.br/atividade-legislativa/comissoes/comissoes-temporarias/especiais/55a-legislatura/denuncia-contra-a-presidente-da-republica/documentos/outros-documentos/ParecerDep.JovairArantes.pdf.

Avritzer, L. (2016) *Impasses da democracia no Brasil.* Rio de Janeiro: Civilização Brasileira.

Balán, M. (2011) "Competition by Denunciation: The Political Dynamics of Corruption Scandals in Argentina and Chile" *Comparative Politics*, vol. 43(4), 459–478.

Boydstun, A. (2013) *Making the News. Politics, the Media, and Agenda Setting.* Chicago, IL: University of Chicago Press.

Cabral, E.D.T. (2017) "Mídia Concentrada no Brasil: Até Quando?" *Revista Latino-Americana de Ciencias de la Comunicación*, vol. 13(24), 49–59.

Comaroff, J. and Comaroff, J. (eds.) (2006) *Law and Disorder in the Postcolony.* Chicago, IL: University of Chicago Press.

Datafolha (2017) *Avaliação do Congresso Nacional, novembro 2017 – PO 813942.* São Paulo: Datafolha.

Falcão, J., Hartmann, I.A., and Chaves, V. (2014) *III Relatório Supremo em Números: o Supremo e o tempo.* Rio de Janeiro: Escola de Direito do Rio de Janeiro da Fundação Getulio Vargas.

Feres Júnior, J. and Sassara, L. (2016) "O cão que nem sempre late: o Grupo Globo e a cobertura das eleições presidenciais de 2014 e 1998" *Revista Compolítica*, vol. 6(1), 30–61.

Galtung, J. and Ruge, M. (1965) "The Structure of Foreign News" *Journal of Peace Research*, vol. 2(1), 64–91.

Habermas, J. (1989 [1962]) *The Structural Transformation of the Public Sphere.* Cambridge, MA: MIT Press.

Hansen, H.K. and Flyverbom, M. (2014) "The Politics of Transparency and the Calibration of Knowledge in the Digital Age" *Organization*, vol. 22(6), 872–889.

Hendricks, V. and Hansen, P.G. (2016) *Infostorms. Why Do We "Like"? Explaining Individual Behavior on the Social Net.* 2nd edition. London: Springer.

Kristensen, N.N. and Mortensen, M. (2015) "Amateur Sources Breaking the News, Meta-sources Authorizing the News of Gaddafi's Death: New Patterns of Journalistic Information Gathering and Dissemination in the Digital Age" *Digital Journalism*, vol. 1(3), 352–367.

Latinobarómetro (2017) *Informe Latinobarómetro 2017.* Santiago de Chile: Corporación Latinobarómetro.

Mainwaring, S. and Welna, C. (eds.) (2003) *Democratic Accountability in Latin America.* Oxford: Oxford University Press.

Pederiva, J., Alves, D., and Rincon, F. (2016) *Laudo Pericial.* Brasília: Senado Federal. Retrieved from www12.senado.leg.br/noticias/arquivos/2016/06/27/laudo-da-junta-pericial.

Pereira, C. and Mueller, B. (2000) "Theory of Executive Dominance: The Committee System in the Brazilian Congress" *Revista Brasileira de Ciências Sociais*, vol. 15, 45–67.

Peruzzotti, E. (2006) "Media Scandals and Social Accountability. Assessing the Role of Scandals in Argentina." In E. Peruzzotti and C. Smulovitz (eds.), *Enforcing the Rule of Law. Social Accountability in the New Latin American Democracies* (249–271). Pittsburgh, PA: University of Pittsburgh Press.

Porto, M. (2011) "The Media and Political Accountability." In T. Power and M. Taylor (eds.), *Corruption and Democracy in Brazil* (103–126). South Bend, IN: University of Notre Dame Press.

Power, T. and Taylor, M. (eds.) (2011) *Corruption and Democracy in Brazil.* South Bend, IN: University of Notre Dame Press.

Pring, C. (2017) *People and Corruption: Latin America and the Carribbean.* Berlin: Transparency International.

Seligson, M. (2002) "The Impact of Corruption on Regime Legitimacy: A Comparative Study of Four Latin American Countries" *The Journal of Politics*, vol. 64(2), 408–433.

Smulovitz, C. and Peruzzotti, E. (2000) "Social Accountability in Latin America" *Journal of Democracy*, vol. 11(4), 147–158.

Taylor, M. (2011) "The Federal Judiciary and the Electoral Courts." In T. Power and M. Taylor (eds.), *Corruption and Democracy in Brazil* (162–183). South Bend, IN: University of Notre Dame Press.

Thompson, J.P. (2000) *Political Scandal: Power and Visibility in the Media Age*. Cambridge: Polity Press.

Thompson, J.P. (2005) "The New Visibility" *Theory, Culture & Society*, vol. 22(6), 31–51.

Valente, R. (2016) "Em diálogo, Jucá fala em pacto para deter avanço da Lava Jato" *Folha de S. Paulo*, p. A4, May 23.

Villaverde, J. (2016) *Perigosas pedaladas*. São Paulo: Geração Editorial.

Wahl-Jørgensen, K. (2014) "Is WikiLeaks Challenging the Paradigm of Journalism? Boundary Work and Beyond" *International Journal of Communication*, vol. 8, 2581–2592.

Waisbord, S. (2000) *Watchdog Journalism in South America. News, Accountability, and Democracy*. New York: Columbia University Press.

Walgrave, S., Boydstun, A., Vliegenthart, R., and Hardy, A. (2017) "The Nonlinear Effect of Information on Political Attention: Media Storms and U.S. Congressional Hearings" *Political Communication*, vol. 34(4), 548–570.

Wiewiura, J. and Hendricks, V. (2017) "Informational Pathologies and Interest Bubbles: Exploring the Structural Mobilization of Knowledge, Ignorance, and Slack" *New Media and Society*, Article first published online: January 10, 2017 – https://doi.org/10.1177/1461444816686095.

Wink, G. (2017) "Judicialização da política ou politização da justiça? Uma Análise Crítica do Discurso do Libelo Acusatório contra a presidenta Dilma Rousseff no processo de impeachment" *Moara*, vol. 47, 152–177.

Zalis, R. (2015) "E o governo mal começou…" *Veja*, edition #2417, March 18.

Afterword[1]
Lula and Lava-Jato

The current political crisis Brazil is facing has a multifaceted nature, which can only be grasped through a multidisciplinary approach. The coup against Dilma Rousseff itself is a point of contention among political scientists, and between them and law scholars, most supporting the idea of a political coup while a few others resist employing the term, claiming that everything was done according to legal procedure and that no major democratic institution was harmed – a rather doubtful opinion. The event was termed by some commentators a judicial-media-parliamentary coup because it was brought about through the synergetic endeavors of both houses of the legislative branch – the Chamber of Deputies and the Senate –, the judicial system, which promoted the Lava Jato Operation on one side while allowing the case against Rousseff to progress despite its lack of substance, and the media, which fiercely supported the pro-impeachment movement and initiate a campaign against Rousseff, her government, the Workers' Party (PT) and Luiz Inácio Lula da Silva.

From the perspective of media studies, the behavior of Brazil's major news outlets was truly staggering. Putting things in perspective, the fact that the media acted against PT was not at all a surprise. Numerous academic studies have shown, since the return of the democratic regime in the 1980s, that Brazil's big media has shown a marked bias against the left, particularly PT and Lula (Aldé, Mendes, and Figueiredo 2007, Azevedo 2017, Feres Júnior and Sassara 2018, Kucinski 1998, Miguel 1999, Miguel and Biroli 2011, Rubim and Azevedo 1998). In election after election, they have employed a variety of means to undermine left-wing candidacies and promote its conservative opponents, from the manipulation of television debates to heavily loaded framing of key political themes, to agenda-setting that exploits bad news for the left while hiding information that could harm conservative candidates, to highly speculative news that border what today we call fake news, to the outright fabrication of scandals.

Most of the academic work done in the field of media and politics in Brazil focused on elections. Thus, the impression one might get by becoming acquainted with this literature is that the media behaves in such manner partly because of the highly politicized climate of the election period. That is certainly no excuse for the general behavior of Brazilian media during elections, but there hadn't been much evidence about its behavior in non-electoral years. This all changed with project Manchetômetro,[2] which was established to analyze the media coverage of the 2014 presidential election but then continued until this day, producing sentiment analysis of the big media coverage of chief political figures, parties, and themes, and of the economy.

Our data shows, for example, that after her 2014 victory in the presidential election, Dilma Rousseff enjoyed the opposite of a honeymoon (Feres Júnior and Sassara 2018), a concept some American authors define as a period of truce between the newly elected president and the political opposition, including the media (Dominguez 2005, Johnson 1983). The number of negative news items about her doubled in January, the first month of her second term, and practically tripled two months later, while her neutral coverage declined. Rousseff's negative coverage kept on peaking in September and December 2015, when it reached around 300 negative news items per month in the three newspapers and *Jornal Nacional* – in other words, an average of ten negative items a day.[3] In March 2016, the same month Lula was unlawfully forced to testify by Judge Sergio Moro, and when the same judge, Moro, illegally leaked to Grupo Globo a wiretap containing a phone conversation between Rousseff and Lula, Rousseff's negatives reached the historical mark of 373. We can see here what this volume's author, Mads Damgaard, termed lawfare in Chapter 4, borrowing the concept from anthropology and from the writings of Lula's attorney, Cristiano Zanin: the strategic use of politically loaded legal procedures combined with biased media coverage in the pursuit of political ends. President Dilma Rousseff was actually the first target. The intensity of her negative coverage only subsides when she is removed from power.

A similar pattern of coverage is shown when we examine the variable federal government. The figures are even larger. In March 2015 the government received almost 500 negative items. This massacre continued on a similar level until Dilma Rousseff was removed from power in May 2016. Proving a point Mads Damgaard makes quite well in this book, despite the numerous accusations of corruption against Michel Temer and the meager popular support he enjoys, the media gave his government a perennial honeymoon, with a brief interruption in May 2017 when a recorded conversation between him and Joesley Batista, the owner of the meat-packing giant JBS, in which the president condones bribery, and a video showing one of his assistants receiving a suitcase full of cash were leaked to the media. After a couple of months, however, the scandal was practically forgotten by the news outlets, which continue to treat Temer in a very benign manner, fully supporting his agenda of neo-liberal economic reforms.

But the replacement of Dilma Rousseff by the neo-liberal Temer is just half of the story. The other half, probably the most important one in political terms, is the persecution of Lula by the same judicial/media-organizational dispositive that produced the impeachment. The behavior of public prosecutors, judges, and Supreme Court justices has been so flawed and politically loaded that it is impossible to speak of it here without extending this text beyond what is advisable. It suffices to say that Moro sentenced Lula even without sound material proof of his guilt, that the verdict was affirmed by the appellate court, which extended his sentence just enough to force his imprisonment, and that the Supreme Court refused to grant him a *habeas corpus* even though the Constitution expressly forbids imprisonment until all possibilities of appealing are exhausted, which is Lula's case.

Lula's political stature can hardly be overstated. During the last 30 years he has been a chief protagonist in Brazil's presidential elections. He passed to the second round of the 1989 election, to be defeated by Fernando Collor the Mello after a massive media campaign that accused PT of being involved in the kidnapping of a famous businessman, which turned out to be false, and the broadcasting of a heavily edited and manipulated version of the last debate of the campaign by TV Globo's *Jornal Nacional*, which portrayed Lula losing the debate to Collor. Lula was also the runner-up in the following two presidential elections, 1994 and 1998, and finally won in 2002 and 2006, defeating PT's main political adversary, PSDB. With his popular approval rating approaching 80 percent, he managed to elect Dilma Rousseff, his hand-picked successor, twice, in 2010 and 2014, again defeating PSDB candidates. Now he keeps a clear lead in 2018's presidential race but will most probably be unable to run given his conviction and detention.

In other words, the coup did not stop at Rousseff, cancelling the popular mandate transferred to her through popular vote: it is going all the way to block the majority of the people to choose their favorite candidate in the next presidential election. But lawfare is not complete if we do not factor in the role of the media. And in the case of Lula it has exceeded itself. The numbers of his news coverage, produced by Manchetômetro, are staggering. Without holding any office, Lula started to become the target of a fierce media smear campaign about the time Dilma Rousseff was starting her second term. In January 2015 he received 50 negative news items in our database. This figure almost doubled in the next month and by October it had already tripled. But nothing compares to the peak of March 2016, when Moro had Lula forcefully conducted to testify. That month Lula received 352 negative items from the three newspapers and *Jornal Nacional*.

The numbers can hardly be more extreme. If we take into account only the opinion items (editorials, op-ed articles, and signed columns) of the three newspapers, Lula received from January 2015 to April 2018 an average of 66 negative pieces per month. This is almost eight opinion pieces per day per newspaper. Since his prosecution was controversial, given that besides all its political import it also involved important constitutional matters, one would assume that the media cared also to publish pieces that would comment on the facts from perspectives other than those of the accusation. But that is not the case. Positive pieces, that is, texts that put into question the dealings of Moro, the prosecutors, and were keener to the arguments of Lula's defense averaged 3.5 throughout the period from January 2015 to April 2018: almost 20 times less frequent than negative texts. Just to keep the comparison similar, their frequency was close to one piece per newspaper per month.

Quantitative analysis such as the one I have been expounding here gives the reader a rather cold and detached image of what really goes on. So, we will delve a little bit more into details to flesh out the analysis. Right after Lula was arrested, his attorneys filed a *habeas corpus* petition at the Supreme Court claiming that the arrest was illegal because the constitution forbade it before the case went through the three stages of Brazil's judicial system: first instance, regional appellate courts, and the federal Supreme Court. How did the big media approach this event? Let's see how the two most important Brazilian newspapers, *O Globo* and *Folha de S. Paulo*, covered the Supreme Court ruling on the day of the verdict, April 4, 2018.

The cover of *O Globo*, the newspaper of the family Marinho, owners of Grupo Globo, the largest media conglomerate in Latin America, makes quite an impact. Three-fifths of its area is covered by items referring to the Supreme Court ruling. The headline, in huge letters on the top of the page reads: "For Dodge, the excess of appeals annihilates justice." It is a reference to a declaration given by the Chief Federal Prosecutor Raquel Dodge. Below the headline there is a title that says that the Supreme Court will rule over intense pressure. At the bottom of the column there is another title saying that Commander-in-Chief of the Army, General Vilas Bôas, tweeted that impunity should be rejected at all costs, a clear threat against the Supreme Court in case they decide to suspend Lula's arrest. Then, on the right-hand side of the page there is a column containing snippets of text pointing to opinion pieces inside the newspaper. The top one is the editorial entitled "Lula at the Supreme Courts represents impunity." This is followed by a teaser for the column of Miriam Leitão, a known detractor of President Lula, with a threatening tone, saying that the Court will give Lula the *habeas corpus*. The next snippet is authored by Merval Pereira, another self-declared enemy of Lula and his party, saying that Justice Rosa Weber will have the responsibility to decide upon such an important matter, that is, putting pressure on her to decide against Lula. The next snippet is by Elio Gaspari, which has the clear intent of delegitimizing Lula's *habeas corpus* by saying that poor convicts do not have access to so many appeals. Underneath these columns there is a large photograph that takes the entire center area of the first page, showing people in São Paulo protesting against Lula's *habeas corpus*. The title reads "pressure from the streets," followed by the information that "thousands went to the streets in at least 23 states and the Federal District to ask the Supreme Court to confirm the arrest of president Lula." This is the whole coverage of the event on the first page: That is, *O Globo* did not allow in its first page a single mention of an opinion in favor the *habeas corpus*.

The opinion pages are no different. The editorial, as its title announces, is fiercely against the *habeas corpus*, arguing that its acceptance by the court will benefit all corrupt politicians. In the same page there is the article by *O Globo*'s columnist Élio Gaspari saying that the *habeas corpus* is a privilege of the elites, not enjoyed by the poor. The following opinion page contains a text by Zuenir Ventura, which despite its vague tone argues that there are reasons to believe that if the *habeas corpus* is accepted, the fight against corruption will be endangered. At the bottom of the page, an article by Jorge Maranhão, the director of a right-wing NGO Instituto de Cultura de Cidadania, who argues that the Supreme

Court cannot overrule the will of the people in the streets. This phrase is in line with the picture on the first page of the newspaper, and both are examples of how mainstream media often approaches fake news. Simply, there were not masses of people in the streets demanding the Supreme Court to withhold Lula's imprisonment. Finally, there is a cryptic text by Marco Lucchesi which does not touch directly the subject in question but suggests that there is a new ethical Brazil rising from the wreckage of the old society, a soteriological and messianic discourse very much in line with that of the evangelical prosecutors of Lava-Jato.

The first page of *Folha de S. Paulo* is quite similar to that of its counterpart from Rio de Janeiro. The space dedicated to the topic is a little smaller, but still quite sizable: roughly half the page. The titles are inverted. The highlight of the headline is given to the tweet of the commander-in-chief of the Army, who warned the Supreme Court against accepting the *habeas corpus*. To Rachel Dodges's declaration against the excess of appeals, the newspaper gives a smaller box of text. Also similar to the first page of *O Globo* is the disposition of a column on the right side of the page displaying snippets leading to opinion pieces inside the newspaper. The first one comments on the reaction of the general's comment in the Supreme Court. The second states that the government of Paraná is already finding a proper place to incarcerate Lula. The third snippet, by columnist Hélio Schwartsman, is a cryptic note saying that the Supreme Court's decision will not alter the political context. Next is the same text by Élio Gaspari, who published in both newspapers. And finally the editorial of *Folha de S. Paulo*, entitled "It is not about Lula," is announced.

The first opinion page is topped by the same editorial. The point is clear: if the Court accepts the *habeas corpus*, corrupt politicians would avoid prison. Thus, the justices must reject it. On the right-hand side of the editorial, there are three columns. The top one by Schwartsman replicates the cryptic tone of the snippet, but is clearly ironical toward Gilmar Mendes, a STF judge who switched his previous opinion to vote in favor of the *habeas corpus*. The second text, by Bruno Boghossian, accuses the court of privileging Lula, suggesting that it should reject the *habeas corpus*. And finally, columnist Ruy Castro openly advocates the imprisonment of the ex-president in his article, calling him an ingrate. The second opinion of *Folha de S. Paulo* contains a section called Trends and Debates that often pitches contrasting opinions on the same topic. This time the topic was Lula's request to the Supreme Court. The text on the top is authored by the Prosecutor-General Raquel Dodge herself, defending the position that Brazil should follow other advanced democracies around the world and adopt the imprisonment of people convicted after the first appeal. The text below is authored by a lawyer named Augusto Arruda Botelho, who defends the Constitution against the innovation forcefully advocated by the Lava-Jato supporters. There is one important detail, however. Dodge's text is not only on top of his, but it is three times larger.

Completing its second opinion page, *Folha de S. Paulo* has another fixed section, the Readers' Panel, which reproduces emails sent from alleged *Folha*'s readers. Four of them deal with the *habeas corpus* case. The first simply states that a 2016 statute interprets the Constitution allowing for Lula to be arrested after the sentence if confirmed at the appeals court. The second is supportive of STF President Cármen Lúcia, who not only voted for repealing the *habeas corpus* but also arranged the Court's agenda in a way to harm Lula and his defense. The third email echoes the main argument of the editorial and of Gaspari's article, that the right to a third instance appeal in the Constitution only benefits the rich. And finally, a fourth email is a short invective against Lula, saying that he only deceives intellectuals that are not able to think.

This brief summary of what the two main newspapers in the country have published in their first pages and opinion pieces in the day of a momentous ruling in the Supreme Court reveals how profoundly slanted Brazil's big media is regarding Lula and PT and how it is deeply invested in promoting certain legal views in tandem with sectors of the judiciary and of the MPF, a practice that is the core of what Damgaard has correctly identified as lawfare. The Brazilian media promotes a massacre in the realm of public opinion and in order to do that it disregards the most basic principles of professional journalism, first of all to give a fair and balanced account on facts and opinions, and to allow for a plurality of opinions to be expressed.

Brazilian democracy is nowadays tremendously sick, mostly because its institutions of control have been colonized by politics, while the political institutions have been severely devalued in the forum of public opinion – the presidency and Congress are the least trusted institutions in the country (see Chapter 6). The media behaves like a political party, the judiciary and public prosecutors are politically motivated while politicians and political parties seem stunned and unable to provide solutions that would re-energize the polity. The judicial institutions will not fix themselves: They are an elite of highly paid state bureaucrats that enjoy legal protections of all sorts and a great deal of institutional freedom without having to be accountable to almost any institution. The media also enjoy extreme freedom from libel laws, that practically do not exist, and from regulations in general: Brazil has one of the most concentrated and unregulated media systems in the world. The correction must come from outside these control institutions. It must come from the politics itself.

–João Feres Júnior, PhD
Director of Instituto de Estudos Sociais e Políticos at Universidade do
Estado do Rio de Janeiro

Notes

1 Editor's note: This Afterword, provided by João Feres Júnior, reflects upon the Brazilian media system's coverage of the final steps of the trial that led to the incarceration of ex-President Lula in Curitiba on April 7, 2018.
2 Manchetômetro, literally "headline meter," is a research project conducted by the Laboratory on Media and the Public Sphere (LEMEP), led by me, focused on the daily publication of data concerning the news coverage of politics and the economy done by the most prominent Brazilian media outlets: newspapers *Folha de S. Paulo*, *O Globo*,

Estado de S. Paulo, and television news program, *Jornal Nacional*, which is broadcast by TV Globo.

3 Manchetômetro's dataset covers the first page and two opinion pages of each newspaper, which contain editorials, signed columns, and op-eds, and the entire content of *Jornal Nacional*, the most-viewed TV newscast in Brazil.

References

Aldé, A., Mendes, G., and Figueiredo, M. (2007) "Tomando partido: imprensa e eleições presidenciais em 2006" *Política e Sociedade*, vol. 10, 153–172.

Azevedo, F.A. (2017) *A Grande Imprensa e o PT (1989–2014)*. São Carlos: Editora UFSCar.

Dominguez, C.B.K. (2005) "Is It a Honeymoon? An Empirical Investigation of the President's First Hundred Days" *Congress & the Presidency*, vol. 32(1), 63–78. doi: 10.1080/07343460509507697.

Feres Júnior, J. and Oliveira Sassara, L. de (2018) "Failed Honeymoon: Dilma Rousseff's Third Election Round" *Latin American Perspectives*, vol. 45(3), 224–235. doi: 10.1177/0094582x18767429.

Johnson, K.S. (1983) "The Honeymoon Period: Fact or Fiction?" *Journalism Quarterly*, vol. 60(3), 869–876.

Kucinski, B. (1998) *A síndrome da antena parabólica: ética no jornalismo brasileiro.* 1a edn. São Paulo, SP, Brasil: Editora Fundação Perseu Abramo.

Miguel, L.F. (1999) "Mídia e eleições: a campanha de 1998 na Rede Globo" *Dados*, vol. 42(2), 253–276.

Miguel, L.F. and Biroli, F. (2011) "Meios de comunicação de massa e eleições no Brasil: da influência simples à interação complexa" *Revista USP*, vol. 90, 74–83.

Rubim, A.A.C., and Azevedo F.A. (1998) "Mídia e política no Brasil: textos e agenda de pesquisa" *Lua Nova: Revista de Cultura e Política*, vol. 43, 189–216.

Index

Page numbers in **bold** denote tables, those in *italics* denote figures.

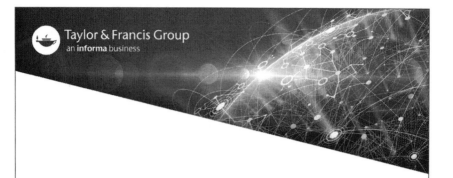